Old Tales and
New Truths

Old Tales and New Truths

Charting the Bright-Shadow World

James Roy King

STATE UNIVERSITY OF NEW YORK PRESS

Grateful acknowledgment is made to the following publishers for permission to quote from their works:

The Creative Education Foundation, for permission to reprint from "Behavioral Implication of Mental World-Making," by James Roy King, in *The Journal of Creative Behavior*, Volume 23, #1, 1989.

Grove Press, for portions of Shawn and Gregory, *My Dinner with André*, copyright © 1966 by Warner Books.

HarperCollins Publishers, New York, and Chatto & Windus, London, for portions of Aldous Huxley, *Heaven and Hell* and *The Doors of Perception*, copyright © 1963 by Harper & Row.

Penguin USA, and The Octagon Press, London, for quotations from Indries Shah, *Tales of the Dervishes*. Copyright © by Indries Shah. Reprinted by permission of the publisher, Dutton, and imprint of New American Library, a division of Penguin Books USA, Inc.

The University of Chicago Press, for portions of John Ellis, *One Fairy Story Too Many*, copyright © 1983 by The University of Chicago Press; and from J.B.B. van Buitenen, *Tales of Ancient India*, copyright © 1959 by The University of Chicago Press.

Published by
State University of New York Press, Albany

© 1992 State University of New York

For information, address State University of New York
Press, State University Plaza, Albany, N.Y., 12246

Production by E. Moore
Marketing by Fran Keneston

Library of Congress Cataloging-in-Publication Data

King, James Roy.
    Old tales and new truths : charting the bright-shadow world /
James Roy King.
        p. cm.
    Includes bibliographical references and index.
    ISBN 0-7914-0853-1 (CH : acid-free). — ISBN 0-7914-0854-X (PB :
acid-free)
        1. Fairy tales—History and criticism.   2. Fairy tales—
Psychological aspects.   3. Tales — History and criticism.   4. Tales —
Structural analysis.   I. Title
    GR550.K56   1992
    398.21—dc20   90-26345
                                                                            CIP

10   9   8   7   6   5   4   3   2   1

for Judith
a most congenial Fellow Traveler through the
bright-shadow world

Contents

Acknowledgments   ix

1. Hearing Tales: The Behavioral Dimension   1

2. A Way of Proceeding   11

3. On Reading the World: Jus' Settin' 'n' Rockin'   16

4. Some Structural Possibilities   27

5. Edges   45

6. The Ambiguities of Enchantment   63

7. Power   78

8. Moral Ties   94

9. Personal Identity   112

10. The Experience of Knowing   138

11. Some Typical Bright-Shadow-World Problems   161

12. Nimble Riding—a Question of Style   183

13. The World of the Bright Shadow   199

Appendix 1: Analysis of the Structure of Situations   211

Appendix 2: Assessment of Life-Enhancing Themes   219

Notes   223

Index   257

Acknowledgments

Thanks are due to a number of my colleagues at Wittenberg University for their willingness to discuss the material in this book: Imogene Bolls, Leonard Brown, Kent Dixon, Arthur Faber, Barbara Kaiser, Allen Koppenhaver, Terry Otten, Kathleen Schulz, Eugene Swanger, and John Wing. During a Fulbright year in Cairo I learned much about Egyptian culture and folk narrative from Andrea Rugh. A former student, Marcus Bales, was the most critical reader of this manuscript and thus one of the most helpful. Many of the ideas discussed here began to develop over a decade ago at an NEH Seminar on Old Testament Narrative conducted by Jack Sasson at Chapel Hill. I am also grateful to David Appelbaum, the College of New Paltz, for patient reading of a number of drafts of this manuscript, and to Sabra Webber, the Ohio State University, for encouragement. My wife has rescued me from problems with our word processor, informed me about the most esoteric reaches of science fiction, and done a hundred other supportive things. Nancy Miller, Sandra Freshour, and Rosemarie Burley have been patient and helpful typists.

1 Hearing Tales: The Behavioral Dimension

A major task in times of rapid cultural change is to develop images applicable to the personal dimension of the process, new models of humanness, emergent possibilities for specific individuals. I mean a truly imaginative grasp of what may be hoped for, expected, of Tom, Dick, and Harriet: increased sensitivities, the expansion of capabilities (including intelligence), more productive relationships with others and with the environment, the enhancement of mental and spiritual well-being, the development of individual creative capacity. Futuristics, a discipline intensely interested in change, has devoted itself primarily to technological, political, and social progress, and for the most part writers of science fiction have populated their worlds with creatures too strange to serve as actual models of human development. The problem has been exacerbated by the contention of the postmodernists that none of the great classic scripts by which we have lived is any longer available for our guidance.

My purpose is to suggest that there is a *role* here for traditional narrative—fairytale, folktale, legend, religious teaching-story. These genres are usually regarded as bearers of tradition. But they have also played—and continue to play—a significant role in stimulating the intellectual, spiritual, and psychological development of human beings, breaking rather than simply reinforcing the bonds of tradition. Jack Zipes has studied the transformation of fairytales in contemporary Europe into instruments of political subversion, and Ruth Bottigheimer has examined, among other feminist issues, the treatment of women's conversational patterns in the Brothers Grimm. (Fairytales have stimulated, if not supported, liberationist thinking.) So we can say that traditional narrative has sometimes been used to call attention to, dramatize, clothe with a certain imaginative grandeur various still-scantily recognized possibilities—places to go (including within), powers to develop, new moralities to explore, relationships to nurture, weaknesses to assess, sensibilities to refine.

That is to say, fairytales and folktales, which are so often grounded in the bizarre, the abnormal, even the supernatural, carry out certain creative functions as they summon their hearers out of the normal, the accepted, the rational, the modern to possibilities that are speculative but also experience-enhancing. The popular tale enormously expands our repertoire of possible behaviors—both by suggesting alternative patterns and by describing other worlds where these patterns might be tried out.

Our experience of the world as Westerners of the twentieth century (and that is all I have any claim to know about) is for the most part geared to very restricted purposes. Our sense of what is consequential embraces much but leaves out even more. The modern educational enterprise—a major determinant of all our later experience—is both inclusive and exclusive. In the eyes of many (local school boards, for example), the principal purpose of education is to control what immature individuals allow into their experience, even to restrict their selection to what is acceptable to the community or to some group of experts, and to limit sharply the range of acceptable responses. A very narrow map of reality is offered. Twentieth-century education has stressed the development of individuals with a strong sense of self, whose capacity to seek out and accept new experiences is distinctly limited, who are confined to what Emily Dickinson called "a world of circumstances." Such individuals are at home in an area of proven and generally accepted physical and social facts, and the personality itself is seen as rigid, formed early, relatively unchanging. "Real-world" individuals have become accustomed to acquiring knowledge through the senses and by reasoning and kept records, and efforts to secure a place for intuition, dreams, and "voices" are rarely successful. The world for which they are trained finds its power in wealth, vocation, family, status, progress, but impulses to what is beyond the here and now are weak, and the possibility of other realities, or experiences radically different from what they are trained for, is denied or passed over by influential thinkers. Morality is seen pragmatically, as whatever keeps the system going, and individuals who depart from the norm are ignored or condemned. So much is left out! so many limitations accepted! so many resources ignored![1]

For some few individuals, however, education means enlarging the range of data which they admit to their mental files, encouraging responses well beyond those acceptable to the community, giving to their experience dimensions which even their teachers may know nothing of.[2] Within certain more daring frameworks it is acceptable to redirect reflection, to reimage truths thought to be fundamental, to alter the method by which basic data are collected, even to challenge (by suggesting alternatives) the assumptions that may lie behind reflection itself. It is such possibilities that we can think of as enhancing experience, and it is in this area that the human potentialities movement of the 1970s flourished. But in the rubble of deconstruction and postmodernism, the liberal—and often liberating—assumptions of that decade seem overly optimistic, too rigidly patterned.

Various tools are available for broadening experience beyond the limitations of the traditional curriculum or academically acceptable images of the mature personality. These means include poetry, intentional exploration of altered states of consciousness, contacts with other cultures, the crafts, and travel. And, as I have suggested, the sharing of legends, fairytales, and folktales has always had a place of special importance in this process, alerting readers and listeners in highly personal ways to *other* arrangements and interpretations of the stuff of experience. Such narratives have summoned both children and adults to forgotten or neglected possibilities of experience and have suggested the extraordinary potential of even the simplest situation to take on life-enhancing or transcendental implications. But above all traditional narratives have generated in certain readers and listeners the firm conviction that other worlds (i.e., patterns of experience) exist, the worlds where these stories take place, beyond the world in which most of us spend our lives, and that it is possible to enter these worlds and draw strength from them. Michael Metzgar speaks of the power of fairytales to induce an individual "to change his own way of being."[3] When this concept is firmly planted, a significant shift in perception occurs—away from judging fairytales by how well they conform to our world, to judging our world by how well it measures up to the possibilities offered by certain other realities.

Perhaps the most celebrated study of fairytales in recent decades has been the late Bruno Bettelheim's *The Uses of Enchantment*. This book has sold widely and has been acclaimed by both parents and experts in child training and therapy. And many of Bettelheim's analyses have literary importance as well—I am thinking especially of his remarks on Sindbad, on the frame story of *Thousand and One Nights*, and on "Tales of Two Brothers." But it must also be observed that the pronounced Freudianism of Bettelheim's work has raised many eyebrows.[4] Part of my own quarrel is with Bettelheim's view that there comes a time in the maturing process of every individual when he/she moves away from the fairytale mentality toward an adult view of the world.[5] Adults, I believe, continue to benefit by the enrichment and expansion of experience that popular tales offer. There is no time at which this material can be put aside as irrelevant. Old stories can call individuals at any stage of development to higher or richer experience.[6]

Closely related to this problem is Bettelheim's apparent acceptance of the values of the "modern world" as normative. His view that "fairy tales do not pretend to describe the world as it is" (25) reflects "modern" rational attitudes. The interest of this material—for me, anyway—lies precisely in the way it challenges norms and opens up new possibilities. Bettelheim, by contrast, stresses the importance of achieving a mature consciousness (23), enjoying "a rewarding, good life" (24), and finding one's place as an individual. He speaks of the need to develop the superego, learning to live in accordance with the reality principle, gaining "true" answers to one's questions (47), and finding out "what the world is really like" (45). He notes the importance of learning to view reality "in an adult way" (51), integrating the personality, and developing a self of which one can be "unambivalently proud" (69). The point is not that we are ready to reject these values now—nothing very solid is in place yet as a substitute. But we must recognize that they represent a *modern* way of thinking being challenged today by various postmodern thinkers and deconstructionists, whose views promise to introduce new elements into the debate about the use of traditional narrative.

I am aware that these terms—*postmodern* and *deconstructionist*—have many meanings, and many of them I welcome to this discussion. I am taking 'postmodernism' to represent, in its most essential form, the view that all the constructs/assumptions/philosophical positions/metanarratives that have been laid on us by the modern world are to be opened up to question once again. They are to be seen as no more valid than any of a number of other assumptions that might be accepted or adopted. This seems to imply that we are all becoming aware of the fragility of any narrative we construct or of any position we might assume from which to look at our world(s). And it suggests that myth speaks from a broad, authoritative point of view; fairytale more tentatively and with a narrower focus. 'Deconstruction' I take to mean the rejection of not only old patterns but the very notion that we must depend on patterns, the search for alternate possibilities. This does not mean—to me, anyway—cynicism or negativism. Rather, it evokes a hopeful, optimistic frame of mind, the faith that various ministructures can be found within which satisfaction lies and creative work can be carried out.

Now it may be objected that traditional narrative seems to be based on some rather rigid patterns. For the narrator this is in some sense true, although he/she can never know what positions an audience will bring to the hearing of the story. But the story itself invariably describes individuals who are *feeling their way*, who have not heard their own stories, and who have absolutely no way of knowing how they will turn out. So the premodern ignorance of how things are blends with the postmodern insistence that the patterns we thought were there are not really there, after all.[7]

Something more needs to be said about this process of blending the old and the new, and I make the following points:

1. Many of the important concerns of contemporary scholarship (especially in religion, psychology, social psychology, and ethics) as it studies emergent human experience are linked with motifs that also figure prominently in traditional narrative. The human will, the ongoing interpretation of everyday data which we all engage in, dreaming, problem-solving, networking, social behavior, the structure of the personality, relations with the environment, and all kinds of negotiating procedures are areas that have attracted the interest of both modern thinkers/researchers and traditional storytellers. As Maria Tatar observes, "fairy tales translate (however roughly) psychic realities into concrete images, characters, and events."[8] This state of affairs suggests that many of the possibilities described in traditional stories are open to human beings in our world. This issue I will deal with throughout the book.

2. Another way of drawing the link between traditional tales and modern needs is to suggest that the structure of the situations described in old stories often replicates and intensifies the structure of ordinary experience. This may come as a surprise to those who believe that traditional tales are dominated by the supernatural or otherwise nonrealistic material. At the structural level, however, everything seems very sober indeed. Structural factors transcend the truth/fiction dichotomy. And when we grasp the structure of a story we may also grasp that story's life-enhancing implications. More about this in chapter 2.

3. We recognize that the characters, settings, events described in popular narrative also constitute a coherent world of their own, a world many fantasists have described and many very real individuals have chosen to inhabit. When such a choice is made, that other world can quickly envelop an individual and his life-goals.

In dealing with this third point, this third kind of connection between human experience and traditional narrative, I may be allowed certain personal reflections. My own initial experience of world-expanding beyond the obvious things on the "maps" being supplied me was the result of contact with *My Bookhouse*, a collection of poems, fairytales and folktales, legends and biographies, illustrated delicately and evocatively, which was popular children's fare in the 1920s. I came into possession of a set at an extremely tender age, when emotions ruled my nature and when the closets and backstairs and attic rooms of my grandparents' house were all invitations to other realities. I still turn to these precious, battered volumes for orientation, refreshment, and inspiration: to open any volume of that set has always meant entering another world. No context I have inhabited has gone untouched by it. Among other things, *My Bookhouse* nurtured certain sensibilities which made particularly meaningful to me, when I was very young, the return of an uncle from the Middle East after many years' absence, and a further broadening of my sense of the range of experience that might be open to me. That man spoke often of a distant place called "Angora," and it is in Ankara (the more modern form of the name), strangely enough, that I write these words, over half a century later. No one else on the scene knew about the lines of force that were passing to me, a tiny five-year-old, from that splendidly romantic individual. Yet his appearance began to open up power sources I have continued to exploit all my life, and over the years he broadened enormously the physical context in which my life has been lived. These early experiences, all belonging to what Gendlin has called the "preconceptual" stage of development,[9] motivated my later "professional" interest in old narratives, and they meant, inevitably, that professional concerns were never uncolored by personal involvement.

Since those very early days I have encountered many versions of what was so moving in *My Bookhouse* and my uncle's reappearance, none more poignant, more capable of enhancing the ordinary than a passage in C. S. Lewis's autobiography, *Surprised by Joy*. Lewis has been discussing certain early childhood experiences that gripped him with extraordinary power and pushed out the bounds of his own experience—how the flowering of a currant bush stirred thoughts of the Garden of Eden; how Beatrix Potter's animal stories helped him "possess" the idea of Autumn; and how Longfellow's sagas and the music of Wagner aroused in him a sense of the North—something "cold, spacious, severe, pale, and remote."[10] These "stabs of Joy" finally coalesced into a settled way of looking at the world when he read George MacDonald's *Phantastes*:

Even when real clouds or trees had been the material of the vision, they had been so only by reminding me of another world; and I did not like the return to ours. But now I saw the bright shadow coming out of the book into the real world and resting there, transforming all common things and yet itself unchanged. Or, more accurately, I saw the common things drawn into the bright shadow (*Surprised by Joy*, 181).

"Bright shadow" goes back to Shelley's "Alastor" and was picked up from MacDonald by Lewis. It seems an appropriate designation for the transcendental region this book deals with, a world that embraces searches and quests, secret doors and casement windows, poverty and wealth, puddles and lamps, twilight and dawn—as well as grandmothers, flea-market types, craftsmen, poets, third sons, and sometimes encountered individuals who resemble Mozart. All for the most part very ordinary beings, but all messages from another world (if one chooses to postulate such a reality and so populate it), strangely, incomprehensibly significant to some real-world individuals.[11]

A compelling case for admitting various abnormal dimensions to our experience has been made by contemporary social scientists. For example, it has been argued that anything like full integration of the human personality is possible only for those who can envision and move easily within multiple worlds. Thus the anthropologist Gregory Bateson has suggested that transcontextual gifts (the ability to move between different levels or types of reality) are a vital element in creativity and that inability to move across contexts is one of the roots of schizophrenia.[12] The Iranian analyst Reza Arasteh has observed that "all Western and Eastern ways of attaining maturity in the adult personality have recognized as an essential quality the ability to become aware of multiple realities." The individual who knows only one world lacks psychic material of sufficient richness and complexity; he/she cannot achieve a level of personality integration appropriate to the demands of the modern world.[13] And the philosopher Paul Feyerabend argues that only by inventing dream worlds can we *"discover the features of the real world we think we inhabit."*[14] Traditional world views, he feels, "can be used to modify, and even to replace the 'scientific' cosmologies of a given period" (46).

Traditional narrative describes many points of entry into other worlds. A careful examination or close reading of one's environment, such as modern education rarely equips individuals to undertake, is the initial experience-broadening activity for some people, allowing them to examine the unusual capacities for observation demonstrated by many characters in traditional narrative and bringing to their attention many important but easily overlooked elements of their own worlds (chapters 3, 4). For others an expansion of experience is tied to various moves along whatever "edges" their worlds offer them, of which, of course, travel is an obvious symbol (chapter 5). For still others, the enhancement of experience means primarily the struggle against enchantment and all that threatens consciousness and alertness (chapter 6). Certain individuals realize this broadening and transcending and deepening as they come into contact with peculiar forms of power the bright-shadow world offers, especially the power of the will (chapter 7), or as they make various moral commitments that differ from those we make in this world (chapter 8). One price of the enlarging of experience which I am postulating may be a certain reimaging of the nature of the human personality, the unsettling realization that it is not nearly so stable as had been imagined (chapter 9), but one of the rewards is the discovery of rarely exploited sources of knowledge (chapter 10). Problem-solving techniques related to rarely used mental abilities are described in chapter 11, matters of behavior and style in chapter 12.

My sources for this study of some of the broader, more exotic ranges of human experience are traditional tales—folktales and fairytales, especially those that have reached us through Europe from South Asia and the Middle East. Occasionally I have cited analogues from East Asian and American Indian lore, as well as from various modern fantasists for whom other worlds are more than mere fictions. I have made considerable use of the great ethnic collections of story, such as *Ocean of the Streams of Story*, *Jataka*, and *Thousand and One Nights*, and more rarely of literary compilations, such as those of Basile and Boccaccio, most—if not all—of whose stories have a popular origin. However, I must emphasize that I am not writing here as a folklorist but as one interested in the structure of experience—in studying the elements of their lives that human beings deem significant and how they put these pieces together. This means sometimes using the most authentic available folkloric texts but at other times turning to material that is modern or literary in nature. (I am aware that the dichotomy I have set up here may not be to everyone's liking.) My chief criterion for including material is that it has appealed for extended periods of time to a variety of listeners, children and adults, naive and sophisticated, who have used these tales in thinking about their experience or in making their own imaginative reconstructions of reality. The key I use is not truth about origins (important as that may be in other areas of narrative study) but the perception of many (as revealed by the broad acceptance of a tale) that bizarre as the events narrated may be they do say something profoundly important and appealing about the way we humans organize the material that life offers us. I could be more specific if I knew, myself, why certain of the original Oz books by L. Frank Baum fire the ardor and imagination of so many young readers whereas the continuations by Ruth Plumly Thompson make little if any impression at all—or why the Dr. Seuss books, for all the wisdom they offer, seem to have little of the charm or magic of Beatrix Potter. Perhaps the contrast has something to do with the distinction between fancy and imagination, or between what is "made up" and what is somehow always there.[15]

I am not the only one to have grappled with this question. The problem runs all through Roger Sale's *Fairy Tales and After*. Robertson Davies makes a distinction between genuine fantasy and "faked fantasy."[16] In his book on Gandhi, Erik Erikson observes that a parable may have "an intrinsic *actuality* much superior to any question of *factual* occurrence."[17] Jalal ad-Din Rumi, the great Islamic poet-mystic, notes in his *Mathnawi*, "I (had) found the reality: what (use to me) is the clue?"[18] And Lewis observes, in his preface to MacDonald's *Phantastes*, that reading a certain text added nothing to his grasp of a particular theme since he had already "received the myth."[19] Once a myth becomes part of a person's belief-structure, it takes on a life of its own and its point of origin as a moral/psychological truth is of less importance than its power over that particular individual. Our interest here is in material that contributes to the experience-enhancing process of the individual whose life is surrounded and continuously enriched by traditional narrative, and truth here is a matter of proximity to actual human experience rather than source.

A question may be raised about the validity of any challenge to our normal, rational view of experience constructed from such a range of sources as I have just outlined. Can there be any agreement among widely scattered individuals about the nature of human experience, about other dimensions of reality that might be available to us? As George MacDonald observes in *At the Back of the North Wind*, "the fact is, we have different reports of the place from the most trustworthy people."[20] On the other hand, children's games, which always replicate or anticipate some adult reality, follow similar patterns around the world. When we examine the folk arts, we observe that given similar materials and similar limitations of technique, similar products emerge in widely scattered parts of the globe. Certain Turkish and Tunisian tapestries of mine are invariably identified by my friends as American Indian in origin. It has often been observed that mystics, whether Christian, Hindu, or Muslim, share similar experiences. Moreover, Jungian psychology pursues the collective unconscious around the world, and the Aarne-Thompson *Types of the Folktale* is a staggering monument to the existence of cultural parallels among folk of the most diverse regions, a convincing demonstration of the worldwide "migration of tales" so assiduously pursued by nineteenth-century scholars. A tale is not accepted into another culture unless it speaks to some important reality in that culture.[21]

I believe that the material I have collected may be of interest to cognitive behaviorists, who make connections between the picture we have of reality and our response to it, and who believe that we can act creatively on the basis of data that we receive. To those interested in children's literature, since I make a case for the continuing importance of certain genres normally associated only with the very young. To religious thinkers, who should always be listening for "rumors of angels." To futurists, who need to be reminded of the humane aspects of their discipline. And to general readers, who may find something here to encourage their continuing exploration of all that can enhance their own experience.

2 A Way of Proceeding

Lessing has said that, if God held all truth in His right hand, and in His left the lifelong pursuit of it he would choose the left hand.
—S. Kierkegaard, *Concluding Unscientific Postscript*

Methodology is what should come here now, what I tell my students to do next. It is a grand-sounding concept, too grand for this spot or this book, which makes much of the Feyerabendian hostility to method and advocates an informal (though certainly informed) inspection of the world, as well as various ways of knowing and problem-solving that are never taught in the schools. Nevertheless, the problem of procedure merits some attention. As already noted, I plan to give considerable attention to parallels between the concerns of contemporary scholarship and motifs in traditional tales, to the way the structure of old stories replicates the structure of our experience, and to the possibility that we have enough material about "reality" in the fairytale to construct a "world" out of it. But right now we need an instrument for looking at specific tales.

Since the publication in 1958 of an English translation of Propp's *Morphology of the Folktale*[1] there has developed a vast semiotic and narratological literature on the structure of fairytales, folktales, and other traditional narratives. The ultimate goal, it is said, has been the development of a universal narrative grammar or lexicon; that is, a descriptive classification of all existent narrative events, a formula that would enable students to detect immediately the structure of a given tale. Among biblical scholars, many of whom have espoused this movement enthusiastically, a somewhat more modest goal exists—the elucidation of the meaning of texts. While a detailed examination of this critical technique would seriously divert us from our purpose here, it is important to describe, however briefly, the instrument Propp devised, working with Afanas'ev's *Russian Fairy Tales*. Propp sought to identify the laws according to which folk narratives are constructed or to which they adhere, and he approached this problem by identifying some thirty-one "functions" (activities of characters) that appear in folk narrative and seven "spheres of action" (such as villain, helper, dispatcher, and hero) "who" carry out these activities. The analysis of a particular tale meant an examination of the way elements of both of these factors were combined. No later approaches to the structure of the folktale have been made without Propp in mind, and many, including the proposals of Lévi-Strauss, Greimas, and Kongas and Maranda, have sought some kind of mathematical formula through which to depict symbolically what is going on in a given tale and to suggest the common structure of all tales.

A repeated criticism of Propp has been that while his lineal diagrams—"strings" as they are sometimes called—may reveal the external form or shape of a narrative action, this so-called syntagmatic approach does little to illuminate structural elements that may lie beneath the surface of a text. Such submerged elements often enter into rich and complex relationships with each other and may ultimately determine the "meaning" of a narrative. This problem the so-called paradigmatic approach, associated with Lévi-Strauss, sought to deal with. Lévi-Strauss argued in a well-known article, "L'Analyse Morphologique des Contes Russes," that Proppean formalism neglected or sacrificed content, whereas his own structuralist approach saw form and content as inseparable elements in a literary text.[2]

Any scheme by which the structure of narrative is analyzed must be simple to record, bring out forcefully the essential elements of a given story, facilitate some kind of classification of stories, and clarify similarities and differences between existing versions of the same type. The symbolic equations through which linguistic analysts often present their results have proven to be baffling and frustrating to many students of traditional narrative. So I serve up my results in narrative form, keeping the narrative very brief so that contrasts and comparisons, where required, are readily made. Finding the appropriate abstraction level at which to work is tricky business, and I keep my key instruments of analysis at a high level of abstraction, hoping thereby to avoid the overspecificity (thirty-one, seven) of Propp's scheme. The categories on which I base my analysis are actors, vectors, power sources, physical context, and denouement. These elements, plus our sense of the relationship between them, constitute a phenomenon that is appropriately called "narrative structure."

1. *Actors* are the key element in every story-situation, and there seems to be almost no limit to the roles that may be identified. They are a key determinant in the general situation being studied.[3] I prefer

to make actors rather than functions (Propp's term) the centerpiece of my analysis, if only because the former does not suggest the need for any limiting of their possible number. Each of these actors may perform a variety of acts in a given tale. Actors may be fathers or mothers, sons or daughters, thinkers or fighters, dragons, foxes, soldiers, third sons, kings, princesses, witches, trolls, etc. There is no point in distinguishing between animals and humans, and it is easy enough to think of cases where some mechanical device also becomes an actor. Actors initiate or respond to the goings-on in a particular context; they have experiences and they reflect on experiences; their lives are damaged or enhanced, and they damage or enhance the lives of others. Actors in both our world and the worlds of the popular tale perceive, guide, initiate, withdraw, wound/threaten, tease/riddle, quest, suffer, resist, rescue, imprison, withdraw, plan/scheme, yield, defy, deceive, warn, comfort, etc. The possible activities are limitless but within a given writer's work somewhat consistent. (Kafka's actors as a group perform actions that differ from the actions of the actors of Dickens and Hemingway.) Separating the major from the minor actors and actors from their masks and describing how actors relate to each other and how they function solitarily can be complicated and productive tasks.

2. *Vectors* are the lines of force that pass back and forth between the actors (and other elements in the situation), influencing, pressuring, communicating—in short, connecting. The image is an arrow. A splendid example is to be found in the Grimm Brothers' story "The Juniper" as birds who saw a mother kill her son drive her mad by reminding her endlessly, "My mother, she killed me."[4] Under vectors I would place ideas, concepts, and facts that are exchanged; feelings of every variety; understandings and misunderstandings; efforts to clarify, persuade, or confuse; whatever hurts or relieves, penetrates or elicits, evokes trust or doubt; acceptances, rejections, expectations, confusions and uncertainties, resentments, judgments, controls, etc.—in short, the myriad thrusts that make up human negotiations. These pressures are among the most important elements in the structure of any situation, whether real or fictional. In their potency lies the possibility of some enhancement of the lives of certain "actors"— and the further possibility that images of this potency may be passed along to those who read or hear a particular story.[5]

3. *Power sources* provide the motivation and energy through which a given situation works itself out and into which the individuals involved may tap. The image is a mine—coal or gold, perhaps—or an electricity-generating plant.

4. *The physical context* includes all the material elements in a given space that assist, impede, or simply exist in a situation, that make action possible, and around or through which individuals must somehow make their way. This dimension suggests how powerful is the human sense of space.[6] A mountain range is an appropriate image.

5. *The denouement* is the dramatic moment of coming together or unraveling of events that emerges from the interplay of the four previous items, tying them together. This is the part of the story that makes children scream with delight or mock terror and that even adults who have heard the tale a thousand times never cease to enjoy.

These five elements constitute a paradigm that enables us to analyze fairytales and folktales productively, that is, to grasp the basic pattern of experience a given story is presenting and the human interactions being described. This is a simple, direct scheme that does not rely on symbols and supports a conventional reading of texts: it focuses on content but insists as well on seeing the structural implications of content. It works by stimulating active thought about the structure of a situation, the elements that are central to it and their interplay with each other. Its peculiar emphasis brings out effectively the dynamic elements in the story, and the five elements that are central come as close to universals as anything I can imagine. This formula is particularly well suited to traditional narrative since it emphasizes external factors, being less concerned with inward experience than the formula linked with Dilthey, for example.[7] It is an experiential rather than a literary mode of analysis, according well with the purposes of this book. That is, it permits discussion of narrative without imposing any presumed structure on narrative. And it seems to ease a narrative problem noted by Ruth Bottigheimer in her book on the Grimm Brothers: the fact that similar plots can be made to tell quite different stories. When we identify actors, vectors, power sources, physical context, and denouement, there can be little doubt as to the intent of a particular narrative. At the very least, we can identify clearly the source of any ambiguity.[8] And if, for purposes of contrast or classification, we set several such analyses side by side, in the most succinct form possible, we can see at a glance where various versions take the story. Appendix I provides a detailed analysis of the major combinations of these elements in traditional narrative. There seem to be many more functions than Propp recognized, combined in a variety of ways that produces the kind of bewildering array of possibilities that would have delighted Kierkegaard and continues to be dear to the hearts of postmodernists.

It is tempting to argue that Lessing's statement, quoted by Kierkegaard, implies that the chase is worth more than the prize. But I think it means more than that. Lessing seems to offer us a kind of Whiteheadian God, really committed to being part of the process, not much interested in the prize itself but in the way the nature of the prize shifts about as it is pursued. This accords well with the spirit of traditional tales and with the program of postmodernism.

3 On Reading the World: Jus' Settin' 'n' Rockin'

I had often seen pilots gazing at the water and pretending to read it as if it were a book; but it was a book that told me nothing. A time came at last, however, when Mr. Bixby seemed to think me far enough advanced to bear a lesson on water-reading.
>—Mark Twain, *Life on the Mississippi*

I loaf and invite my soul.
>—Walt Whitman, *Leaves of Grass*

In days of old, every sound still had sense and meaning.
>—The Brothers Grimm

One of the key "actors" in traditional narrative is the observer, the onlooker, the quiet and informal assessor of everyday affairs. Today he may assume the role of a country newspaper editor enjoying his rocking chair, a baseball manager studying a pitcher's delivery, or a farmer noting the weather. But this role is not as important as it once was. We prefer to receive our information in print, already digested, and centuries of reading have made it difficult for us to draw significant conclusions from observation. But lovers of fairy-tales and folktales are familiar with something quite different: the quester who must find a way into the heavily guarded castle with no advice from anyone, the courtier seeking a clue about his fate in his monarch's face, the bright young rogue determined to escape a pattern that has doomed others before him. Like the modern scientist, the editor, the manager, the farmer, the loafer, the quester, and the rogue have a feeling for "an infrastructure of some kind, that is, a patterning of activity, a structural formula that is repeated throughout the course of [an] activity" (Goffman, 493). Of course such insights are implicit rather than explicit, subconscious rather than conscious, informal rather than informed.

In the bright-shadow world careful observation can be highly productive, for that world proves enormously legible when approached in a quiet, attentive manner with a minimum of preconceptions, when the eyes are allowed to roam and be "true windows"[1] and the soul is "invited" by a loafing body. I am not talking about absolute legibility but about a legibility relative to one's own culture, the ability to grasp its elements and their relationships, a legibility even certain constructive forms of postmodernism would be willing to concede. For example, the lines of postmodern architecture are sharp and clear, but the "message" of the building may be very puzzling. The concept of "writerly reading" is relevant here, a process that, according to Mary Wiseman, is characterized by a constant changing of the lenses through which one reads and the starting points to which one has grown accustomed (Shapiro, 30).

It was the life-work of John Dewey, a Vermonter, to draw human thinking away from abstract theory toward the world of real experience—"the planted field, the sowed seeds, the reaped harvests, the changes of night and day, spring and autumn, wet and dry, heat and cold, that are observed, feared, longed for."[2] George Lakoff has called our attention to a "psychologically basic level" (Lakoff, 33) of reality, where things are perceived holistically and remembered more easily. Another important spokesman for the field of everyday psychology was Fritz Heider, whose work has been described as an "investigation of the naive psychology implicit in everyday language or expressed in literary, philosophical, and common-sense propositions concerning interpersonal relations."[3] Heider himself said, "We note the properties of objects, their visibility, appearance, and underlying reality; we are aware of mediating conditions and factors within the person that influence perception. We may be concerned with the circumstances or underlying conditions of these conditions. The knowledge of these conditions bears upon our actions."[4]

Michel Foucault has described his interest in the code of knowledge obeyed by "errors (and truths) . . . old beliefs, including not only genuine discoveries, but also the most naive notions." The field of Foucault's concern includes taxonomies or classifications other than those we are accustomed to, a recognition of the possibility that the orders we are taught are "perhaps not the only ones or the best ones." Some of the classifications and categories developed by traditional world readers may be implied here. Paul Feyerabend, with a sense of the importance of physical realities that rivals Dewey's, praises Galileo for his use of "the whole rich reservoir of . . . everyday experience" in developing his astronomical theories and for "a style, a sense of humour, an elasticity and elegance, and an awareness of the valuable weaknesses of human thinking" unequaled in the history of science. Like Dewey, Feyerabend suggests that the purpose of any interpretation of reality should be to establish contact with actual phenomena. And Adriaan D. de Groot, in discussing the development of theories of intelligence, has suggested the importance of "looking around" at various creative processes for data. Relaxed (but directed) observation can yield data of importance even in the most formal contexts, he asserts.[5]

D. C. Dennett criticizes folk psychology as inferior to the rational, goal-oriented attitude he advocates in *The Intentional Stance* (1987). Yet he deals at length with folk material because it does exist and thus is a fact of anthropology; because it embodies certain of the myths we live by; because, like much of folk science, it may be incorporated into academic psychology. He also notes that in certain areas it may be "extraordinarily reliable in its predictive power." "Folk psychology," he concludes, "might best be viewed as . . . an idealizing, abstract, instrumentalistic method that has evolved because it works and works because we have evolved."[6] It works because we treat each other as rational, and indeed "we are pretty rational" (50).[7]

The view of many modern observers that the "real" modern world and its methods enjoy some metaphysical priority over worlds that naive people notice from their quiet posts has been held by only a very few people for a brief period of time. Its results have been far from uniformly life-enhancing. Countless other worlds have been imaged throughout history and have functioned effectively for those who worked them out. Each has its own claims to reality, claims generally disregarded today because in solving certain problems the scientific or objective method has proven enormously successful. Happily, there are signs that for other kinds of problems, other kinds of solutions are being considered or reconsidered, solutions that take into account the wisdom of even preliterate peoples.

To open up this important topic, I turn to an examination of the simple act of observing in three very different contexts in which several very different individuals found themselves. My claim is that direct observation, even though it may be untrained (as it usually is in traditional narrative), can provide valuable resources for the reconstruction of our experience along new lines. In *The Book of Proof*, al-Jahiz, the great ninth-century Iraqi exponent of *adab* (humanistic belles lettres), tells the story of the loss of a great jewel in a public square. A frantic search is made by the owner and her friends, and two nearby ascetics are accused of the theft. They face bodily harm until a casual passerby asks about the problem. He observes an ostrich in the square and concludes that it has swallowed the jewel. The bird is slaughtered, and the jewel is indeed found in its stomach, smaller in size but with a color marvelously heightened by the bird's digestive processes.[8]

In *Old Deccan Days* Miss Frere, a nineteenth-century collector of Indian stories, recounts an anecdote from the life of the great Indian hero Rama, who is traveling about with his friend and wazir, Luxman, and generally missing all the important sights. Rama fails to see that a banyan tree under which they are passing is about to fall on the road, and he is saved only when Luxman, remembering the warning of an owl, whisks him to safety just in time. Rama is also blind to danger when he rests at the base of a tottering stone wall, and later, when the wazir licks cobra venom off the forehead of the prince's wife, Rama thinks the wazir is kissing her.[9] Despite his high repute in Indian mythology, Rama in this version from the Deccan is depicted as totally inept at picking up hints, noting signs, making connections, sorting out possibilities, grasping the dynamics of situations—in short, at making sense of his world. But of course there is always the possibility that Rama was at work on another taxonomy!

A third example comes from the nineteenth-century Scottish fantasist George MacDonald, who has delighted both children and adults with his imaginative powers. I have already noted C. S. Lewis's tribute to him. At one point in *At the Back of the North Wind* Little Diamond, a young lad familiar with out-of-body experiences, is struggling to put the saddle, collar, and yoke on a horse much too big for him to manage. But he is making a valiant effort, and certain men who are watching him do not interfere, for "they were so anxious to see how he would get over the various difficulties" (220). It is not that they are unfriendly—eventually, they do come to Diamond's assistance—but at this point curiosity about some tiny detail of the world, how one human being will manage, dominates their thinking.

How different these three physical contexts are from ours, and yet how keenly the actors carry out their acts of perception in each! Certain Iraqi villagers stare at a scene uncomprehendingly, various women search frantically for the lost jewel, two ascetics wonder how they ever became involved, and one passerby studies the situation intently. Luxman's eyes are open to any harm that may befall his imperceptive master as they travel casually about. And certain men lounging in a London stableyard study coolly a young lad's problem-solving technique.

The structural contrast between the observer/actor and all the other figures on the scene in the al-Jahiz story is striking. He is an assured person too, for it is a big and risky leap from the possibility to the actuality. His is a simple context, and when he accounts for all the possibilities, he can act. Luxman's eyes are open to any harm that may befall his master, who is not even aware of the care being taken of him as he stumbles imperceptively through his context. Little Diamond lives in a world that is somewhat benign, even though he is forced to do a man's work and is doomed to a short life. As they watch him, his friends also watch out for him; they are willing to let him struggle, as we might not today, but they are there to help, and they watch intensely for his signals. Diamond may see them there, at the side, and perform for them.

The structural pattern in all of these stories is quite similar: the physical context is diffuse, poorly defined, crowded with people who are uncertain about their roles and with objects whose purpose is unclear, requiring definition by those involved. The premodern world was this way, and the postmodern world is too. One actor stands out by virtue of his intensity and his ability to see the *significant* details—why is the ostrich wandering around here? why does the wazir seem to be kissing the woman? is the boy able to manage that strap? The denouement of each anecdote is linked to these questions. The power source in every case is insight, and the vectors are projections of aid and curiosity into the situation. Such factors are helped along by the rocking-chair mentality, and sometimes, too, by low levels of literary education, highly restricted fields of activity, a lot of opportunity to "shoot the breeze." I link skill in this kind of world-reading with practical people whose capacity to observe and make connections has not been damaged or destroyed by literary culture.[10] What has been learned? The power of the educated guess. That things are—and are not—what they seem. That everyone has his or her own approach to a problem.

Among educated modern adults, this kind of reflecting is usually encountered through the language of gamesmanship and conflict resolution. Only in the last few decades, with the work of Eric Berne and Thomas Schelling, among others, have we begun to understand conflict situations, where the vectors do seem particularly clear. Something of this world-reading spirit may be found, too, among computer hackers, who delight in exploring possibilities and sharing their discoveries, even when they cannot see the full significance of them. These young whizzes have alert minds, share a considerable amount of data among themselves, and operate easily within networks of great complexity, where new pathways are constantly opening up.[11] It may be that our lack of interest today in world-reading is one reason why we find ourselves so constantly pressured by events, experiencing inner chaos, missing the possibiliites for transcendence that open up to us. To this inability, too, may be traced our limited repertoire of possible behaviors in difficult situations and our lack of experience of other realities.

But in the popular literature under discussion here, we constantly encounter bright people like Luxman and the Iraqi traveler, reflecting on their worlds, observing structures, examining cases, developing their own classifications. The "folk" are born phenomenologists. Thus from a well known collection of Middle-Eastern teaching stories, I glean such expressions as "to extend his experiences of life . . . try conclusions . . . the greater ranges of existence . . . the inexplicable contrariness of the world . . . the inner correspondence of things . . . essential qualities of a situation"—all of which suggest the world-reading mindset.[12] And even today one still hears, especially from older people, questions like "Have you ever noticed how . . . when?" or "Why is it that worrying about something seems to ensure that it will never happen?" Such questions bring to mind the figure from *Thousand and One Nights* who was always fascinated by the "strangeness" of things.[13] My students, who have not amassed the quantity or quality of experience needed to think about such structural problems, are stuck with the far less productive question, "How can I be sure that this is right?"—a question that seriously limits their experience and effectively wipes out all the rich possibilities inherent in being wrong. Or, if one is an academician, "How can I be sure that my methodology is sufficiently sophisticated?"

I do not want to make a case for the importance of naive psychology by distinguishing it absolutely from more sophisticated ways of viewing the world. We all are "folk," and no matter how great our expertise in a given area, we do revert at critical times to absolutely basic ways of dealing with problems. How does a physician deal with an illness that threatens his own life? A clergyman with his own crisis of belief? An art-museum director with the problem of decorating his own house? If a need to revert to basic responses did not exist, there would be no point at all in arguing for the importance of fairytales and folktales.

Naive world-reading is of course more than a question of picking up information. Like phenomenology, it means "a certain way of patterning the world" (Merleau-Ponty), or, as Heider observes, it involves also the kind and degree of one's contact with the world (how deeply is one embedded? for example), the awareness of another's needs, the kind of mediation (i.e., how what you perceive makes its effect upon you) available, the capacity of the receiver to process information and fit it into his/her own construct, and the way he/she interprets and gives meaning to the data (p. 23 ff.). Productive naive reading also means being attuned to a very special kind of information—lots and lots of free-floating data that is still largely unprocessed. In the past, country folk, whose knowledge grows largely from their contact with sky and soil, seem to have carried on this kind of reflection quite naturally, gaining thereby most unusual insights. I suppose one could argue that the staggering variety of fairies and goblins with which the folk have populated their world is the result of just such a process of reflecting and reading, for every kind of creature has its own characteristics and responsibilities—be it banshee, black dog, blue man, bodach, brownie, church grim, cowry, derrick, elf, ratchet, kobol, phooka, shriker, or troll.[14] But even more significant than such products of the fertile imagination and unspoiled observations of the folk is the very careful manner in which they arrange or structure their world. Are not the ballads that have come down to us from so many sources products of endless organizing and review of the same material until it is just right—the dramatic moment firmly established, the characters both individuals and representatives, and all the available pathos wrung from the event?

An anthropologist friend, Andrea B. Rugh, describes how the poor women of Bulaq, a district of Cairo rich in history, go over and over their life stories, combining recurrent patterns, clarifying roles of various people, streamlining and highlighting narratives. This process resembles writerly reading, reading that is always responding to, rearranging, a text, refusing ever to accept its finality. It is this kind of fully informed but nonexpert intelligence that inspires comedians and creates almanacs and superstitions based on observed connections between events, some of which prove to have considerable reliability when they are scrutinized scientifically.[15] Computer hackers pin up on bulletin boards the observations they have made, the use of which they may not yet perceive, in the hope that someone else can fit them into a developing pattern. And a similar *modus operandi* has been observed in the international intelligence community today.

World-reading at its most skillful is frequently depicted in that great collection of South Asian folktales, the *Jataka* tales or Buddhist birth stories—anecdotes about the various incarnations of the Buddha. Here can be found shrewd advice about getting on in the world and picking up hints about one's situation even when almost no solid information is provided and when the operative reality can only be inferred. For example, a physician examines an elephant that has been behaving badly, finds no physical problem, and concludes that it has overheard human conversation and thereby been perverted. This is a daring leap at possibility, though not perhaps in the direction we would take today. The dominant actor, a highly observant individual, identifies issues (vectors) in the physical context no one had yet thought of.[16] A partridge, mule, and elephant live together until they begin to lose mutual respect because they "had no ordering of their common life." Clearly all three are intelligent enough to spot some strains and take action to remedy their situation, a splendid example of individuals caught in a situation able to rise above it and view it objectively. A traveler sees a tree in a village, laden with fruit, and concludes that the fruit is poisonous; he warns his companions not to touch it, but some do and die. The wise man realized that had the fruit been good, the villagers would already have eaten it. The dominant actors could be expected to know well the power available in their context. And another Bodhisatta concludes, after learning that a servant has scrupulously returned to his master a straw from the master's roof (which stuck to his clothes), that the servant has stolen something of real value. Whence such striking insights? Heider observes that being in "direct contact with things and persons" in an environment is of great help in reading that world (22). Merleau-Ponty says that "sense experience is that vital comunication with the world which makes it present as a familiar setting of our life" (52). And M. Esther Harding asserts that it is possible to "summon feeling at will" and to "learn to feel correctly about a situation" (271). Common to all three analyses—Merleau-Ponty's, Heider's, Harding's—is the suggestion that the dominant vectors by which we gain knowledge in the modern world need to be reconnected to the actors and the physical context out of which they spring.

What structural elements stand out in these anecdotes that may relate to a productive reading of situations in general? Perhaps foremost is the importance of grasping the context of a problem, its setting, how the individuals involved in it must feel, what they are observing. Apparently the physician worked his way through several important assumptions: that animals have pure minds and spirits, that their only contacts are with other animals and with humans, that human beings are corrupting influences, and that mind and body—even in animals—are closely linked. Then he moved as surely to his conclusion as did the observer in the story of the ostrich. But how did he know that he was correct? Indeed, he may not have been sure, being confident only that if he changed one factor in the complex situation he might produce some overall improvement. The guess that elephant, mule, and partridge make about their problem is only a guess, but an intelligent one, and it again suggests the importance in all structural analyses of identifying the operative structural factor. In its context the unpicked fruit on the village tree should have been a red warning flag for any traveler, and the thieving servant actually seems compelled to call attention to his wrongdoing. But once again the leap of the observer from straw to something more serious is nothing short of brilliant. All of these stories conclude with the sudden click of insight confirmed.

Individuals who lack an awareness of the concatenation of events (as revealed in the cases of the physican and the traveler) find themselves shortchanged, mistreated, or dead; at best, they persist in responding to patterns they would have done well to see yesterday. But those who are skilled in world-reading can make adjustments to changing patterns that will elicit positive responses from those around them. Tiidu, a young ne'er-do-well in an Estonian tale, is contemptuous of older people and their ways and finds the world quite a hostile place. Acquiring a set of pipes, he discovers the joy of playing them and senses a world of kindness opening up before him. "For the first time the thought came to him: he had without knowledge and purpose wronged his parents in leaving his home, forsaking his family, and roaming like a tramp." But fortunately he has discovered the rich network of relationships in which he lives and is able to transcend such nonproductive relationships.[17] The story of Tiidu seems to point to the importance of recognizing and positioning oneself in a structure which may not, in computer language, be user friendly and then acting in accord with the vectors of that situation.

The key, of course, is to uncover the operative element, "the hierarchy of factors that influence people's actions."[18] For Heider, the student of commonsense psychology, these factors include our own perceptions and our perceptions of the perceptions of others, a sense of life-space, affects, causes, an awareness of one's ability to carry out a certain task, the willingness to attempt something, a period of germination, a sense of belonging, and an awareness of the interplay of obligation and possibility. These factors, which add up to a very subtle way of confronting the world, are frequently noted in traditional narratives. For example, Hasan, in "The Tale of Abu-al Din al-Shamat" from *Thousand and One Nights*, touches several of these bases when he describes the pattern his life has taken: "I went to one of the traders and borrowed of him a thousand dinars, wherewith I bought stuffs and carrying them to Damascus, sold them there at a profit of two for one. Then I bought Syrian stuffs and carrying them to Aleppo, made a similar gain of them; after which I bought stuffs of Aleppo and repaired with them to Baghdad, where I sold them with like result, two for one; nor did I cease trading upon my capital till I was worth nigh ten thousand ducats" (*1001*, IV, 39). In January 1981 I asked an old man in a Cairo taxi how he had made his money: "Commerce," he said without having to think for even a moment, "buying and selling." A capable actor, a physical context, a power source (goods, knowledge of demand), vectors (the joy of trading, ambition) moving back and forth, all linked by the old man's profound satisfaction with his life. No structure could be simpler, and of it my companion was a complete master!

It is hard to imagine the typical product of modern Western education demonstrating this kind of conceptual mastery of experience, reducing his/her career to such a simple pattern or even being aware of patterns. Mastery of a specific field, yes, but I am speaking here of a sense of the rhythms and relationships that have shaped one's total being-in-the-world. As a result has come a certain helplessness in facing the subtler structures of life, and we have little sense that our wills can alter situations. By contrast, in medieval Asia and the Middle East, the source of so much traditional narrative material, threats to personal safety lurked on every side, and only those survived who were astute about reading situations and faces, picking up patterns. Such celebrated classics as the *Panchatantra*, *Tuti-Nama*, and the *Fables of Bidpai* (*Kalilah and Dimnah*) were collections of stories, proverbs, and sundry observations designed to help young princes develop their capacity to read the world and survive in it. Such individuals knew nothing, of course, of "naive" and "sophisticated." This material was intensely practical in their eyes, and it stood at the forefront of human knowledge. World-reading, despite its aesthetic implications, can be practical for us too, at its best opening up a series of structures through which our experience can be enhanced, even remade.

Is it possible to identify some juncture in human history when this critical ability to decipher the world and guard oneself against its threats was lost?[19] It might be suggested that the Book of Genesis records such a moment, for when man was given permission to dominate his environment, he no longer felt any need to comprehend it. Perhaps world-reading stopped with Plato, who urged man to seek truths beyond their physical, material context. Perhaps with the medieval Church, which saw this world as primarily a symbol of spiritual truth. Foucault suggests that *Don Quixote* marks such a watershed (47–48). The process may have ceased with Descartes, who affirmed that his sense of being was rooted in abstract thought, not in contacts and observation. Perhaps the nineteenth-century brought an end to naive psychology, for when man acquired the physical power to "move mountains," he seems to have concluded that the scientific-technological context alone mattered.

When will we start to read the world again? There are many signs today that point to a renewed interest in such activity. It is the argument of this book that a familiarity with traditional narratives can alert us to the actors, the vectors, the power sources, certain physical realities, and the different outcomes of different activities that skilled readers have always been interested in. The traditional science of alchemy was such an effort, based, though, on inadequate data. John Dewey was an eloquent spokesman for an empiricism that studied the world directly, and postmodernists have attempted to quash the Cartesian claim. The same point may be made about sensitive modern science, which listens patiently to Nature, and about the ecology movement, which can be traced back through Rachel Carson to Thoreau, himself marvelously skilled at listening to the natural world. The modern revival of interest in writing and reading poetry reflects this trend too, as do educational curricula that encourage individuals to immerse themselves in other cultures or to make actual human experience the basis of their study, as Denton urges. Curiously enough, the development of a sense of matter-of-factness will also help, the kind of matter-of-factness that lies behind Miss Briggs's account of a chat between a fairy and an English farmer's wife in 1962. The fairy was dressed in green and had a round, smiling face. He didn't disappear, observed the wife; he just wasn't there any more. "A visitor from Hampshire suggested that it was a derrick. Derricks are ill-natured fairies in Devonshire, but it seems that in Hampshire they must be considered friendly."[20] One could go a long way on such a precise and discriminating reading of the world! The power source driving this precision and discrimination is the knowledge of fairy material the visitor from Hampshire manifests. We would call it lore, but in a traditional-rural context it is fact: it works. Main vectors are the sense of puzzlement felt by the farmer's wife and the assurance projected by the visitor. The latter overcomes the former, though the victory is not tested.[21]

4 Some Structural Possibilities

World-reading reaches any number of conclusions about any number of issues, as the preceding chapter has indicated. Certain of these conclusions stand out in a particularly vivid manner, however—motifs running all through traditional narrative; motifs linked in a special way to the enhancement of human experience. Here we consider four such issues: motifs that have to do with counting, with correspondences, with the balancing out of active and passive responses, and with anomalies. In its treatment of these issues, traditional narrative tends to shy away from modern rational responses, from the assumptions that dominate *our* thinking, and promotes instead highly original, spur-of-the moment constructions of the stuff of experience, which sometimes work surprisingly well.

Number Magic

Numbers constitute one of the most important structural elements in the world of the bright shadow, one of the legibilities most often noted, a useful factor in world-remaking. Many children's games involve counting. "It's happened twice, and I know it will happen again" is a bit of naive psychology still taken seriously in certain quarters. Jacob has twelve sons, Jesus has twelve disciples, and there are twelve dancing princesses. Seven has about it an aura of holiness.[1] In tales of the wanderer who picks up companions with special skills, there are often five such individuals, as if to imply that thereby any task could be accomplished, any danger overcome. Basile's *Pentamerone* is a collection of stories told in five days, and the *Panchatantra* consists of five books of animal fables. Forty is a useful way of suggesting a collection that is quite large; it implies that attention is to be accorded to the ensemble, not to individuals.

In all these cases, the modern interest in exact numbers gives way to something much more graphic, to the set or configuration like the six dots on a domino, or the quincunx, which so interested Sir Thomas Browne. The experience of sets, "figural perception," as Heider calls it (182), seems to be quite common whenever we move toward preliterate expertise, naive mastery of some gestalt. When I became familiar with my word processor and wanted to carry out a complicated operation, I no longer watched the screen as I went through a lineal process of key punching; instead I got the desired result by pressing a configuration of keys, much as a musician reduces a difficult rhythmic passage to a pattern of dum-de-dums. But in the bright-shadow world, much more than proficiency is at stake: the problem is to order or organize the world so that it can be understood, exploited, dealt with.[2]

Implied here is the notion that the numbers around which a culture constructs itself arise inevitably from important sets in that culture: Ten is important to human beings because we have ten fingers. Our year contains 365 days because that is the length of time it takes our earth to circle the sun. Were we closer, our year would be shorter, as might our week, our day, etc. Fantasists have imaged worlds based on the most bizarre numerical possibilities. In some cases, reality determines the way we count something; in still others, as I am about to argue, the way we count determines the reality we get.

In the bright-shadow world *three* is an important set, one of the basic elements in reality, a structural certainty to which storytellers return time and again. In popular narrative we constantly encounter groupings we know to be formed of three items without even counting them—sisters, wishes, sons, or trials—and we always know the outcome of the process in which this triad appears. Though the elements in the set are rarely more than slightly distinguished, they follow certain structural rules linked with threes. The third crack at something will succeed, and the third child is always different somehow from the other two. A world is a set of sets (or perhaps a set of set of sets . . .), and to perceive sets is to begin to perceive the world. The central actor (in a story) organizes his physical context numerically in a way that facilitates dealing with it.

In the semitropical regions from which a great deal of this material comes there are often only three seasons, and woman's life is seen as falling into three stages. The central Mediterranean deity is often a triple goddess. Sisters, wishes, fates come in threes. Water, earth, and sky make up the traditional cosmos. Three brothers set off on a quest for the golden bird; three times a questing figure disobeys a helpful advisor; for three nights a long-lost husband tries to penetrate the consciousness of his wife, who is about to marry another; three times a hero battles a giant; three times young men seek the princess atop a glass hill; in stories of the "East o' the Sun" type, the hero must seek advice from three hermits or old hags; in "Beauty and the Beast" tales, the beast-lover visits the young girl on three successive nights; and many jokes are based on patterns of threes.[3]

Thus it would appear that in the bright-shadow world the dynamic and creative qualities we treasure are somewhat reduced (three is not as rich in possibilities as multiplicity), but the creative element is rather more accessible. Tasks are fewer and more precisely defined, more confrontive, but also more quickly accomplished. Reality lies close at hand and appears less strange than it sometimes does to us. But I sense a certain ambiguity here. Part of me wants to be very objective about this and to assert that triplicity is central because the bright-shadow world is indeed built upon threes. But my more subjective side prefers to assert that triplicity is important to that world because people impose such an image upon it, for purposes of emphasis, coherence, even neatness. There is a mindset that sees threes in everything, even if it means cutting out some elements that don't fit or spinning out others that are a little thin. Thus we can suggest that the traditional tale sees reality as very much a product of human will and shaping, where vectors may be admitted or rejected on the basis of the decision of the entire community-as-actor.

It is clear that *objective* and *subjective* are not very helpful categories as we try to work our way into the structure of the bright-shadow world and that some middle ground is needed where "facts" are given a human coloring and feelings are in some way shaped by facts. In reality there may be only two sisters, but a third is needed by the storyteller to intensify the stress that every group of sisters feels. Or there may be four sisters, but three are enough to present the full range of good and evil. Or there may be a whole range of hostile feelings, but three may be all that the audience needs to hear about. In such cases sets may prove more useful than specific numbers, both to storytellers, who do pretty much as they wish anyway, and to observers within the bright-shadow world, who may see threes everywhere, just as Byzantine artists saw the sky as gold and medieval painters saw children as tiny adults. Fairytales can open up to us many new patterns, far more, indeed, than normal education suggests, giving us some confidence that other structures, however imaginative or unfamiliar they may be, are functional. A certain ex-

ultation, even a form of transcendence, may accompany the realization that several disparate elements have clicked into a set that fits
nicely into one's assumptions about reality.

"I Want One Just Like That"

The question of similarities and differences is an endless bother to
world-readers. We teach and learn by comparing and contrasting; we
evaluate and choose by examining similarities and differences; models of all kinds offer a recognizable reality within a new context—and
the same point might be made about poetic metaphors. Language
would not be possible did not we group objects under certain categories on the basis of significant similarities, but languages are difficult
because the environments in which they occur and the thought pro-
ceses out of which they develop differ so radically from people to
people. The sets we have been observing emerge from a powerful
sense that some things belong together; some don't. At certain levels
of abstraction set-making becomes very abstruse, highly technical indeed.[4]

Now we moderns have a strong feeling for similarities, but differences and distinctions are ultimately more important to us: our
education tends to the analytical rather than the analogical. The importance of sets in the bright-shadow world suggests that "there" the
reverse is true: similarities stand out, and objects which are too different are not even taken into account. Differences we might regard as
critical are ignored, and similarities that strike us as superficial become the basis for linking very diverse objects. Emile Durkheim, in
fact, regarded a concern with correspondences and analogies as one
of the basic marks of early religious life.[5]

Thus we find in traditional narrative the view that since lions
have courage, eating their meat will make an individual brave. According to alchemic theory the transformation of one metal to another
is possible through human intervention, because lead and gold have a
fundamental similarity. And similarities between the human and the
inanimate suggest the possibility of transforming minds and spirits as
well as metals. Obstacle-flight is a common motif in traditional tales,
another example of analogical thinking. In tales based on this motif,
the individual being pursued throws behind himself or herself various objects to delay pursuers, the discarded objects turning into natural forms that resemble in some way the originals. Thus earth thrown
at a pursuer becomes a mountain; water, a river; thorns (or a comb), a
forest; etc.

What is more, bright-shadow-world thinking is untroubled by the apples-oranges rule so important to us: categories are confused shamelessly on the basis of similarities that appear important to those experiencing them but hardly capable of standing the test of reality as we know it. A juror at the trial in *Alice in Wonderland* (not strictly speaking a traditional tale) adds together days fourteen, fifteen, and sixteen and converts the total to shillings and pence. A Yugoslavian peasant carries to his druggist the door on which a physician has written his prescription. And an Indian peasant who asks for a *paila* (a measure) of rice is given the weight and tries to boil *it*. More sophisticated individuals are content simply to draw moral parallels from physical facts. For example, in one of the *Jataka* tales, the Bodhisatta watches birds fighting with each other over bits of garbage. "These desires of ours are like pieces of meat," he reflects. "To those that grasp at them is sorrow, and to those that let them go is peace" (III, 67).

One of the most celebrated of all spiritual visionaries, dwellers in the world of the bright shadow, was the American Indian Black Elk (1863–1950), and the most celebrated incident of his life was his recreation as an adult of a boyhood vision, in a great public ceremony with horses and all the original celebrants on hand. Of this remarkable experience of duplication or correspondence extending across the years, Black Elk says, "I saw my vision yonder once again. . . . I knew the real was yonder and the darkened dream of it was here."[6] This experience of duplication sustained the great leader in the difficult work he was doing on behalf of his people against the increasingly serious threat of the white man: no matter what the problems here, this world was only a shadow of another, better reality.

The analogical mindset merits in some fashion its condemnation by the folklorist E. S. Hartland as "childish" and "savage."[7] But Jung discovered in alchemy a useful symbol of human transformation, and Eliot found in the image of the wasteland a symbol of moral decay— perhaps something more than a symbol. Our own wastefulness has indeed rendered our environment a desert. While we may smile at category mistakes like the Yugoslavian peasant's, we discover that some of our own groupings (true/false, good/evil) are not nearly subtle enough. And we recognize in the moralizing of the Bodhisatta the germs of poetic metaphor, without which any kind of subtle communication would be impossible.

It is clear that the issue hinges on the fact that the way phenomena are grouped in the bright-shadow world is quite different from the way things are assembled in our world. This itself is a sensitivity-enhancing realization. In *Alice* all numbers are grouped, without regard for what they might refer to, just because they are numbers, and the recipe for medicine, what it is written on, and the medicine itself are identified. It is awkward to challenge the reality of these positions since they are tied to a reality quite different from the modern world's. The analytic framework has given us modern medicine; the synthetic framework generates a culture dominated by comprehensibility and meaningfulness.

In the bright-shadow world the most important groupings are the following:

1. *The word and its referent.* We learn from elementary modern semantics that words "point"—nouns to objects, verbs to acts, prepositions to relationships. One of our most cherished rules is that the map is not the territory. Postmodern theory goes further, to deny even the possibility of correspondence between words and things out there. Words, the thinking goes, can only point to words. In the bright-shadow world, however, word and referent are two aspects of the same reality—different forms of the same phenomenon. If you know my name, you also control me; your blessing means good to me; your curse, evil (Merleau-Ponty, 178). To act or speak at some "pretend" level assures that something of the same kind will happen at the phenomenal level. In this scheme the actor, who is the speaker, becomes the controller, the creator. The physical facts have to do with the sound and the actual writing of the word, which are just as important as the object or idea to which sound and writing point. The vectors have to do with the passing of words not only into another's consciousness but also into the broad arena of the outer world, where they can affect reality. The power lies in the perceived tendency of two things to merge when they are alike in one significant respect, and the denouement is the sudden experience of dominance.

2. *Roles.* The denizens of the bright-shadow world are normally identified not by their individual personalities but by the roles they play. All third sons resemble each other, as do all stepmothers, wazirs, dragons, and foxes. Actors are noted, therefore, by the way they fit into the structure of a situation, not by their individual traits, and their personalities are formed of elements assembled from the environment (see chapter 9). Of course, we make a certain limited use of such thinking today when we speak of the managerial type, or the professorial type, or the military type. It is a productive, humbling, but also life-enhancing experience for a person who believes himself to be highly individualistic to learn that actually he fits exactly a certain type or role!

3. *Events/actions*. Quests, the escape from enchantment, the careful observance of interdictions—these activities and many like them all tend to follow the same pattern, no matter who the actor or what the goal. Vectors in one story resemble vectors of the same type in another story of the same type, etc.

4. *Messages*. Readers of folktales knew about the medium and the message long before McLuhan fell upon the concept, and lines of force that carry information are among the most significant elements in the popular tale. In the bright-shadow world the content of the message is inseparable from the means by which that content is transmitted. The knife drips blood when the distant brother is in danger. Here is a rich network of relationships that we have been taught to disregard, though there is a mind-enhancing experience (involving communication) awaiting whoever enters the network.

5. *Physical/spiritual/moral ties*. Moral corruption leads to physical decay; breaches of physical taboos have spiritual consequences. Kindness to animals brings unexpected help down the line. Between the private individual and the king there are ties of influence that cannot be severed. On these points the denizens of the bright-shadow world have no doubts; the vectors here are rich and compelling. We may make similar connections (often without really believing in them), but they certainly do not constitute one of the major axes of our thinking.

Strange as these combinations may seem to us, there can be no denying that they create a great network of meanings and insights that help to make the world both understandable and friendly. At least some merit reintroduction into our moral repertoire. But, as I suggested earlier, too much stress on similarities and analogies can lead to a serious blurring and confusing of issues, and this fact is not lost on naive psychologists either. In the *Jataka* collection, for example, there is an account of a man who assumed that a camouflage that deceived his friends would also fool the birds (II, 113). A more sophisticated intelligence would be cautious about such apparent similarities, realizing that camouflage works only among those whose manner of perceiving is essentially similar (i.e., follows similar axes, grows out of common reference points), and it must surely be assumed, even within the context of this very old collection of stories, that human and bird vision respond to very different stimuli. A disguise is best when it hides the fact that it hides (Heider, 64). In another *Jataka* tale, two kings whose chariots have met in a narrow way struggle to find some distinction that would establish some precedence, finally agreeing that one has a slightly greater claim to virtue than the other (II, 3).

In a world whose citizens blend things freely, special importance is attached to specialists in differences. A teacher condemns a student vigorously in these terms: "You made no distinctions, and that is the reason of your mistake" (*Jataka*, II, 185). Rumi tells a delightful story about a parrot who, having knocked over some bottles of oil, was beaten on the head by its master until it became bald. Later the parrot, observing a hairless dervish in the street, shouted at him, "Did you, then, spill oil from the bottle?" (I, 17). And in *Jataka* there is also the story of a man who by looking at a stick could tell which was the root end and which the top; could distinguish the skull of a man from that of a woman; and could identify male and female snakes.[8] But the very stress put here on making distinctions suggests an assumption that things are basically identical, that at every level correspondences dominate possible disjunctions.

Despite our generally negative feelings about a world geared to similarities and analogues, there is much to be said for this mode of perception or world-making. Psychosomaticists have long been drawing ties between body and mind that would have astounded Hartman. Ecologists have identified a man-environment axis rural people never lost sight of. We give cautious assent to the proposition that the moon does indeed influence human behavior. Today even our rational, analytic, difference-noting mindset is being challenged by modern image theory, which asserts that reality is pretty much what we picture it to be. Through these largely postmodern developments a way opens up once again to a sense of the connections and similarities between all things, and the axes of fact, which we have made so important, tend to become less significant than the mental filters and lenses through which we look at these facts. Many marvels lie buried in neglected similarities.

Active and Passive

Another substantial chunk of world-reading data has to do with the dilemma we all face from time to time over acting or holding back, assuming an aggressive role or waiting for things to develop in their own way. Which approach will prove more productive is often far from clear, and traditionally East and West have split philosophically on the issue. Situations requiring a sharp decision on this matter can be fraught with many unpleasant surprises and must be faced with a mixture of caution and daring that may not be easy to work out. To the question "Shall I act?" the world of work supplies one answer—of course—insistently, and the bright-shadow world quite another. Success depends on a very skillful evaluation of the vectors involved. In many folktales, however, the fox is more successful than the other animals in confronting challenges because it is relaxed, inclined to do as little as possible, until the moment is just right. Still other stories present the case of two brothers who amuse themselves at an inn while their younger sibling actively pursues a task or takes the time to help someone in trouble. By contrast, the statement of an Indian storyteller about destiny reflects a widely held view on the importance of action: "*Unless it is aided by a man's personal efforts, destiny is like a bow without an archer, a seed without a sower: it merely exists as a possibility*" (Van Buitenen, 130–31). Similarly, the *Hitopadesa* observes, "Fortune attendeth the lion amongst men who exerteth himself. They are weak men who declare fate to be the sole cause. . . . As the chariot will not move upon a single wheel; even so fate succeedeth not without human exertion."[9]

The case for doing nothing—and it is an impressive one—is frequently made by contemporary psychoanalysts convinced that passivity may produce the surrender of the ego that permits subconscious elements to be heard. In the celebrated "Tale of the Three Apples" a man secures three pieces of fruit for his wife, who is ill, but she cannot eat them. Then he sees a black slave with one of these apples and kills his wife, thinking she has been unfaithful. Later he learns that one of his sons took the apple from his mother only to have it wrested from his hands in the market by the slave (*1001*, I, 186 ff.). Inaction would have been a better course for him. In the Old Testament Moses inevitably fails when he acts in such a way as to advance his own ego, but succeeds brilliantly when he allows himself to be God's instrument. Jesus talked about the lilies of the field. Rumi's famous dictum "We are as the flute, and the music in us is from thee" (I, 35) implies a connection between passivity and faith. Indeed, the general feeling of the *Jataka* tales on this matter is summed up in the quatrain

> If no evil in thy heart
> Prompts to deed of villainy,
> Shouldst thou play a passive part,
> Guilt attaches not to thee (III, 44).

This is a common theme, too, in the teaching stories of the dervishes, one of their most celebrated tales being that of the man of Samarkand who learns that Death is seeking him. In a desperate effort to escape he flees to Baghdad, unaware that Death's intention all along had been to seize him there.[10] On this great anecdote we must pause for a while. Modern readers tend to see it as an illustration of the power of fate: you cannot escape your destiny. Dennett finds in the story questions about how well someone's behavior can be predicted from what is known about him or her. Is there, he asks, an inevitable pattern in human affairs "that will impose itself *come what may*, that is, no matter how the victims scheme and second guess, no matter how they twist and turn in their chains?" Dennett argues that the "fatalists are wrong," for though there are patterns in affairs—the patterns created by "the beliefs, desires, and intentions of rational agents"—that do impose themselves on us with great vigor, they do not impose themselves inexorably (27). But there is yet another way of looking at the story: the central figure might well have escaped what is alleged to be his fate had he simply remained where he was, done nothing. It was his precipitous action, his effort to correct a situation that was best not tampered with, that destroyed him. The real challenge to the victim lay in determining whether or not to act at all, not in where to fly.

Further analysis begins with the physical context: although his city is decidedly unhealthy, not everyone is dying, and other places may be dangerous too. The principal actor, a timid person, is receiving all kinds of messages (vectors) from his world—news of the plague, a natural drive to remain where he is, fear of looking the fool if he runs, the possibility that he will not be stricken, advice and counteradvice. One important power source is his trust in Allah; another, his legs. In his confusion he neglects yet another—his ability to reflect, to evaluate the situation carefully. If he thinks, he will realize that not all vectors point to flight. To reflect, to reach a decision, and then to perish is one thing: this is the human lot, and about it there is a certain grandeur; faith is a factor. But to run like a scared rabbit is something quite different. Foolishly he responds to vectors he should have ignored. How was he to know? Traditional narrative suggests that without compelling opposing vectors, doing nothing may be the best response.

In *Kalilah and Dimnah*, an Arabic collection of animal stories with roots in Persia and India, four companions argue about how wealth is gained. A farmer's son suggests that it comes from toil; he works day and night and makes at least a tiny amount. A second companion suggests that wealth is gained by appearance; the wife of a rich merchant falls in love with him and gives him five hundred dinars. A merchant's son, who argues that money is made through buying and selling, carries out some shrewd trading and actually gains a hundred thousand dinars. But the prince, who happens to reach a certain city on the day the king dies, behaves rather passively in this difficult situation; he does not thrust himself forward, yet at the same time he manages to present himself so favorably that he is given the throne.[11] That there are four participants in this particular situation suggests an array of vectors that renders the situation quite complex. They include all the elements the four individuals adduce in support of their positions—hard work, acquaintances, shrewdness, a productive context, background and experience, personal ability, adventuresomeness, personal restraint, and luck. Who is to say what particular combination will be most helpful? Each of them, however, offers something of value. This is a very typical bright-shadow-world structure, the kind of situation that in that world requires careful reading.

Still another coloring is given the same issue by a story from *Tuti-Nama*, a Persian collection, the hero of which is a parrot. The story, #47, begins when a wise man advises four individuals to seek a means of supporting themselves. They come first to a copper mine, which satisfies one; then to a silver mine, which satisfies another; and then to a gold mine, where another is content. The fourth individual presses on for a hoard of jewels. This quest failing, he returns to the gold mine, but it has disappeared. The silver mine is gone too, as is the copper mine. When he seeks the wise man, he finds that he too has vanished.[12] This story raises interesting questions. We can applaud the man for his aggressive search for something better, but we feel too that there might well have been limits to what he demands of life—perhaps silver would have been enough, or gold at the very most. So there was an aggressive transcending of limits here that seems both good and bad. We are told that the man was miserable because of his obstinacy. However, an adequate reading of his physical context might have suggested that the more he demanded, the riskier his situation became, the more tenuous the vectors on which he was counting. Of course, he may have known this all along and accepted the outcome.

Such stories promote neither stupid indifference nor thoughtless aggressiveness but suggest instead the wisdom of a blend of self-assurance and cautious diffidence, an interest in what may come next and an acceptance of what is already at hand. Popular tales rarely offer something recognizably cognitive, something that can be learned (though this is what the psychoanalytic approach seems to imply); instead they seem to *incline* the personality in a certain direction, alerting it to possibilities, suggesting, activating psychological/spiritual "faculties" that might otherwise have been neglected. In this way the whole decision-making process is enriched. In this process a close, trusting relationship to the storyteller can be of immense importance. The mindset that is a product of story-listening and world-reading avoids the problems inherent in both hyperactivity and complete withdrawal from any activity whatever.

Does traditional narrative make any observations about when to act and when to hold back, offer any insights into operative vectors and power sources and how they intersect in human experience? This is a moral question, and a structural question as well. Some characteristic suggestions:

Avoid acting on appearances, without some data, for appearances smack of a two-item rather than a multi-item world, where insufficient vectors are operating. (This is where rocking and inviting one's soul becomes a critical element in world-reading.) Self-interest is not the best motive for action, though clearly it must not be neglected. This is not a single-valued world where you alone count, but you cannot depend on another party, since dualism is not the rule either.[13] In other cases the vectors at work are numerous and complex; some may even be invisible. Making too quick a decision can get you into trouble, but equally dangerous is waiting too long. Of particular importance are signals from your subconscious; you need the input of your *daemon*, just as Socrates did. Do not try to manipulate events, since power sources of which you are not aware may be operating. As Islamic devotional literature never tires of noting, with a delicious shudder, among skillful manipulators Allah is the most skillful. The man who traveled to Baghdad found this out.[14] Be aware of ironic possibilities (vectors that are working in ways opposite to your assumptions), for they can overwhelm you. This is a difficult area, and the information we have about its structure is hard to sift out: even the brightest heroes have serious problems with world reading here. Nevertheless, when these suggestions appear to work, we do get some important insights into the nature of the bright-shadow world.[15]

"How Did You Get in Here?"

The discovery of functioning patterns should be one of the chief products of any effective reading of the bright-shadow world. We have identified some of these patterns as numerical sets, a sense of similarities or relationships we might tend to miss or reject, a certain feel for productive modes of action or nonaction. Many of these patterns we dismiss summarily as superstitions, though when they seem to work we may refer to them, patronizingly, as examples of "folk wisdom" or "naive psychology." The fact of patterns, however, must also alert us to the possibility of anomalies, surprises, unexpected breaks in pattern, to the realization that the next item in a series may be quite unexpected. In a rational scheme everything possible is done to eliminate such elements, but the heroes of fantasy worlds are not motivated by such a need or lulled by repetition. To witty persons experience offers surprises, introjects, and other unexpected and sometimes nasty elements—for which they are by their very nature not unprepared. The dull and unobservant, by contrast, find themselves constantly being overwhelmed by factors for which they are quite unready and by which they are destroyed. This is a favorite theme of popular tales, and it reflects an experience that some dismiss as unimportant (because it cannot be charted), while it yields up to others clues to much enhanced realities.

In a Sufi tale three fish of varying intelligence struggle to elude capture by a fisherman. The first fish, an inventive individual, gets away by a bold and original move—he pretends to be dead and is thrown back into the water. The second fish, impressed, copies his predecessor's strategy and just saves himself. The third fish, a typical product of linear, patterned thinking, too stupid to grasp the dynamics of the situation (that the fisherman is learning from experience), copies the behavior of the first—and lands in the fisherman's hamper.[16]

The fisherman, who apparently overlooks the impossibility of dead fish snapping at his line, actually assists his first catch to escape. Of course, the fisherman has very little information about what is happening, but by the time of the second catch, he has spotted the pattern, though still he cannot bring himself to take home an apparently dead fish. The third fish is caught right in the middle of the pattern, now quite clear (to the fisherman, anyway), and can survive only if it creates another anomaly, which it is unable to do. One actor copies another, the last two relying on the same vectors that saved the first, failing to realize that the fisherman's growing awareness of the situation is rapidly becoming another crucial vector. The power source is witty intelligence. The physical context is the water, which means freedom; the land, which is an area of negotiation; and the fisherman's hamper, which is captivity for anyone who cannot quickly master the situation and all its contradictions.

The problem of working within a pattern without being aware

that one element in a situation has changed is brilliantly illustrated in a Sudanese folktale, "The Poor Man's Bowl." A wretched individual is fired from his job by a rich neighbor; he secures work on a ship, taking with him only his rice bowl, and during a storm is tossed onto an island, where the ruler is intrigued by the wooden bowl. Indeed, the ruler puts it to use as a hat and rewards the original owner with splendid jewels. So impressed is the rich man by the jewels the poor man brings home that he goes to the island with rich gifts—and is given the rice bowl in exchange.[17] Why did he not actuate a greater variety of vectors in the situation, perhaps talking to the poor man? we may ask; why didn't he too take a rice bowl? The same/different problem arises again, and once again we see how difficult it is to determine the axis along which someone else is thinking. Our assumptions limit the reference points available to us, and like the third fish and the rich man we find ourselves surprised when others make connections we had not considered. The rich man was thinking only along the jewels-gifts-pride axis and failed to consider the crucial anomaly presented by the dirty, battered rice bowl. The third fish was thinking along the play dead–escape axis and never considered the possibility that the fisherman's mind had taken another turn; its reference points were limited by its own assumptions.

One very common type of surprise, which careful world-reading can anticipate, is to be found in the so-called accumulation stories, which reflect what Max Lüthi has spoken of as the delight of fairytales in sheer repetition.[18] Like us, individuals in popular tales are constantly getting caught in chain reactions. Vector after vector is actually the same vector. Somewhat more technically Jean Houston describes the process, which she calls "sequential verbalizing," as involving some of the more passive areas of the brain, in particular those highly "susceptible to patterns, symbolic processes, and constellational constructs."[19] Such are the elements, of course, on which traditional education builds, and this training makes very difficult the kind of world-reading that might notice and escape the structural traps here. In the simplest form of this motif, a young man has a goose; the innkeeper's daughter touches and sticks to it; her sister tries to release her and sticks; the priest intervenes, and then a coppersmith. Nancy tries to quiet her cow with a fist; it sticks; Rory tries to pull Nancy away; he sticks; Shamus tries to free Rory.[20] And in a *Jataka* tale a hare wonders what would happen to itself if the Earth collapsed, sees a leaf fall from a tree, flees in panic, and is soon joined by other animals, till there is a procession a league long (III, 50).

Vector after vector repeats itself, and the power source that operates in most situations to introduce some new element is, quite surprisingly, inoperative.

An important variant on this theme is to be found in the many folktales in which some wretched creature piles one imagined success upon another in fantasy. In *Thousand and One Nights* a fakir dreams about the fortune he will amass by selling his daily allowance of butter and honey, and about his marriage to a beautiful woman, and about the birth of a son who will, however, prove disobedient. The fakir raises his hand as if to strike the son and of course smashes the butter jar (IX, 40). Alnaschar, dreaming of the wealth he will accumulate through some just-purchased glassware, reaches out to embrace the daughter of the wazir, who is coming to greet him, and smashes his merchandise.[21] In Aesop a dreamer kicks over his stock of eggs, in *Kalilah and Dimnah* an ascetic ruins his hopes by upsetting his jars of rice and honey, and in *Panchatantra* a pot of rice on which another fortune was riding is lost. The common element vis-à-vis the actors? Mindlessness, I think; the loss of autonomous involvement in a pattern that might actually have led somewhere, the failure to pay adequate attention to the structure of things. Vis-à-vis the vectors? The entry into a situation of a single tiny element that had been neglected. I think again of the women of Bulaq, who rehearse their stories tirelessly in terms of the context they actually inhabit, checking them constantly against real daily experiences.

Warnings that seem to come from nowhere and yet prove curiously relevant are common in popular tales; it is always a surprise when they prove accurate, when the possibiliies they suggest are fulfilled in unexpected ways, breaking some established pattern. In an Indian tale, "A Lac of Rupees for a Bit of Advice," an individual is warned not to close his eyes in a strange house, to approach his married sister with pomp rather than humility, and always to act strongly and fearlessly. The advice is surprising, apparently irrelevant, yet by heeding it the young man saves himself and his friends, having taken these strange warnings and filed them away until there comes a time for their use.[22] This story, and many like it, suggest that the bright-shadow world (just like our world) is criss-crossed by networks into which human beings can tap, networks that have very little to do with cause and effect, before and after (at least as we understand these dimensions), networks in which problems, solutions, means, ends, spirit, and matter coexist in clusters, ready to be exploited to serve human needs. Possibility and actuality blend to form structures to the nature of which we have very few clues, and outcomes are often surprising, arranging themselves on axes to which those involved in the drama have given too little thought.

Irony is a special kind of anomaly or disjunction, a situation in which the "apparently fortuitous incongruities in life . . . are discovered to be not merely fortuitous."[23] Irony implies a situational misalignment, a jog or a kink in the linear pattern, a serious contrast between dreams or hopes and actual reality, which strikes the individual who had hoped to straighten it out with special poignancy *because of some distinctive quality he thought to bring to it*. So it can be said that a productive reading of the world must also involve a fine sense of the possibility of ironic entrapment; being aware of the many ways the vectors of a situation can twist about, out of your control, when you least expect it; protecting yourself from being an unwitting victim; maintaining a range of perspectives in any particular context; keeping your reference points under control. But in traditional tales we see repeatedly that even a careful reading may fail to reveal the scope of one's situation, one's context, since only a small portion of the world may be apparent. Human expectations are met or frustrated in surprising ways. So it is that echoes of the story of Oedipus are often heard in this material: steps are taken to eliminate an infant who, it is predicted, will marry the king's daughter and/or kill the king. By sheer force of will the infant survives, however, and through a series of intricately connected steps fulfills the prophecy. Rumi describes how Moses was engendered, despite all of Pharaoh's efforts to prevent it, by Hebrews who actually lived in his own palace, and how later Pharaoh killed thousands of infants outside the palace in an effort to eliminate Moses, who all the time was safe within its walls (*Mathnawi*, II, 49–55). And the infant Moses was saved by the very river in which it was intended that he perish.

Irony takes yet another form in stories about the helpful animal that repeatedly knocks a cup from its master's hand until the master in exasperation kills it, only to discover that the creature was trying to prevent his drinking poison. And in another important pattern a woman who tried to replace a legitimate wife is asked to suggest appropriate punishment for an unnamed malefactor who has done the same thing. Of course she unwittingly prescribes her own doom.[24]

One intent of such stories seems to be to warn and to instruct, to advise hearers about being alert to other dimensions of reality where important events are occurring, or to the fact that other persons may have other designs. Another purpose, structurally the most important, is to point out that certain forces are at work in every situation manipulating that situation with greater skill than humans can bring to bear upon it. Here we get into genuinely religious issues, if indeed we have not been there all along!

All of this is a long way from the beautiful simplicity of triplicities and my Cairo friend's easy summary of his life as "buying and selling." The bright-shadow world can get very complex, and for this complexity there seems to be but one answer, expressed in the material before us in many ways, an answer that prescribes always a certain openness and adventuresomeness, which I find quite appealing, and which often prove a productive way of meeting the inevitable disjunctions of life. Thus Walter Benjamin observes, "The wisest thing—so the fairy tale taught mankind in olden times, and teaches children to this day—is to meet the forces of the mythical world with cunning and high spirits."[25] A young man wondering which way to go blows a feather into the air and follows it. Someone else wanders into a bazaar, or knits, or simply sits rocking in a posture of quiet receptivity—often with surprising results. The general attitude is well put by Rayon-de-Soleil in the Rumanian tale "Jouvencelle-Jouvenceau": "*Si tu la prends, tu t'en repentiras; si tu ne le prends pas, tu t'en repentiras de meme; donc, prends-la*" (If you take it, you will be sorry; if you don't take it, you will be sorry; therefore, take it).[26] The world offers various possibilities, and movement, activity, and a stance of openness will invite these forces that lead by so many diverse paths to the enhancement of experience. But it is hard to escape from patterns into what is fully random, which is why mathematicians have tables of random numbers and why psychoanalysts must work so hard to persuade patients to allow subconscious forces to operate as they tell their stories.[27]

In these last two chapters, to cite again Shah's *Tales of the Dervishes*, we have watched individuals extending their experience of life, trying conclusions, observing the inexplicable contrariness of the world, noting inner correspondences, and determining the essential qualities of certain situations. I have argued that what is to be observed is the way the bright-shadow world proceeds by "subtle ways, and slow ones, and queer, risky ones."[28] And I have suggested, too, some of the ways that popular narrative can extend the experience of life: by increasing or calling attention to the legibility of its context, helping us to gain that sense of meaningfulness and wholeness that comes from thinking in sets; by reminding us of certain powers that lie in a sense of similarity; by suggesting the values inherent in passivity; and by calling our attention to various anomalies as phenomena to beware of—but also to put to good use, if one has the requisite imagination.

5 Edges

The wildest dreams of Kew
Are the facts of Katmandu.
               —Kipling

The desert threatens the sown; the forest comes up to the very gates of the city; the ocean laps at the beach; dreams and insanity distort everyday reality; context yields to context. Human beings have always lived along edges, and any attempt at world-reading, whether in "real" life or in fiction, inevitably produces ambiguous passages, regions that demand annotation or translation because they can mean this *or* that; pages that will be clear only when the reader passes to the next stage of his or her own development; passages whose import may be surprising, bizarre, unacceptable in the psychic midlands where most of us dwell. Even in our everyday world, which we have organized to pieces, we encounter surprises involving cultural distinctions, changes in physical status, personal relationships, attitudes, technology, the nature of beauty, and the very structure of knowledge itself. Edges are an important source of the moments out of which experience is constructed and life is enhanced. And in the transition from modern to postmodern, which we are now negotiating, edges all too often become true break-boundaries, where one grasp of reality is deconstructed, grows unrecognizable. Postmodernism is the most colossal edge that has ever yawned on the cultural history of mankind![1]

Alfred Schutz observes that we humans abandon one image of reality for another only when we have experienced a "specific *shock*" (*Multiple Realities*, 231). We have, in fact, developed a number of ways to guard the edges these shocks create so as to buffer ourselves against most efforts to push us beyond or outside. Social classes. Academic degrees. International boundaries. Psychoanalysis. Retirement ceremonies. The paraphernalia of death and dying. And we quite agree with Kipling's witty couplet—that given time we can tame the wildest dream into sober fact, get used to anything! In all these ways we ensure that the unknown and the unexpected do not threaten the orderly processes, the rational understanding we cherish so deeply.[2]

The experience of marginality, which figures so prominently in traditional narrative, has considerable importance, too, in postmodernism. As contact with oppressed peoples, it is a (or the) means, says George Yúdice, by which typically sheltered Westerners have discovered otherness and realized the extent of their own ethnocentricity.[3] Through the experience of marginality, of which foreign travel is only the most obvious form, thought has been in some sense liberated and the struggle against oppression aided. Postmodernism has vigorously affirmed the importance of retaining the particularity of various positions marginality uncovers—their distinctiveness from what lies on either side of them—and has urged caring individuals not to turn aside from otherness but to embrace and enter into it. Yúdice, in fact, goes so far as to find the basis for a new moral code in the Christianity of the oppressed poor of the Third World.

Traditional narrative can contribute to this unfolding discussion not only certain techniques for dealing with/entering into marginal situations but also the suggestion that some situations are more or less permanently unassimilable, fit only for actors attuned to vectors that are strange, bizarre, unexpected—individuals who have been or are being permanently changed by encounters with other worlds, by contacts with chaos.[4] The Old Testament Moses, Tolkien's Hobbit, and MacDonald's Little Diamond, for example. These individuals, like so many from the bright-shadow world, suggest that it is possible to encounter the strange and the unexpected, not to tame it, but to experience it to the full and learn from it. To their group also belongs that wazir of *Thousand and One Nights* who was fascinated by "the strangeness of things" and the supposedly silly third sons of so many folktales who are nevertheless always ready to "do the next thing," to move toward entirely undefined goals.

What are world-edges like? Has anybody ever been out to one? and returned? I suspect that this is an area where breakdowns in patterns are common, sets shifting about into new forms it is impossible to make any sense of. Careful analyses, established frames collapse. The interplay of activity and passivity in a situation grows confused. Powers that one had counted on dissipate and new powers are felt—but undefinedly. Vectors become more and more tenuous and finally are exhausted. There is a dreadful dropping off into nothingness, with the real possibility that the person at the edge may not be able to forge from the new materials he or she finds anything that will support him or her. Physical facts fade away, but this does not render passage any easier. Many children's games exploit the edge phenomenon, in particular the various forms of Prisoner's Base, in which one is vulnerable to capture while crossing an open area. In fact, David Winnicutt has observed that a very special environment can be observed in the play between mother and child. He calls it a "transitional phenomenon"[5] lying somewhere between the objective and subjective, a precarious zone of "illusory experience" (3) that nurtures both inner reality and a sense of the external world, between which it takes place. At this point traditional narrative and traditional play reinforce each other in developing the child's awareness of a kind of reality for which the adult world has very little use.

To open up this topic, which is such an important adjunct to any discussion of world-reading, such a useful corrective to the illusion of overlegibility (from which we all suffer), we look at a figure less familiar than those just cited, the distinguished Brahman quester Saktideva, whose lengthy story is told in the Indian anthology *Ocean of the Streams of Story*.[6] Unfamiliarity may be tempered by the fact that Saktideva's story bears some relationship to the more familiar "East o' the Sun, West o' the Moon."

In the city of Vardhamana, Kanakarekha, a lovely princess, has just come up against one of life's edges: she has become a woman, and her parents seek a suitable husband for her. But the girl refuses to consider marriage; she will not be separated from her mother; if she marries, she will die. The king, her father, advances all the usual reasons for marriage, seeking to lure her into his network, and she finally agrees, but it will be only to a Brahman nobleman who has visited the City of Gold. So the king, suspecting that his daughter is of divine origin, has the marriage conditions proclaimed throughout the city. No one responds, however, except Saktideva, a young Brahman who has just gambled away his fortune, his power source, and has nothing else to lose by a new adventure. Moreover, he believes that no one can check his story. He is one of Mary Esther Harding's average persons, a man "who assumes that his conscious ego represents the whole of his psyche, believes that he is really as civilized and cultured as he appears to be" (18). Yes, he says, he has visited the City of Gold. But a few questions, which he answers casually, reveal that he knows nothing at all of any such place. The princess believes that this young man is trying to deceive her, though her father thinks his daughter's position unjustified. Saktideva, gloomy over his rejection, decides that his life is worthless until he does indeed see the city, and so, making a solemn vow, he sets out. His life has begun to darken and deepen.

On his way across the boundaries of his familiar network, he passes through a forest where vicious deeds are done and through untamed deserts where the air quivers in the heat, and for seemingly endless days he has no water. He is breaking many significant frames (Goffman, 345 ff.). Finally coming across a hermit, he bows to him and reverently explains his mission. The hermit observes that he has lived on this spot for eight centuries and has never heard of the City of Gold. Evidently this is to be a transcontextual experience, one that will take the protagonist across different levels of reality, into new networks. But the hermit has a brother farther down the road who may have the necessary information. Another long and perilous journey takes the hero to the second hermit, and he too disclaims any knowledge of the city that is Saktideva's goal. It must be very remote. Go to an island in the ocean, he suggests, and there visit Satyavrata, the Fisher-King. He travels a lot and may know something. The network background is clear—everyone knows someone at the next junction and can pass you on a bit farther. But Saktideva is unaware of how rapidly contexts are changing around him as he moves from point to point of his journey.

So the young man, focusing his powers ever more sharply, sets off to the port city to seek passage, and here he meets the merchant Samudratta, who proves friendly. They embark together, but once at sea they are overtaken by a violent storm that capsizes their boat. The merchant drowns, but Saktideva is swallowed by a sea monster, from which he presently gains release, alive and well. More suffering, a second gestation, more growing. The network grows ever more complex; perhaps, indeed, a new network is being penetrated. And now, as luck would have it, Saktideva finds himself on the very island of the King, Satyavrata, whom he has been seeking. The Fisher-King has never visited the City of Gold, but he knows of its existence on the fringe of the archipelago. The storm and the experience inside the sea monster are opening up new worlds to our hero. While Saktideva is visiting this friendly island, he establishes kinship with a monk from a nearby monastery, and then the young Brahman begins to await his chance to make the next stage of his voyage. During this time he also hears an important—and highly relevant—story about certain women from his own city who offended a hermit and were condemned to live as mortals until rescued by a hero. Two great networks begin to coalesce. The king takes Saktideva to a great festival on his island to introduce him to someone who can help with information, and on the way, in a small boat, they pass near a banyan tree under which a maelstrom rages. The king dies, sucked under the water, while saving Saktideva. Disconsolate, the young man clings to the tree; while hanging there he overhears two birds talking. One of them, he learns, is flying the very next day to the Golden City.

By tying himself to the back of the bird, Saktideva secures passage to his long-sought destination and at once gains an audience with Princess Chandraprabha. She sighs deeply as she listens to his tale, for her father, the King of the Golden City, has four daughters, herself and three sisters. The three were cursed by a hermit whom they offended (Saktideva has already learned of this incident) and doomed to a state of mortality (dying to the spiritual world and losing all power to remember their former condition). Now Chandraprabha lives alone in the palace and is determined to marry Saktideva. But she must be gone for two days, seeking permission from her father. When she returns, they will marry; meanwhile Saktideva may wander at will through the palace, always avoiding, however, the middle level. (This motif of the forbidden room is common in traditional narrative, perhaps the best known instance being found in "Bluebeard." It seems related to the prohibition in the Psyche story against looking at a particular face; does it suggest ultimately the interdiction against entering the biblical Holy of Holies?)

Saktideva explores his new home and cannot, of course, resist crossing the edge into the forbidden zone. When he does, he finds a woman lying dead there on a bier, wrapped in fine clothes. This proves to be the spiritual form of Princess Kanakarekha, the very woman he was hoping to marry back in Vardhamana, the princess whose question started this long process. Other apparently dead girls lie in other rooms—the other two sisters—and the young man is convinced that he is being enmeshed in the snares of a delusion. The network he is exploring is vaster than he had thought: it is linked to many other systems. We must assume that our hero is undergoing complete and permanent disorientation.

Now he observes outside the palace a lake, and beside it a horse. When he approaches, the horse pushes him into the lake, despite his struggles, and when he rises, he finds himself back home. Reunited with his family, he once again hears the proclamation about the princess and the Golden City, and this time he can truthfully proclaim "I have seen it"—a statement that is confirmed when, at the palace, he sees the Princess Kanakarekha alive (in her mortal form) and asks, "How can I see you alive here and you were dead there?" The question, not any particular answer, was the proof of his visit. As a vector of enormous power, capable of transforming the lives of those it touches, it marks the high point of the narrative.

This is also the very question that releases the young woman from the spell imposed by the hermit and permits her to return to the spirit world. The question is critical in that it indicates that Saktideva has noticed and grown curious about the tensions between the world of the spirit and the world of matter and the way one passes between them. Now the princess proclaims to her father that Saktideva will marry her and her sisters: he has been their way back, their means of remembering their former life. So she disappears, and the Brahman hero is frustrated again; he remembers his lessons well when he is in the Golden City but less well at home. Indeed, when he is at home the reality of the Golden City seems to fade, just as a sense of the reality of fairyland often fades for Prince Anados in *Phantastes*. And it is heartbreaking to think of making the long return journey again, for both home and the Golden City are now beginning to look very strange. Nevertheless, out of his despair comes courage, for he remembers that Kanakarekha said he would succeed. So once again he summons resolution and sets out, reaching the same port, seeing the same merchant, and in time arriving at the island of the Fisher-King. Now he is accused by the king's sons of having caused their father's death. For a night Saktideva is imprisoned, but the daughter of the Fisher-King, Vindumati, falls in love with him, gains his release, and marries him.

Now Vindumati tells her new husband that she is actually a Vidyadhari who fell into the world of men for a certain offense (her mouth touched the dry sinew of a cow) and was condemned to the material world. (Actually she is the third of the four sisters.) She also tells Saktideva that he will marry again soon and that he must rip that wife's child from her womb. And indeed he does marry Vindurekha, the fourth sister, and at the appropriate time rips open her belly. When he does, the infant becomes a sword and Saktideva becomes an aerial spirit. So our hero, by the power of his sword, is able to reunite these young women with their father and marry all, restoring them to their original spiritual condition. He himself becomes an air spirit, a "Man of Light," and all enter the City of Gold, "which is the pennant of the realm of the Spirit," and the city itself blazes in splendor.[7]

Here is a classic, highly suggestive account of human beings moving across edges of the most challenging and dramatic variety! It embraces experiences of which most of us rarely catch anything more than glimpses, and it describes a long and complex process of life-enhancement with rare fullness and detail. At the beginning Kanakarekha is facing the problem of moving into womanhood, a difficult edge, involving her in conflict with the wishes of her parents, who are quite conventional people. Good Hindu that her earthly father is, he intuits that his daughter has ties with another world, and the conditions for marriage she lays down seem to imply that she herself has not completely forgotten the other realm.[8] But this earthly Kanakarekha is attracted to the familiar (her earthly mother) and not toward the strange adventures across other levels of consciousness it is clearly her lot to experience. The seriousness of her distaste for an earthly sexual relationship is indicated by her threat to kill herself if she is forced to marry. But ultimately it is revealed that she has been making transcontextual moves far beyond the capability of a mere mortal, facing strange experiences that are all the stranger because of their gloss of familiarity. There are mighty vectors at work here.

When Kanakarekha agrees to take a step into the unknown, as proposed by her parents, she stipulates actually that her husband be a like-minded actor, another willing to confront the strange and un-defined, ready to enter realms she herself only dimly remembers. Otherwise she cannot experience release from the hermit's curse. She seeks a very special kind of power. Saktideva is himself ready to move to another level of experience, to enrich his network of contacts. His bravado seems to mask a wish that the risks he is taking may really lead somewhere, and the folly of his response to the royal invitation is blended with something much deeper (of which he is unaware). Let us call it yearning. But at the conscious level Saktideva is still a very superficial young man, quite unprepared for the challenges he will face, and for a long time he sees only parts of the truth. We are not told exactly what inner powers Saktideva is able to call upon as he sets out, to penetrate deep into his network, but surely there is a suicidal streak here, along with life-enhancing themes. In jungle, across desert, at sea he encounters dimensions of reality he never before dreamed of.

Saktideva is very much on his own as he travels, for the guides and advisors he meets know nothing of the new experiences he has been encouraged to seek out. The geographical remoteness he attains matches his psychological distance from all that he believes really matters. He must recontextualize constantly. There are unavoidable casualties on the way, but one must go to certain places—islands, ports—and meet certain people—merchants, hermits—when one is on such a quest (Deutsch and Krauss, 39, 45). Awareness of the vectors in one's context is critical, and it is essential to generate some luck. Physical prowess is a requisite too, if one is to escape threatening situations. So in new context after new context, Saktideva makes connections and weaves his own network, gradually learning how to open himself up to still more information. It will take a long time to piece together the story of the young women who sinned so grievously but delicately, and they must remain trapped between two worlds until this edge-strider can rescue them, by acts that are a strange mix of obedience to an inner voice and defiance of conventional wisdom.

When he reaches the very remotest place, the "marches" of medieval literature, he finds himself in a kind of upward spiral leading him back again and again into similar situations at higher levels. He returns to old realities, seeing them in a new light, and he finds himself relaxed enough to begin to explore, though he continues to have doubts about the process in which he is involved. Ultimately, as a result of his response to bizarre and forbidding vectors, he becomes a being whose life is lived at a wholly new level.

Physical context is the major issue here, as the principal actor—and several secondary actors—moves back and forth between a variety of "places," crossing edge after edge in the process and taking in a great mix of impressions (vectors), impressions that suggest to Saktideva how different this all is—and how similar to what he's been through before, warnings, threats, advice, perceptions of every kind. The breach of the interdiction against entering a certain room has been seen as an example of the trouble that curiosity can get a person into (Tatar, *The Hard Facts*, 157 ff.). My own view would be quite the opposite—that is, it is possible for a person of courage to survive the most harrowing threats and emerge intact. So much of what any child sees is determined by that child's basic nature—the vectors dominant in its personality. Pediatricians seem bent on placing the source of these vectors at earlier and earlier moments! In any case, as long as Saktideva keeps moving, continues to "go back," he seems invulnerable. The essential experience provided by this great tale is a realization that one context is just like the previous context, just like it, that is, until all the contexts are totaled up and you realize what a vast change in perspective has actually occurred. Power sources are inner strength and determination, as well as luck and aid from people and animals along the way.

The Shapes of Strangeness

Vulnerability

Accepting the possibility that one may be hurt seems a common trait among march-stalkers like Saktideva and an experience to be shunned by those who above all crave safety. A number of real-life figures come to mind, albeit individuals certainly well established in the bright-shadow world. Emily Dickinson merits citation for her exquisite capacity to be touched by beauty and pain. In a positive vein she speaks of the arrival in Massachussets of the morning mail from Tunis (74); she thinks of home while imagining herself abroad (37); and she notes that the arrival of spring fills the village with "a Tyrian light," deepening the twilight on the lawn, imbuing untraveled roads with "fern-odors" (69–70). More darkly she speaks of the sweetness of knowing the worst (4); the divine sense inherent in madness (7), the charging of the "cavalry of woe" on "one's own bosom" (10), and "the narrow fellow in the grass"—the glistening snake.[9]

I do not see Aldous Huxley as vulnerable in the same way as Dickinson, though he too positioned himself on many edges—the drug world, the future, war, the threat of undisciplined technology. But here I am thinking of a stunning moment in London described in *The Doors of Perception*, in "The World's Biggest Drug Store," when, as he stood browsing through a shelf of art books, his eye was caught by a jewel painted onto the folds of an angel's garment, in a painting by Botticelli. Instantly he found himself transported to another world:

> What the rest of us see only under the influence of mescalin, the artist is congenitally equipped to see all the time. His perception is not limited to what is biologically or socially useful. A little of the knowledge belonging to Mind at Large oozes past the reducing valve of brain and ego, into his consciousness. It is a knowledge of the intrinsic significance of every existent. For the artist as for the mescalin taker draperies are living hieroglyphs that stand in some peculiarly expressive way for the unfathomable mystery of pure being.[10]

Contrast, the experience of edges, dominates the incident. At the level of context: between the crassness of the store and the glory of the painting; the size of London and the tiny detail of drapery. At the level of the actor: between artist and ordinary person. At the vectoral level: the gleam of jewels; the tawdry drugstore. What of power? the stunning image of Universal Mind oozing into individual worldly minds here and now. And the denouement? Ecstasy.

Betwixt and Between

Many storytellers have evoked the strangeness of the bright-shadow world by describing various halfway states, positions or conditions that are undefinable because they exist apart from all definitions or at some point between normal definitions. The ambiguity, the in-betweenness, the undefinability of such states seem to cry out for a third mode, a radically different way of talking about the situation. Apropos is the suggestion of Rosemary Jackson that oxymoron, "a figure of speech which holds together contradictions and sustains them in an impossible unity," is "the basic trope of fantasy" (*Fantasy*, 21). The classic presentation of this motif is to be found in the Hindu myth of Hiranyakasipu, whom Vishnu, in his fourth incarnation, Narasimha, the man-lion, was sent to destroy. The demon seems to be invulnerable, since according to a decree issued by Brahma, he will die neither by night nor by day, neither indoors nor out, at the hands of a being neither mortal nor immortal. Vishnu evades the conditions of Brahma's decree by assuming the form of a lion and attacking the demon at twilight in a doorway.[11] In this story the actor becomes a number of different actors in order to meet a series of very different threats (vectors) hurled at him by his environment. His chief power source is his essential Vishnuhood, which in this case means finding a place from which to operate that is as yet not staked out, not defined.

A similar theme dominates the celebrated *Tibetan Book of the Dead*, which for centuries has offered Buddhists instruction in what they will meet in the moments and days after death in *Bardo*, between this world and the next. It is assumed that the believer will maintain full consciousness during this period, and the text is designed to enable the one passing through this state to manage all the new experiences he or she faces in a way that will promote the soul's well-being. He/she must learn not to fear a certain "bright, dazzling, transparent white light"[12] by maintaining a resigned and trusting mind; he/she must shun his/her own intellectual faculties so as to "abide in the mood of non-thought formation" (123); and he/she must not fear when he/she hears Truth reverberating "like a thousand thunders" (129). And, perhaps most interesting of all, as he/she goes through a series of vast and unexpected changes, he/she must continue to be conscious so as to recognize his/her own "thought-forms" (147). P. W. Martin suggests in *Experiment in Depth* that all those who seek to pass beyond the limitations of the world of time and matter must experience a similar "maze of contraries" but that a person can learn to steer a course, "*his* course, the way appropriate to that man as a unique human being."[13] The path inevitably lies "between opposites."

Many analogues point to the importance of this motif. In the English folktale "Childe Rowland," a moment is noted that is "not exactly dark, but a kind of twilight or gloaming."[14] In a German tale, "The Clever Peasant Lass," a king orders a girl to come to him "neither clothed nor naked, neither riding nor driving, neither on the road nor off the road." So she wraps herself in a fishing net and forces an ass to drag her across ruts (Magoun and Krappe, 348). In "The Wise Little Girl," the tsar asks that a girl be brought to him "neither on foot nor on horseback, neither naked nor dressed, neither with a present nor without a gift." What he gets is a seven-year-old female dressed (again) in a net, sitting on a hare, carrying a quail. Of course, when she presents the quail to the tsar, it flies away. This motif also appears in the Greek story of Agamemnon and in the story of King Llew Llan in the *Mabinogeon*.[15] It seems to point to the inevitable open spaces in any network, where a clever actor can escape the dominant vectors and generate powers of his or her own.

Yet another coloring is added to this theme by a story from the *Jataka* collection about a girl whom a Brahman has raised very carefully, but who has been having an extended affair behind her stepfather's back. When she is accused of immorality, she swears that no man's hand has touched her and agrees to submit to fire to prove it. A pyre is constructed and lit, and as the girl is about to throw herself on it, her lover rushes out to restrain her. At this point she swears that no man has ever touched her except her rescuer, but she notes also that her original oath is now invalid, and she is exonerated.[16] Inbetwixities are clearly places to hide in as well as to exploit; they are power sources because they are empty spots no one has bothered to attend to.

So we have in this motif some tricks—verbal or otherwise—and a concept of major importance. This is the possibility that realities exist outside the famous Aristotelian categories, new categories of enormous potential, which we, given our limitations, can only talk about *in terms of* objects that we have identified and pinned down, categories that lie between the reference marks by which we normally function. Castaneda speaks of seeing "two separate worlds; one that was going away from me and the other that was coming closer to me. . . . I . . . had two realizations without the unifying conclusion." Here life-enhancement means discovering a completely new mode of being, set apart from the choices one has been presented with. Doris Lessing compares the experience to suddenly seeing something completely new in "words spoken casually in the next room, familiar music heard with particularly close attention, a passage in a book one would normally class as commonplace." And George MacDonald's North Wind observes that "behind my back and before my face things are so different!"[17]

Nowhere is there a more poignant development of this concept of realities that exist between normal categories than in the great Rumanian tale "The Fairy Aurora."[18] The story draws on the motifs of the quest and the dragon fight to spin a rich set of variants on similar tales—"The Golden Bird" and "Bird Grip" tales in particular—to describe how a sensitive individual can enter, be enveloped in, and actually survive demanding but poorly defined situations, situations that remain unresolved until the end.

There is an emperor who weeps out of one eye and laughs out of the other. His three sons learn that he will be able to laugh with both eyes only when he can bathe them in water from the spring of Aurora, the Dawn Fairy. Apparently the father's intention is to test the courage and integrity of his boys. The first two fail completely, of course (this being a fairytale), and now it is the turn of Petru to try, though his only piece of equipment is a pair of badly decayed reins for a nonexistent horse. Not to worry, for a little magic will provide the animal and also splendid equipment to go with it. Like Saktideva, Petru is inventing his world as he moves into and through it. When his mount asks Petru at what speed he wishes to travel, the youth suggests not too fast, not too slow. Horse and rider first enter a copper forest, and Petru stares about speechlessly, never having seen anything like it before: he is facing for the first time a tiny segment of the wholly other. Flowers beg to be picked, and Petru succumbs, though his steed has warned him against touching anything. As a punishment Petru must fight a Welwa, itself a highly ambiguous creature, having something like, but not exactly like, a head. "Are you afraid?" asks the horse, and Petru replies, "Not yet." A terrific battle ensues, during which Petru bridles the beast, which then turns into a handsome horse.

Much the same thing happens in the silver wood through which they next must pass—the interdictions, the battle, and the hard-won victory. During their passage through a golden wood, Petru and his horse are enveloped in a thick fog, and they approach a river that is not exactly a river, facing a battle that is something like what one might—or might not—see in a dream. Then Petru must pass through a region of terrible cold, without seeking to warm himself, and through a region of great heat, seeking nothing cooling, and finally through a region of soft airs, neither hot nor cold. He must face questions without knowing whether to answer truthfully or not and fight a dragon in a misty garden, which seems different every time he passes through it and which belongs to the Dawn Fairy, to whose identity he has no clues. And at last, having secured the water sought by his father, he must fight off the wiles of his brothers, who want to take credit for meeting their father's needs. But at the last moment, when he is about to yield to them, he realizes what is happening and makes his way home with the treasure in his grasp.

The heart of the problem motivating this sequence of events seems to lie in the kingdom itself, in the inability of its king, a too passive actor, to develop any sense of the ambiguity of contexts or any capacity for self-transcendence. Surely more complex responses than laughing and weeping are demanded of life! The water that will rescue him from his plight is the water of ambivalence, the capacity to dwell on the edge, the product of many conflicting vectors; the goddess who controls this water lives between night and day. The first two brothers are as rigid as their father, but the third, who has never allowed himself to be wedded to one situation (a deconstructionist who shuns the safety of fully charted positions), can move in and resolve the problem. He can forge his own equipment from bits and pieces lying around, because he has no preconceptions about what may be useful. His advice to his mount indicates that he recognizes the wisdom of some middle ground, as well as the wisdom of Nature. His prescription may look like indecisiveness, but actually it is the result of a valuable capacity to tolerate ambiguity, to live along the edge of things. He succumbs to neither hot nor cold and is rewarded with soft airs. He fights ugly monsters and prefers rendering them harmless to killing them. Having passed so many tests of his edge-dwelling capabilities, he must fight off one final threat—the claim of his brothers to credit for the success of the mission. But the claim is too blunt to be considered seriously; a softer, compromise position might have succeeded.[19]

We may say, then, that an edge is not simply the place where something definable terminates or commences; it is a place—or a state of mind—or a reality—in its own right, between blunt physical facts that most people regard as the only reality, a place where certain rather subtle people choose to be and where they accept vulnerability, out of necessity or because of the rewards it may bring them. The truth of the matter is reflected in the Frisian word *Skimerje*, "to sit in the twilight enjoying doing nothing in particular." "The Fairy Aurora" is a marvelous story for children—and adults—to hear as they move into a world where clear markers are missing.

In yet another kind of inbetwixity, a splendidly trained individual performs acts of marvelous skill in the cracks of reality that most of us cannot ever penetrate. In a *Jataka* tale a teacher of the lute, in a contest with his pupil, breaks string after string but continues to play entrancing music when all the strings are gone, on the body of the instrument (II, 176). An archer pierces a falling arrow with another arrow and cuts off a mango with an arrow, catching both mango and arrow before they hit the ground (II, 61–63). And in "The Three Brothers" (Grimm), one son learns to shave a hare running at full tilt; a second learns to shoe galloping horses; a third flourishes a sword so quickly that raindrops cannot touch it. In each case, gross vectors/acts are reduced to their tiny components, each of which is so small that it seems to exist outside time. The clever person finds his place between existence and nonexistence; he or she freezes a continuing action and deals with each segment separately; analogue movement becomes digital. The archer is successful because he splits up the movement of his arrow into a series of steps during each of which the arrow is halted. The swordsman flashes his arrow so quickly that by contrast with its movement the raindrops stop. The shoemaker brings the pace of his work up to the point where he actually stops the horse in midstride. Out of continuous movement each creates an edge on which he/she can perch however briefly!

Alteration/Metamorphosis of the Person

Striking changes in the personality constitute one of the most common manifestations of edge-dwelling, and of it we will have more to say in chapter 9. This is a phenomenon that we are called upon to recognize frequently, not just a fairytale theme. The motif goes back to Homer and Ovid, and it is to be found in India and China (vampire stories, the theme of catalepsy). Under extreme pressure, some inner mechanism that has been trusted or taken for granted ceases to function; the creative part of the personality breaks down. Sometimes, however, the pieces can be reassembled, though often in quite unusual ways. In many fairytales and folktales the ugly beast, the helpful fox, and the white swans become handsome men through the inexplicable devotion of a young girl, or the ugly hag turns into a beautiful woman when the questing prince marries her. Those who experience the actual alteration seem to take it in stride, but the experience produces a dizzy feeling in those who witness it: one of the basic realities, our sense of the permanence of identity, is challenged. This is an experience with transcendent overtones popular narrative seems to exist to encourage.

Orgies, the Witches' Sabbath

This theme belongs essentially to myth rather than to fairytale or folktale: it concerns the cosmic theme of fertility, it tends to horrify rather than intrigue or even interest young children, and by its gross sexuality it appears to threaten order rather than support it. It has been treated seriously by many Western artists—Euripides, Goethe, Hawthorne, Mann, Berlioz, and Bosch—and it appears in Indian vampire literature. Sexual aberration was taken seriously in the 1960s as a means of escape from middle-class morality, and many different forms were advocated. The particular strangeness to which it points is, I suppose, the strangeness of total sexual exposure, the breakdown of the decorous surface of things, and the revelation of demonic forces lurking beneath. Nowhere else are certain destructive urges that are part of all of us so powerfully combined with the desire to celebrate life in the most positive way possible. In the 1960s many people experienced new and exhilarating freedom; many others realized their vulnerability—or were actually destroyed.

Distance

Sometimes the strangeness of the bright-shadow world is expressed in terms of its distance from our world. It is an enormously long way to and across the edge. Heider discusses the distance dimension in the larger context of desire and pleasure, and that makes sense: the quest is a common element in both. He observes that this dimension "includes such relations as having or being in contact with *x*, not having *x*, possibly getting it, possibly losing it, and almost getting or losing it" (Heider, 138). Deutsch and Krauss, as has already been noted, discuss the concept in terms of "goal regions" and tension reduction: it is an aspect of Lewin's "field theory" (*Theories in Social Psychology*, 39), and since the distance is often (especially when we are dealing with edges) undefined, we face here yet another element of interest to social psychologists, *cognitively unstructured situations* (45). This motif and modern comment on it add to our discussion a critical element. The only travelers we really respect are the explorers, who move into not only the unknown but also the untenable, who seek some kind of distance, psychological as well as geographical, from the normal.

In the great Norweigian tale "East o' the Sun, West o' the Moon," the North Wind observes that he does not know where that land is, for "once in my life I blew an aspen-leaf thither, but I was so tired that I couldn't blow a puff for ever so many days after."[20] Here, as in the tale of Saktideva, a series of hermits urges the quester on. In an Egyptian version of the same motif, Yousif, who is seeking Louliyya, is told repeatedly by a series of ogres to "keep on going" (El-Shamy, 57). Of course, as one "goes on," the whole complexion of one's experience changes—ever so subtly. New vectors emerge out of old ones. One adopts new roles, learns to speak new languages.

Inwardness

Clefts in mountains, wells, pathways into the earth, and various subterranean regions also serve in popular narrative as symbols of strangeness, ways across edges. The motifs of walking down a long corridor with closed doors on either side and of opening a set of boxes within boxes touch something so deep within us as to deserve to be called "archetypal." In folktales we encounter hares within coffers, ducks within hares, eggs within ducks, seeds within eggs. In a city there is a lake, and in the lake a dragon, and within the dragon a boar, and within the boar a pigeon. Or there is a hind on an island in a lake, and a hodie in the hind, and a trout in the hodie, and an egg in the trout. Within the egg is a maiden's soul—linking this motif with the theme of the external soul. One *Jataka* tale describes a needle that can be reached only by penetrating six other needles within needles (III, 180). Modern electron microscopy has brought to our attention a very similar phenomenon, and whether or not we will ever reach the end of the line, where there is nothing smaller, is not apparently known at this time. Here is one of the most potent of all confirmations of the view that *the scale* at which we function is a basic constitutent of reality.

In other stories the idea of interiority as an unfamiliar state/mode/place is developed through the idea of a microcosm. In "The Tale of the Tontlawald," a girl shakes drops of water from her cloak onto the ground, and the earth is swallowed up forthwith in a great ocean (*Ehstnische Märchen*, 64), and in a similar Russian tale, "Go I Know Not Whither," a goblet in a man's pocket contains the entire world and a tiny box holds a splendid garden (Afanas'ev, 518). Such stories, Wendy O'Flaherty suggests (with regard to a familiar Indian version), appear designed to teach "the philosophical doctrine of illusion to nonphilosophical, worldly Hindus who dwell in the common-sense world of materialism, the world in which reality is defined by normal, social, conventional human existence."[21] I would prefer to say "substitutes another reality for the one we commonly accept."

The underground is another common symbol of inwardness, and plunging into a lake or river is often the means by which another world is attained—the Jordan, the Styx, the Nile, and Ocean have all been seen as means of passage. Aladdin enters an underground treasure chamber by raising a stone slab; Judar finds a golden door with two metal rings; Ma'ruf comes upon an entry as he plows the farmer's field (VI, 217; X, 28). Uprooting a tree can also provide entry, as can a pond, a well, or even some deserted building. Curdie, the stout-hearted young miner in MacDonald's *The Princess and the Goblin*, finds his way into another world through a mine shaft. Hoffmann's "The Mines at Falun" and Verne's *Journey to the Center of the Earth* are other successful evocations of the experience of inwardness.[22]

Time

Time is another edge across which fantasy-world travelers must sometimes move, and distortions of time (i.e., our sense of sequentiality) serve as useful symbols of significant psychological edges. Mann's Hans Castorp (*The Magic Mountain*) is a complex, modern version of Rip van Winkle caught in a mysteriously expanding time frame he cannot deal with. It seems clear that normal time (i.e., the "clock time" that all of us—if only for convenience—agree to accept) is a basic axis of our perception of reality, one of our fundamental reference points. Any warping of our time perception creates major discontinuities in our experience and may easily induce a sense of transcendence. Despite the impact of jet lag upon us, we have managed to limit sharply the negative results of such disorientation by increasing the penalties for nonobservance of established rules regarding time. In stories of the Rip van Winkle type, a period of sleep separates a person not only from his normal world but also from normal ways of keeping track of time.[23] How does one recover or reestablish the basic reference points? That is a real-world question hardly germane to the bright-shadow world, whose inhabitants choose to explore as far as they can beyond the reference points provided them.

A nice case of time-induced other-world creation is the legend of the Seven Sleepers of Ephesus—early Christians who refused to offer sacrifices to idols, as demanded by the Emperor Decius. After giving up all their possessions to the poor, they retreated to a mountain cave, the entrance to which was walled up by imperial command. Almost two hundred years later, at a time when many people were denying the resurrection, God awakened these sleepers and caused the cave to be unlocked. One of the group went into the city and was puzzled by all the changes that had occurred: it was now a Christian community. For bread he offered an ancient coin and was immediately accused of stealing imperial treasures. But with the help of a bishop the truth was uncovered, a miracle was declared, and the sleepers were embraced by the emperor, who was, we must hope, impressed by the transcontextual experience that had occurred.[24]

Out-of-Body Travel

In other cases, out-of-body travel is the issue. From Islamic tradition comes the story of Muhammad's night journey or *miraj*, which took the prophet from Mecca to Jerusalem, through the heavens, where he saw Allah on his throne, surrounded by angels. As he was spirited out of his tent, his horse knocked over a vial of water. When the Prophet was returned to the tent, the last of the fluid was running out of the cup. There is a familiar, similar medieval tale about a monk who ventured into the forest to listen to the birds sing; centuries later he made his way back to the monastery, which he found in ruins (Lüthi, 42).

These are some of the most important kinds of edge-events described in popular narrative and characteristic of the bright-shadow world. They open up a world of undefined situations in which "the consequences of behavior are seemingly unpredictable or uncontrollable" (Deutsch and Krauss, 45) and for that very reason can enhance normal experience in unusual ways. Each is in some way related to real world experiences (we too face time problems, personality changes, travel to distant places), but each is accorded a life-enhancing dimension (we watch travelers being changed, traditional definitions giving way to definitions that incorporate new experiences), and each is in some way tied to the great network of experiences in which the individual lives out his life. Such experiences seem to occur most often to a certain personality type—witty, nimble, adventuresome, free of the need for definitions and precise goals. We will observe this personality type repeatedly as we explore other facets of the bright-shadow world.

6 The Ambiguities of Enchantment

Strangeness may flower into delight, but it can also darken into evil destructive of both life and values. Fairytales make clear that even the tiniest life-passages demand care and caution, lest in being caught up in some unfamiliar situation one is trapped in dark processes that quickly destroy whatever potential for life-enhancement a particular context may offer.

Every great culture, every major thinker, reaches some understanding of the nature of evil. In traditional narrative, which generally reflects bourgeois values, evil is represented by dragons, dungeons, witches, cruel stepmothers, and arrogant older siblings—all symbols of malignant forces over which ordinary actors are powerless, forces that tend to engulf victims, dehumanize them, and rob them of control over their lives. The various networks within which individuals learn to function offer many possibilities for life-enhancement, but they can also squeeze, lull, and strangle those moving within them. Of these experiences traditional narrative offers many vivid representations that further enrich our sense of the structure of important human experiences.

Through this chart I suggest that concepts of evil fall into a continuum that moves from essentially physical or external explanations (on the left) to inward, even spiritual explanations (on the right):

| Physical Deficiency | Ignorance | Poor Environment | Isolation from Others Alienation | Arrogance Manipulation of Others | Loss of Control One's Life | Dominance by Primitive Forces | Willed, Conscious Malignity |

The biblical view of evil as a transcendent force, the manifestation in our world of malignant forces, occupies the right; modern, secular views, which seek control and rectification of evil, the left. Modern events such as the holocaust, the Vietnam War, the development of nuclear power have convinced many that terrible forces consciously seeking to do evil are indeed at work in the world. In their sheer horror, such events seem to transcend any rational understanding human actors might work out. In grasping the implications of such events, the imagination plays a critical role.[1]

Both Freud and Jung concentrated their efforts in the area of the dotted circle. Jung identified evil with "the unavoidable destruction of [one's] individuality," the lapse into unconsciousness, and the choking up of society's spiritual progress. This is Dostoevsky's territory. Jung made no place for the supernatural, asserting that by "God" he meant "the independence and sovereignty of certain psychic contents which express themselves by their power to thwart our will."[2] Marie Louise von Franz, a Jungian, went a step further in suggesting that as a result of the ignorance of "the folk" about what passes as knowledge of the natural world there is a tendency among them to regard some vague IT as the source of evil, "a kind of overpowering nature phenomenon."[3] Freud touched on evil in the notion of the Id—the raw, uncivilized elements in the personality; in his accounts of various manifestations of the mishandling of infant sexuality; and in terms of the problems inherent in civilization he characterized as "discontents" (*unbehagen*, malaise). And Harding, following Freud, underscores the importance of "aggressive and vengeful impulses" (*Psychic Energy*, 19, 88). Like Freud, too, she notes the importance of holding in check the ego "with its desire to possess and control" (78) and its various negative impulses (228).

Reflection on evil in the bright-shadow world focuses on the circled area, though it moves out from there, especially toward the right when it develops a theological coloring. Certain modern theological fantasists such as C. S. Lewis and Charles Williams have made an impressive case for the reality of the right side of the continuum, that is to say, the presence of malign forces in the universe. And in their great tale "The Juniper," the Grimm Brothers come right out and speak of "the Evil One" (Magoun and Krappe, 169). This understanding of evil embodied in a person or persons tends to become important whenever traditional narrative is influenced by Christianity, Islam, or Hinduism. But our material also moves toward the center of the continuum and sees malignity working itself out as enchantment—the loss of ability to control one's own life or the effort to dominate others and work them harm. Enchantment dulls one's sense of positive vectors at work in one's life; it separates one from power sources; it obscures network paths; it renders the world illegible. By its very nature, Harding observes, life has a stupefying effect on individuals, and it is all too easy to drift into a pattern that dulls the perceptions and eventually destroys the consciousness, so that nothing can penetrate it (Harding, 39), whether or not "beings" help along the process.

This is a very negative understanding of *enchanted*, given the positive connotations customarily attached to its participial and noun forms. Certainly the use of the word (or some form of it) in the titles of such useful books as Bruno Bettelheim's *The Uses of Enchantment* (of course) and Morris Berman's *The Reenchantment of the World* enforces positive rather than negative connotations. Both Bettelheim and Berman argue that something of value can be learned or shaped or recovered through what is taken by them to be the central, positive experience of the fairytale world. Stated briefly, Bettelheim's thesis is that an awareness of how fairytale figures form productive interpersonal relations can help a child toward maturity; Berman's, that the achievement of harmony with the natural world should be an important human goal. Bettelheim, as I have already suggested, reflects a modern position; Berman speaks for postmodernism.[4]

In the bright-shadow world, however, to be enchanted is to experience delusion, to have one's heart and mind captured by evil forces offering some alluring but insubstantial prize; to be lured to one's death by powers one is too weak to oppose; to be turned to stone because one's own personality structure is weak; to have one's head stuck up on some Baba-Yaga fence; to be obsessed, like Sindbad, with distant and difficult places; to be drugged, diverted, put to sleep, or otherwise rendered forgetful; to be incapable of distinguishing true from false. It means to be overwhelmed, as the American Indian seer Black Elk was, by a sense of helplessness: "I, to whom so great a vision was given in my youth,—you see me now a pitiful old man who has done nothing, for the nation's hoop is broken and scattered. There is no center any longer, and the sacred tree is dead" (270). Being enchanted means to seek some easy, readymade solution to a serious problem, a solution like the one Mephistopheles offers Faust.[5] To work willingly at some soul-numbing task, missing an obvious way out of difficulty.[6] To withdraw from active relationships. To be neither alert, awake, nor decisive. To give oneself entirely to what is trivial and insignificant. To surrender to the "autos," the mechanical processes that are all too ready to take over life.[7] Whatever it is that makes the actor act has been destroyed. What is more, the intensity level of the bright-shadow world is so low that the will to be active, alert, conscious is constantly undercut. World-making takes energy.

In stories about enchantment, the traditional actor is no longer in charge; rather, he is overwhelmed, rendered incapable of response; his powers of discrimination are destroyed; he loses all sense of his place in the network that is his context and all contact with power sources. The vectors he once counted on prove insubstantial, go nowhere. Enchantment stories are dominated by powerful physical facts (which may, of course, symbolize various psychological forces) seen always as quite overpowering in size, scope, and impact, and quite beyond the ability of human actors to control. These physical facts quickly dominate the various power sources—intelligence, wakefulness, imagination, luck, will—the individual relies upon, rendering human actors passive, helpless. These physical forces, symbolized by wicked wazirs, unfeeling stepmothers, the jinn rising in a huge black cloud above the bottle that was its prison, unsympathetic wives and husbands, ogres, witches, and dragons, quickly overwhelm the actors, permanently if they are unlucky, or temporarily if opposing forces (i.e., heroes who can brush aside illusion and break out of paralyzing traps) can be assembled. In that case, the negative forces that threaten the actor are reversed, and power once again starts to flow from him or her against the hostile forces. Dominant feelings are numbness and insignificance—and a sense of relief over escape.

Sexuality

The fact that children have traditionally been the most common audience for fantasy and fairytale has forced narrators and editors into all kinds of bowdlerizings of their material when sexuality has been at the heart of the enchantment theme. It is impossible and quite undesirable to convey to children the powerful grip orgasm can hold over those who have experienced sexual intimacy, or the need to possess another or to be possessed. So precisely what Odysseus was doing in Calypso's cave or with the Sirens (whose "lovely voices came to [him] across the water")[8] has been left to whatever imagination the child possesses (which, I think, Bettelheim persistently overestimates), the story of Circe becomes the tale of Hansel and Gretel, and the nymph Calypso is seen as Odysseus's nurse rather than his sexual partner. The actual power source must be concealed, the actors rendered incapable of even noting the dominant vectors. In fact, not only the perversions of sexuality but also accounts of normal sexuality offered in traditional narrative are beyond the reach of children.

Nevertheless, the theme of degrading transformation is clear enough to children when they hear the story of Circe, even if they miss the sexual implications. This luring witch, who lives deep in a forest, turns all—or nearly all—who visit her into animals. Odysseus arrives forewarned and not only saves himself from Circe's spells but actually restores the woman's earlier victims to their proper human form. Sometime later, when the hero returns to Circe after visiting the underworld, he lives quietly and soberly with her for a year as her husband. This presumably was a rational choice on his part, based on foreknowledge and power to make a choice of his own, not a manifestation of any sexual bondage. The same theme is treated in Apuleius's *The Golden Ass*[9] and in the Hindu collection *Ocean of the Streams of Story* (I, 342 ff.). Somada, a beautiful Brahman woman, is actually unchaste and a witch. She fastens a ring around the neck of Bhavasarman, who has struck her, and he becomes a tame ox. The symbolism is hard to miss. Another witch, Bandhamochini, sees the sorry state of Bhavasarman and by magic loosens the string from his neck so that he becomes a man again. (Does she offer him a less demanding type of love, a love that takes into account his own wishes?) The witch Somada demands to know why her sister witch has thus freed her victim and threatens to kill both. (Sisterhood has broken down; Somada herself is now trapped in the net of sexuality.) But Bhavasarman, armed, knows what to do the next morning when Somada, in the form of a black mare, attacks Bandhamochini, who has been changed into a gray mare. While the two are biting and kicking, the hero comes at Somada from behind and slays her, presumably, like Odysseus, freeing himself forever from sex as bondage. "When I was freed from fear, and having escaped their calamity of bestial transformation I never again allowed my mind to entertain the idea of associating with wicked women."

Here is support for O'Flaherty's view that certain forms of Hinduism "regarded women, particularly demonic women, as the root of all evil. Women were considered illusion incarnate, the sexual power that deludes and maddens otherwise sane and rational men,"[10] a source of highly negative vectors (right of chart) all too easily overwhelming weak male actors. Malignancy darkens to perversion in the story of Sidi Nu'uman, in *Thousand and One Nights*, who notices after marriage that his wife merely picks at her food. One night when he finds her missing from his bed, he follows her to a cemetery, where he observes her meeting a ghoul and enjoying with that demon a banquet of human flesh. When he lets her know the next day that he is aware of her nocturnal behavior, she sprinkles water on him and transforms him into a dog. Later Sidi Nu'uman is given magic spells to cast at her, so that he escapes from enchantment himself and administers appropriate punishment (*1001*, Suppl. IV, 325 ff.).

Sleep

In the bright-shadow world, as in our real world, sleep is the focus of highly ambivalent attitudes. Some of these relate to the theme of evil as illusion or to entrapment; others support the idea that through sleep life can be effectively enhanced. Dreams, which occur in sleep, are seen as a source of knowledge and insight; sleeping after a time of great tension or sickness often suggests that healing is taking place; and we are learning to "sleep on problems," so as to let unconscious or subconscious forces take over whatever creative tasks have to be carried out. Such themes suggest a recognition of other dimensions of reality, other modes of being. But the Bible depicts Yahweh as the One Who "slumbers not nor sleeps" and foolish man as the one who "cannot watch one hour." Thus it is that sleeping is customarily condemned by moralists and spiritual guides as a sign of torpor, a sign of deadness to the world of ultimate reality, and, in the material we are looking at, a serious form of enchantment. In his *Dynamic Psychology of Religion* Paul Pruyser comments on the timeless, revelatory quality of sleep but adds, "The numinous character of sleep is no longer celebrated with the same thoughtfulness that used to give it status in ancient myths."[11]

This position has widespread support. In Zen and Sufi practice, it is always the rule that one cannot grasp inner truth unless one is awake. Gilgamesh, in what is apparently the oldest epic in our Western/Middle-Eastern tradition, searches for answers to questions about death and immortality but falls asleep and misses important truths. From medieval Islamic Spain and the pen of Ibn Tufayl comes an intriguing fantasy on the theme of the young child who grows up alone on a desert island. As he matures, he learns by deduction all the world's important philosophical truths. This charming story, which was published in an English translation in 1708, is thought by some scholars to have been one of the inspirations of Defoe's *Robinson Crusoe*. The lad's name? Hayy Ibn Yaqzun, "Alive, Son of Awake."[12] Much later, Thoreau spoke to the same point when he observed, "Morning is when I am awake and there is dawn in me. . . . We must learn to reawaken and keep ourselves awake not by mechanical aids, but by an infinite expectation of the dawn."

In our day M. Esther Harding has pointed out the terrifying dangers inherent in following unconscious processes. Reza Arasteh argues that any aspirant for final personal integration will find it essential to "wake up, to shed illusions, fictions, and lies, to see reality as it is. The man who wakes up is the liberated man, the man

whose freedom cannot be restricted either by others or by himself."
And Alfred Schutz has observed that "the wide-awake self . . . realizes itself as a totality in its working acts."[13] All of this said, we quote
Pruyser again, "There is still something sacred about sleep" (199). The
verdict of fairytales, however, remains largely negative. Asleep, the
actor almost ceases to exist, though unusual power sources may be
tapped by an actor whose unconscious continues to be alert.

Stories about enchantment as sleep take as many forms as there
are ways of inducing it—by combing the hair, placing a ring on the
finger, passing magic wands near the head, or ensuring that the
intended victim is pricked with a spindle or thorn. No doubt the best
known of all such stories is that which the Grimm Brothers published
as "Briar Rose" and Perrault as "The Sleeping Beauty in the Wood."
These stories are important because they combine the malevolence
and the illusion themes. A slight has been done to a powerful woman
in not inviting her to an important wedding. Her gift to the new-
lyweds is vengeance: in her fifteenth year the princess born of this
marriage will prick herself with a spindle and fall dead. However,
another goddess intervenes and insists that the princess will only fall
asleep. When the time comes, the princess finds her way to the loft-
iest part of the castle, where an old woman is spinning, and does
indeed prick her finger. When she falls asleep, the whole castle sleeps
with her.

The original Grimm manuscript is very brief on the critical moment: "Da auch in dem Augenblick der König and der Hofstaat
zurückgekommen war, so sing alles, alles im Schloss an zu schlafen,
bis auf die Fliegen an den Wänden."[14] This bare original was ex-
panded by the Grimm brothers in later editions, as John M. Ellis and
others have shown, becoming, in the sixth edition:

> The moment that she felt the prick, she fell down onto the bed
> that stood there, and lay in a deep sleep. And this sleep spread
> over the whole castle: the king and queen, who had just come
> home and had entered the hall, began to fall asleep, and the
> whole court with them. Then the horses in the stable slept, the
> dogs in the courtyard, the doves on the roof, the flies on the
> wall, even the fire which was flaming on the hearth became still
> and fell asleep, and the roast meat stopped sizzling, and the
> cook, who wanted to pull the hair of the cook's boy, because he
> had neglected to do something, let go of him and slept. And the
> wind died down, and in the trees in front of the castle not a
> small leaf moved any more.[15]

What an amazingly lyrical, convincingly soporific passage! All vectors have died. Around the castle springs up an impenetrable hedge, reinforcing the enchantment theme powerfully, and the princess becomes a legend—quite a trap for a living human being. Many try to rescue her and the other sleepers, but all perish in the attempt until a prince penetrates the impenetratable and with a kiss brings the girl back to life.

We know now that this version by the Grimm Brothers has come quite a distance from German folklore, being the brothers' own highly romanticized expansion of the bare bones that came down to them. Nevertheless, what the authors do with the theme of enchantment is touching and, for us, not unilluminating. They are guides to the bright-shadow world of no less stature than MacDonald or Lewis, Castaneda or Black Elk, for they grasped as well as any explorers of the bright-shadow world the essential structure of that place, the interplay of actors, vectors, and power sources in a particular physical context. Enchantment here takes the form of something very much like death, a death in the midst of life shared by many, and all those who appear dead are set off from life by a terrifying physical barrier, penetrable only by the chosen one. The analysis here is simplicity itself: a physical context has closed down because life-giving vectors have been unable to reach it; but a strong actor does, finally, make his way into the situation, driven by a power source—love—no lesser actors have thought to tap.[16]

In another kind of story involving sleep and enchantment a deer (or some other gentle animal) makes an appointment with the hero, whom it is trying to help, for the morrow in a church or at an inn. The helpful figure comes and goes while the protagonist (who has brushed against the frame of a door or broken some other interdiction) sleeps soundly. The same thing happens the next day, the protagonist too sleepy to realize that help is again passing him by. This misfortune occurs a third time, and then the help ceases to be available; the helpful figure passes on forever, leaving the hero to make his own way as best he can. Some spiritual treasure has been missed, probably for all time, because of lethargy; life has passed someone by, and certain values can never be recovered; physical facts that can no longer be avoided close down on the hapless actor.[17]

When the dangers of sleep are recognized, attempts are made to develop techniques that will hold it off: in "Six Make Their Way in the World" one of the company uses a horse's skull for a pillow, the discomfort constantly awakening him. In a Swahili tale a boy rubs corn grit in his mouth as a stimulant-irritant, and in "The Snake

Prince" an Arab uses harsh oil for the same purpose.[18] Potentially painful vectors are introduced which will "automatically" dominate existent physical forces.

This material suggests that most actors in the bright-shadow world (like the inhabitants of our world) are helpless in the face of sleep and generally stupid, negligent, and imperceptive. Rarely do they pit their will to consciousness against the forces of drowsiness and illusion, and consequently these forces are constantly reaching out tentacles to draw in even the individuals who should be most alert. Sleep is indeed a natural state but not therefore any less threatening as a form of enchantment. It can bring loss of self-awareness, loss of the ability to take advantage of opportunities, loss of a capacity to defend oneself. There is no fairytale lightheartedness about it at all; it is a form of enchantment that victimizes everyone, sometimes at great cost. Life-enhancement takes two forms—waking up and learning to use sleep itself creatively.

Forgetfulness

Forgetfulness must figure, too, as a form of enchantment at least as important in the bright-shadow world as it is to us—indeed more important, since the individuals we are considering enjoy few of the *aides memoires* that we have developed and live in an environment far less stimulating to the senses than ours is. When we forget, we lose track of the vectors that keep us in touch with what is important in our networks, a theme picked up in a famous Gnostic narrative.[19] The central figure is a young prince who leaves his father's palace for "Egypt" (i.e., the secular world), where he promptly, in the face of all its glitter, forgets his origins, his promising future, and the honor and power that once were his. As an actor, he ceases to function. These blessings he recalls only after messengers from his father (vectors) finally succeed in penetrating his consciousness, reminding him of the life he has blotted out of his memory. Then he can return to his father and his father's joyful welcome, recovering his place in the only network that can sustain him adequately.

Being Diverted

This is a form of forgetfulness and a type of enchantment of special concern to questers. A lack of focus, of concentration, perhaps even of high seriousness is implied, and perhaps also some deficiency of ego stability, as well as not knowing what one really wants. The actor is unable to control the vectors that are supposedly his responsibility. Harding observes that the ability of modern man to carry out difficult tasks that require months or years for their completion "has come about only through the development of the ego—that is, through the concentration of consciousness under a ruler we call the I" (219). Her implication is, of course, that this level of consciousness can easily vanish, especially if the task seems too hard or the inertia is too great (242). Dörner lists important ways of turning aside from goals in an essay on heuristics: redefining the goal to one that is less demanding, replacing the final with an interim goal, "muddling through," repeatedly swinging from goal to goal, changing one's area of pursuit "instead of deciding on a crucial course of action," sticking to one theme obstinately, or refusing to listen to any challenges to one's dogmatic position.[20]

This theme takes a prominent place in the story of Psyche and Eros in *The Golden Ass*, by Apuleius. As punishment for disobeying the command of her nocturnal lover not to seek his identity, Psyche is ordered to carry out a series of apparently impossible tasks. Her unanticipated success, however, assures her maturation into adulthood. The most famous of these tasks, sorting out a huge pile of seeds, is carried out with the help of friendly ants. The final task involves a trip through hell to fetch from Persephone a box of beauty secrets. Psyche is warned that as she makes her way she will be faced by calls for help from many wretched creatures, but that if she is to succeed in her task, she must not heed these calls, must not allow herself to be turned aside from her mission. She succeeds, but only with great difficulty, for she is a person of compassion, and by running this difficult and unusual gauntlet she avoids the dissolution of her ego that might have resulted from a demonstration of pity.[21] Here the actor is required to play a frustrating, passive role in the face of powerful vectors directed at her particular vulnerability.

The widely distributed "Golden Bird" or "Bird Grip" or "Blind Padishah" stories are also based on this motif.[22] A ruler has lost his sight, and it is learned that the power to heal him lies with a golden bird, or parrot, or the some other winged creature—perhaps in just a feather of this bird. A challenge is issued to three brothers to secure the healing talisman. The two older brothers set off, but neither gets any farther than a nearby tavern, perhaps even being turned to stone there. Seeing what has happened, the youngest heads out, not stopping to carouse with his siblings, and he enters a dark forest where a dead man is shrieking. Paying no attention to this individual, the prince makes his way onward with a girl and meets a friendly fox, which, learning of his quest, offers to help. The bird through which the king will be cured is in a nearby castle, and the prince can steal it if he will refrain from stroking its feathers. Of course the young man cannot resist such a tactile pleasure, and he quickly finds himself a prisoner. The fox turns up again, chiding him for not obeying instructions and offering further advice: his client must kidnap the princess, and this he can do only if he refrains from kissing her. Again the suggestion is a powerful motivator, and again the prince finds himself a prisoner. Now he is advised to steal a horse with four golden shoes, but he must, as he nears the stable, refrain from touching the golden saddle. Sorely tempted, he stretches out his hand toward the soft gleaming leather and is dealt a hard blow. But he gets the horse shod and heads home with the princess and the bird, warned this time not to ransom anyone's life on the way. But as he travels, he encounters his two brothers, about to be hanged for debt, and out of pity he pays what they owe. This kindness they repay by casting him into a pit, but even now the fox is waiting to be helpful. The claim of the two brothers that the bird was their find is rejected, the younger brother is duly honored, and the father is healed. At this point the fox commands the prince to dismember him, for he is actually an enchanted prince seeking to recover his true form.

The various forms of this story that have come down to us suggest that the average human actor is oriented to the world around him, not to some inner center,[23] so that every blandishment the world offers (i.e., the vectors it thrusts out)—places to enter, things to hear or see or touch, opportunities for wealth or simply for rest, even chances to be a good samaritan—becomes a powerful distraction. Thus the characteristic disturbance to which such stories point is not neurotic brooding on the self but distraction, the scattering of the personality to the winds. We may surmise that the handsome prince is making use of his time as a fox to pull his own personality together, and that he is to do this by working hard at a difficult assignment— trying to get the third son to stop reaching in so many directions, to focus or concentrate his efforts on his own inner strength. When the fox/prince has learned this lesson himself, he can suffer dismemberment because he will have achieved integration. And when the young quester has learned the lesson, he will secure the bird and heal his father—achievements that at one point must have seemed totally beyond his reach.

An important corollary to stories about diversion is to be found in stories about heroic persistence in the face of great danger, the refusal to yield to hostile forces, no matter what the cost. Of course this situation is often the result of having willed oneself to be in the spot where the danger lies. This point is reflected in the familiar story of the lad who set out to experience fear.[24] In the vetala tales of *Ocean of the Streams of Story* the fear of which I speak grows from the need to maintain oneself overnight in a dark cemetery with the flames of funeral pyres on all sides and the screams of demons filling the air. But a great hero like Vidushaka will emerge unscathed the next morning.[25] In other cases a church or churchyard is the scene of the challenge, and one wonders whether there may not be here some memory of the original Indian version. Herbert Giles, in *Strange Stories from a Chinese Studio*, describes the adventures of Mr. Yin, who spends the night in a haunted house, and Mr. Yu, who waits for death in a lonely room besieged by poltergeists.[26] The German version has clever Hans taking a job ringing churchbells at midnight, even though all previous ringers have disappeared. In the belfry he is attacked by a headless creature whom he fends off and whose life he spares. As a result he is told about buried treasure. How does an actor come into being? Not, surely, simply by being born, but rather by learning to cope with the threatening vectors his world, his physical context, directs against him.

Entrapment in Mechanical Processes

In traditional narrative, stories about a broom that will not stop sweeping or the churn that will not stop turning or the mill that grinds out endless amounts of salt are familiar. Also common are accounts of the dance that will not stop until all the dancers are dead—or perhaps not even then, as the Dance of Death seems to suggest. Sometimes the dancers are as comic as the broom-dancers who trap the sorcerer's apprentice or as talented as the Irish king of pipers, Michael Connor, who after a few drinks can make even the fish dance. Often, of course, dancing is a life-affirming process, though generally in our material it becomes purely mechanical, a form of enslavement of those too weak to resist certain rhythms. The same vectors flash by endlessly. The dance thus becomes another important reflection of the distaste of bright-shadow folk for processes that lie beyond the control of the human mind and will, for various sequential traps. As Ken Kesey observes of "the Daily *Dance* with the wilder step, . . . you can never really have much notion where you are headed. You can trip off to places so wild and so wiggy you don't know where you are until you get back."[27] Yet dancing is also one of the ways the generally loose and tensionless structure of the fantasy world can be organized into a powerful instrument for keeping human experience under some kind of control,[28] and indeed its communal, ego-submerging elements offer a ready form of life-enhancement.

Petrification

Metamorphosis into stone is a form of enchantment familiar through the biblical story of Lot's wife (Gen. 19:26), another case of the most casual act—the gesture of looking back—having the most awful consequences. In such cases, the victim is arrested at one stage of development, drained of vital juices, deprived of the capacity for further movement. Vectoral movement ceases. Such is the fate of a young man in the story of the "Two Brothers," as he travels through magic forests (Magoun and Krappe, 241), of a whole set of brothers in "The Giant Who Had No Heart in His Body," (Dasent, 62), and of a rajah's son and all his brothers in the Indian tale "Punchkin" (*Old Deccan Days*, 8).

The psychological implications of this type of enchantment are spelled out by von Franz: one of the tasks facing all modern persons in a time of overcrowding, she says, is to "separate ourselves and solidify our own personalities." But weak people who cannot submit to creative transformation "harden instead outside and display a psuedo-superior, hard, unrelated, bitter exterior to the outer world."[29] Before the shaping can start, forms, material, and process have all congealed. As we will see when we look at the bright-shadow concept of the personality in chapter 9, this type of enchantment has even more serious implications in that world than in ours. In our world, anyway, there seems a certain justification for the development of a rigid interior and a stiff, durable exterior, and a variety of processes constantly summon overly rigid individuals to something looser, more flexible.

Avoiding Enchantment

For every form of enchantment we have mentioned there are accepted methods of escape or avoidance: the worst results of sexual enchantment can be sidestepped by anyone whose sense of personal identity is strong; entrapment in mechanical processes may be avoided by keeping the consciousness awake; triviality, by a sense of the real significance of things; etc. And in a general way, the interdictions and taboos that play such an important role in popular narrative serve much the same purpose—interdictions against marrying someone or going somewhere or saying or touching something. These interdictions reflect the myths and rituals that so often lie far behind the fairytales that have come down to us, but even in traditional narrative they bespeak a world where the sacred has significance (there are rooms too holy to be entered, sights too awesome to see), a world where mysteries must be approached humbly, a world that can very easily slip out of one's grasp. Gestalt therapy has now occupied a good deal of this territory, not to make us aware of the sacred quality of life, but simply to make us conscious of the way the tiniest parts of our behavior make up a totality. As the boundaries of consciousness expand, the power of illusion and enchantment must shrink. Thus in *My Dinner with André*, it is said of Roc that at Findhorn he

> used to practice certain exercises, like, for instance, if he were right-handed, all today he would do everything with his left hand. All day—writing, eating, everything—opening doors, in order to break the habits of living, because the great danger for him, he felt, was to fall into a trance, out of habit. And he had a whole series of exercises, very simple ones, that he invented to just keep seeing, feeling, remembering.[30]

Such a position nicely establishes the connections between enchantment and interdictions (on the one hand) and many of the important themes of modern therapy (especially Gestalt) and the meditative life (on the other). A major rule of such disciplines: retain conscious control! Keep awake!

One essential feature of interdictions is that no reason for obeying them is ever given, yet many forms of empowerment are clearly related to another's following directions carefully. Why is this? Because coping with a new and difficult situation, whatever it is, requires trust in some wiser individual. One actor must yield control to another. This point is brought out clearly in the story of Psyche and Eros: the girl must trust the male who has told her not to try to determine his identity; in a sense, who he is for her is a function of the attitudes she holds about him. Similarly, when an elf-maiden agrees to marry Wild Eldric, she warns him never to ask her to explain her absence. When he breaks the agreement, she disappears (Briggs, *Personnel*, 41).

Such instructions are also designed to humble the person to whom the command is given, but an even more important reason for the dogmatism of the instructions is the fact that full comprehension of the activity being interdicted may lie only in some other dimension, at another level of reality, in some other context. Its nature is such that it is simply incomprehensible at the beginning of the process. In the trusting and shaping one does, one will come to understand what really is at stake. No single actor can hope to grasp all the vectors at work in a given context, much less identify conclusively the important ones. The Adam and Eve story makes this clear: the couple are so thoroughly bewitched by their own potential, by their own power to act independently, by the possibilities that knowledge holds out for them, that they are unwilling to let the scenario arranged by Another unfold.

Moreover, breaking interdictions also implies a certain brashness or churlishness ("No one is going to tell me what to do"), and such feelings are traps and enchantments. Here we confront a familiar problem again, in a new guise: clearly, intelligence and discrimination are key elements in any human response, but there is a place also for obedience. What is the critical third element that resolves the dilemma? Perhaps it is openness, openness to some larger context than one can see or grasp at the moment, but which in time will unfold. Here lies the strength of the fox in the "Bird Grip" stories; here, too, the continuing hope of storytellers that the hold of illusion over the human personality may in time grow weak and disappear.

Something of this hope is held out in a Middle Eastern story that Amina Shah calls "The Ghostly Miser of Tangier." A bricklayer walls up bags of gold in an old man's house on successive nights. When the house is sold, it is found to be haunted, and the enchantment is broken only when the bricklayer tears down the walls and uncovers the gold, which can now be given to the poor.[31]

I think that we have now accounted for one kind of evil, the loss of conscious control over one's life, that form of evil with which traditional narrative is primarily concerned. This is a form of evil to which we also are subject (more than we realize), and it has clear ties to that other form of evil appearing so commonly in this material, the power of malignant forces. In terms of our formula, we can say that evil is generated when a context so dominates an actor that he or she is unable to reach for power sources or to receive or project significant vectors. At this point a way may open up for some other creative actor, an individual awake and free of illusion, to scatter irrelevant vectors and face boldly the power available in his/her context. When this happens, when the bonds of enchantment are broken, life may be enhanced in glorious ways.[32]

7 Power

Power, the third element of my paradigm, is what myth and ritual are all about, and power-related themes pervade fairytale and folktale, lesser forms as well. In discussing these genres, we are talking about real power, as Durkheim says repeatedly, not about metaphor: power that moves mountains, heals diseases, enchants and disenchants, produces crops, and transports people across great distances. Jack Zipes agrees: "Central to most tales is the concept of power. Where does it reside? Who wields it? Why? How can it be better wielded?" (*Breaking the Magic Spell*, 170). This vast topic embraces sources (on which I will concentrate), the effects of power on individual lives, misuse, and various power transfers. Much of my illustrative material will come from *Thousand and One Nights*, a compilation particularly—overwhelmingly—rich on this topic.

Intelligence

Wit and perceptiveness are important power sources in the bright-shadow world, whether your work is thievery, soothsaying, sword-play, managing a kingdom, or tending a kitchen. Neatly bringing together vectors, actors, power sources, and physical contexts, the Grimm Brothers describe three tailors "whose intelligence was so fine that one could easily thread it through a needle" (Magoun and Krappe, 417). We approve of highly specialized intelligence, carefully trained, thoroughly tested, sharply focused, geared to professional analysis. But in the bright-shadow world intelligence appears diffuse, embraces a wide range of only partially developed abilities. Bright-shadow-world intelligence is largely untrained "street-smarts," evolving from a close reading of one's immediate context, not the absorption of data already digested by others. It is manifest in clever ways of outwitting people by insight into their character; gaining knowledge through hints and clues, devising stratagems, often on an ad hoc basis; thinking in terms of sets and pictures instead of words and numbers; making obscure connections; noting and looking into the cracks in various structures no one else deems worthy of examination; being astute; seeing implications; understanding human motives and human responses. How little of this life-enhancing material is taught in our schools! How stodgy, by contrast, our modern understanding of intelligence!

Embodying many of these abilities is the celebrated serving maid from "Ali Baba and the Forty Thieves," Morgiana (Marjanah), who is described, with considerable understatement, as "shrewd and sharp-witted" (*1001*, Suppl. IV, 378). Her story neatly illustrates the various components of a person's "I-program" as described by de Groot: she grasps completely the situation that challenges her, applying to it her good sense, her dexterity, and her versatility in ways that reveal her native intelligence.[1]

When a robber chieftain identified and marked the home of her master for evil purposes, Morgiana noticed and "marvelled exceedingly at seeing the chalk-marks showing white in the door; she stood awhile in deep thought and presently divined that some enemy had made the signs that he might recognize the house and play some sleight upon her lord" (384). Eagerly she jumps into the game, chalking all the doors along the street, neutralizing hostile gestures with countervectors. The process of attack and counterattack is repeated, and then the robber, disguised as an oil merchant, causes thirty-nine jars, each with an armed man inside, to be deposited in Ali Baba's yard, where he asks to spend the night. Realizing what is going on, Morgiana pours boiling oil into each jar, killing almost all the occupants. Later, when the robber-chieftain/oil-merchant (who comes to dinner to gain revenge on his slain friends) refuses to eat salt (vector and countervector) with her master, she grasps his intentions and appears at their banquet disguised as a dancing girl. Thus she can get close enough to kill the man who had neglected to protect himself from her concealed dagger (a very physical vector) by the traditional response of the guest.

What enables Morgiana to save her master and his property from "hurt and harm" is her extraordinary alertness to the myriad bits of absolutely raw data swirling about her, data that offer opportunities for all kinds of constructs to anyone bright enough to see patterns and organize gestalts. Her activity is a beautiful example of Otto Selz's very pragmatic definition of intelligence as the "insightful acquisition of operative modes" (de Groot, in Groner, Groner, and Bischof, 115). She makes brilliant observations, checks out intuitions, develops hypotheses, controls her own fears, and acts decisively. Of particular interest is her ability to make significant contrasts between the door as it stood yesterday (free of any new marks) and today's marked door, since she really does not know that in the very tiny change (one of innumerable marks of all kinds on the door) lies a hint of disaster to her lord. In computer terminology she is making a "file comparison," and today, as a result of certain analogies that have been developed between computer and brain functioning, we are aware of the importance of developing and maintaining one's mental files. To carry out this process effectively and continuously is an important facet of being intelligent. A computer may be programmed to carry out such a scan at any desired interval; Morgiana seems to be functioning on a twelve-hour cycle. Of course, the computer will have an advantage over Morgiana in that it has been told what to look for. This constant scanning and file comparing are particularly vital to the woman, given her context: in the medieval Middle East survival depended on constant monitoring of one's environment for signs of threatening change. Such a search might well be made at different levels, along different axes; the important resultant that Morgiana gained indicates that she chose an appropriate axis along which to work. No doubt, a person successful in a position like Morgiana's carries out such monitoring subconsciously most of the time. Her success is one of the most productive sources we have of information about the structure of the bright-shadow world and the place of intelligence in it—the importance of the interplay between similarity and difference, the significance of tiny bits of information, the very specific role of quick wit, the place of keen, constant observation. She is alert, and her story can instruct others in alertness. She has power.

Luck

If power questions lie at the heart of the bright-shadow world, luck is close to the very center of the power question. In that world, luck is deemed to function according to certain (apparently) universal principles raised to transcendent significance, understood and intentionally put to use by certain individuals with resources of insight such as we, in the real world, rarely possess. Our impoverishment on this score is suggested by common limiting phrases: "good luck" (usually spoken in quite an offhand manner), "lots of luck" (with an air of resignation), "dumb luck" or "lucky day" (meaning that there is absolutely no reason why something fortunate happened), or "lucky break" (implying that the person has really worked hard to position himself so as to benefit by events). Among gamblers there exists some recognition of *a force* that may be at work in cards or dice. And we do recognize that certain individuals are by nature lucky, perhaps to the extent of urging others to associate with them. In fact, social psychologists identify 'fortuitousness' as a phenomenon of some interest: the possibility that "two or more unconnected and mutually unoriented individuals, each properly guiding his own doings, jointly bring about an unanticipated event that is significant" (Goffman, 33).

What is more, serious attention is given to luck in the Bible as a way of making choices disinterestedly (and staking out some place for divine activity), and no less a theological authority than Dante suggests in the *Inferno* (VII, 73 ff.) that luck was established by God as a way of keeping events moving and assuring the continuing redistribution of divine blessings. A rather more modern—even postmodern—view is voiced by Arthur Koestler, when he suggests that by 'luck' we refer to forces at work in a particular situation that lie beyond reason and analytic understanding and that are more than the chance coming together of certain forces. Koestler cites Arthur Kammerer: "Coincidences, whether they come singly or in series, are manifestations of a universal principle in nature which operates *independently from physical causation*. . . . Moreover, single coincidences are merely tips of the iceberg which happened to catch our eye, because in our traditional ways we tend to ignore the ubiquitous manifestations of Seriality."[2]

By "synchronicity" Jung meant "meaningful simultaneity"—a condition that lay outside the framework of "the probable and rationally possible," outside the bonds of known causality, the contribution of a number of vectors seething beneath the surface of experience over which some control may be exercised. In this situation the psychical state, the readiness or alertness of the subject, played some part. Jung speaks of "spontaneous, meaningful coincidences of so high a degree of improbability as to appear flatly unbelievable."[3]

Some years ago, after reading Klausner's *Why Men Take Chances*, I sat down to write out my reactions. Almost immediately I realized that I needed Koestler's *Roots of Coincidence* as well, and I remembered that some months before my wife had lent my copy to one of her friends. A moment of frustration was followed by a knock at the door, and there was my wife's friend, handing me the book! One can never count on such things happening, though eventually one ceases to be surprised when they do.

The emphasis on lucky breaks and discoveries gives the stories in *Thousand and One Nights* a marvelously buoyant, anything-is-possible flavor. Lucky meetings abound, and life is enhanced at every turn. From many cases I choose the story of Ma'ruf the Cobbler (X, 1–53), to which reference has already been made. The protagonist of this long and complex story is a wretched Cairo journeyman doing what he can with old shoes and enduring a shrewish wife, who beats him when he brings home the wrong pastries. He has no resources with which to bargain for better treatment, no psychic energy to move out, and she torments him so constantly that he has no chance to develop any strategy of his own (Harding, 49, 52n.). Eventually Ma'ruf flees to a garbage dump outside Cairo and sits there dejectedly in the rain. Suddenly a jinn appears before him, ready to do his bidding. The cobbler seeks transport to a distant city, and here, by chance, he meets a boyhood friend from Cairo with whom he works out a strategy—a way to induce luck. Ma'ruf is to claim to be a rich merchant waiting for his goods to arrive, and with this ruse he borrows large sums of money. Eventually his lavish expenditures, which appear at first to be convincing proof of his wealth, dismay even the friend who has suggested the deception, but no matter, since by this time Ma'ruf has attracted the attention of the sultan, another covetous individual. The sultan's wazir has his doubts about Ma'ruf, but the ex-cobbler now takes a daring step, releases a surprising vector—he impresses the sultan by smashing a priceless pearl, declaring it worthless by comparison with the jewels in his baggage. He takes Dunya, the sultan's daughter, as his second wife, and reveals to her the truth about himself. His position is thereby actually strengthened, since she agrees to aid his deception: Mar'uf has her in his power, another piece of luck. The two decide that Ma'ruf must leave the scene until his position can be consolidated. Away from Dunya, however, Ma'ruf experiences total desolation: creative vectors cease to operate on his psyche. Seeking help from a farmer, whom he sends to the village for food, Ma'ruf begins to plow the farmer's field (his offer to do this is a critical vector), uncovers a ring (power source) in the ground, pulls at it, and finds beneath the slab to which it is attached a casket containing a mysterious seal ring, through the power of which Mar'uf calls up a powerful jinn, who provides him with food, wealth, and an army of slaves. From this point his success is assured, though he faces struggles when for a time the wicked wazir is able to gain control of the seal ring.

There is no single way to account for all the good things that happen to Ma'ruf: this is part of the mystery of luck. Much can be attributed to highly subjective factors. Perhaps his personality, like Whitman's, was of "hopeful green stuff woven," so that once he was able to escape from the numbing influence of his first wife, which did not afford him any chance to gain the slightest foothold in life, his naturally sanguine temperament could emerge. This feature of his nature appears in his devil-may-care attitude toward wealth; in his assurance that even if his imaginary baggage does not arrive he can devise some new attack on the problem; in the profligacy with which he spends the sultan's treasure; in the bravura with which he smashes the great pearl; and in the bold way he courts Dunya, bringing her into his scheme, confident that she will side with him.

Ma'ruf projects himself repeatedly into the interstices of the network in which he lives. It is at these junctions that power is to be found. There are no vectors in Cairo strong enough to serve his purposes (the kindness of the pastry seller is not sufficient to propel him out of his wife's sphere of influence, and his dismal Cairo prospects are epitomized by his experience in the rain in the city dump), but the city to which he is carried by the jinn offers a rich grid of possibilities, and Ma'ruf quickly becomes part of an influential merchant group and finds himself caught up in the powerful vectors flowing in and out of the court. Ma'ruf manipulates these lines of force with skill and daring, despite the potent opposition of the wazir. And the wazir's power, great as it may be, is topped by the power of Dunya, who stands even closer to power and is more skillful than the wazir in manipulating it. Carol Channing's famous line in *Hello, Dolly*, "I meddle," might well be applied to the princess. What she puts her hand to turns out well, for psychic energy swirls all around her, as it does around Morgiana.

There is a spiritual dimension here that must also be noted. Sufis never tire of talking about the rubbing of the ring as an act that cleanses it of all impurities. And they find in this act a symbol of the purification of the soul. This suggests that Ma'ruf is actively engaged throughout the story in cleansing his personality of certain blemishes so the psychic energy that is his can manifest itself. In Arabic "Ma'ruf" means "the enlightened one," and Ma'ruf's success suggests that the lucky are both virtuous and endowed with secret knowledge (how to make things happen). For example, he would not have found the treasure in the field had he not undertaken to keep the farmer's work going while the latter sought something for both of them to eat.

This is the final story in *Thousand and One Nights*, and as it ends

Scheherezade is bargaining for her own life. These are your children, she says to the listening sultan as she points to the family she has given him, and if you kill me, they will be motherless (read also: you will hear no more stories, and the world we have constructed together will collapse). This argument is sufficient to save the woman; bargaining processes have dominated the long tale, reinforcing the various manifestations of luck, which are also so important, though a crisis in the life of Ma'ruf was necessary to get the process started.

Magic

In one of the great hero-tales from *Ocean of the Streams of Story*, Maya says to Suryaprabha:

> From undeveloped matter there spring in this world various powers, and subordinate powers. Among them the sound expressed by Anusvara arises from the power of breathing, and becomes a spell of force in magic sciences, when accompanied with the doctrine of the highest truth. And of those sciences which deal with spells, and which are acquired by supernatural knowledge, or austerity, or the holy command of the holy men, the power is hard to resist. So my son, you have obtained all the sciences, except two . . . the science of bewildering, and that of counteracting. (I, 439, and cf. *Jataka* I, 270).

Thus is magic placed on the spiritual rather than the physical side of the ledger, along with powers subtle and mental; with the holy rather than the diabolic. A life-enhancing function, though not necessarily a supernatural one. In fact, Marcel Mauss has argued that magic is a largely "social phenomenon" with the idea and experience of "collectivity" behind it. It belongs in the same category as "law and custom[,] . . . economy and aesthetics[,] . . . language," and religion, he asserts.[4]

I propose to argue here that much of what one culture takes for magic may be accepted as quite normal in another culture (where certain specific powers have been developed) and that a magical act is made up of many separate parts abnormally compressed in time and space. When these same acts are spread out in a time/space continuum they may look less exotic, less magical. Concentration, compression, focusing are significant factors in the generation of psychic energy, an important source of what we call "magic." To explore some of these possibilities, we examine the story "Aladdin and the Magic Lamp" (*1001*, Suppl. III, 51 ff.).

As the story (laid in China) gets under way, Aladdin is pictured as an idle, careless boy who plays all day with other idle boys. His father dies of grief over his son's behavior, and his mother weeps. (Aladdin's world offers him no more power than Ma'ruf's did.) Then a stranger appears, actually a Moor and a notorious magician, introducing himself as Aladdin's long-lost uncle. (He can be seen as a part of himself Aladdin has not yet developed.) He offers to buy the youth fine garments and to set him up in a shop—an offer that few Middle Eastern males can ever turn down. (The evil nature of the uncle is less important than the fact that he provides the initial dynamic element in the story. Yet even though he is a magician, he can do nothing without his nephew's help.)

The magician takes the boy on a long walk through splendid gardens to the mountains, until they reach a spot where the magician makes a fire and throws upon it a magic powder. The earth opens up to reveal a flat stone and a brass ring. (Aladdin is radically reimaging his world, under the influence of another part of himself seeing all kinds of new possibilities.) Upon Aladdin's finger the Moor places the ring—to protect it, he says.[5] (Aladdin is brought into contact with the world he has reimaged.) Then the youth is instructed to lift the stone and descend the stairs, touching nothing, passing through a garden until he finds a niche in which burns a lamp. (Within Aladdin himself there resides a power, which his uncle—part of himself—is tapping.) Actually the lamp is a magically potent object, for "who so possessed it, him it gifted with fairest favor and figure, with wealth and with wisdom." (Such is the power of forming a new picture of oneself.) Wisely Aladdin determines to hold onto the lamp until he is safely out of the cave, but before he can escape, the magician, enraged at his delay, rolls back the stone and traps the lad beneath it. (The individual, lacking any means to express his powers, is trapped within them; part of Aladdin wants nothing to do with the new opportunities being offered him.)

For two days Aladdin remains in the cave in despair (a time of reassessment, realigning the personality), and then he clasps his hands in prayer, accidentally rubbing the ring. This act of cleansing or purifying brings the jinn of the ring to his side. Seeking deliverance from his plight, the youth finds himself back home, all the "fruit" he had collected in the cave having changed into precious stones (as a result of his transcontextual moves). His mother is astonished, the more so when Aladdin, having decided to sell the lamp, rubs it and finds the jinn standing before him once again. (He requires some time to adjust himself to his new powers.) The banquet the jinn produces is the first indication of the power of the lamp to fulfill its potential.

Sometime later, Aladdin falls in love with the daughter of the sultan and orders his mother to secure her as his bride. (The young man's image of what he may achieve is expanding. His rise begins with will and desire.) His mother is frightened by this assignment, but by waiting patiently day after day in the palace she eventually attracts the attention of the sultan, gets a hearing, and astonishes him with her gift of jewels. (The most surprising things are possible if the approach is carefully prepared.) Now Aladdin enters into a competition with the son of the wazir for the hand of the princess. Initially the wazir's son gets the girl (obvious forms of power win the first round), but Aladdin and the jinn so thoroughly discomfit the pair on their wedding night that the young man seeks only to be rid of his bride. (Something that is not to be does not work out.) And by this time the sultan is quite ready to surrender his daughter to Aladdin in exchange for more jewels. (Positive forces are being assembled.) Aladdin further supports his claim by instructing the jinn to erect, overnight, a marvelous palace for his bride. Soon he is placed in charge of the royal armies and by the power of his lamp is transformed into "a finished courtier, warrior, statesman." (His personality has achieved a new level of integration.)

But soon the Moorish magician is back, disguised as a peddler, to recover his lamp. (Aladdin, having reshaped his life and personality, must face a new series of threats at another level.) Now begin a series of breathless transfers of the new palace and the princess to Africa and back again to China (a context for power is being sought), and Aladdin is nearly executed by his royal father-in-law. (The young man has foolishly lost his bargaining chips.) Finally, by trickery, the bride and bridegroom recover the lamp and destroy the magician (power is reassembled), but their troubles are not yet over: the magician's brother, even more powerful than he (a deeper level of hostile power has been identified), appears as an old crone, suggesting that a roc's egg be hung up in the palace as decoration. This suggestion enrages the jinn, since the roc is his master, and realizing now who the old crone is, the jinn destoys him/her and reestablishes peace and security in the kingdom. The jinn finally gets to the root of the problem—the malice which would make all as powerless as itself.

What sense can be made of the magical material that is so common in folktale and fairytale and fantasy—the strange implements, the bizarre activity, of which the story of Aladdin is so splendid an example? Some of it is sheer hocus-pocus from purely fanciful realms that have no basis in any kind of reality we might recognize. We are often invited to allegorize, and this can be helpful—modern science has indeed provided us with magic lamps and seven-league boots, and there are moral forces behind the bizarre surface events. But beyond such possibilities lies the psychological and spiritual power involved in desiring, focusing, and seeking what we can make use of today. For example, the knapsack and the tablecloth that provide all the needed food have in some sense the authority of the Gospels. What is miraculous in one world or at one tempo is quite understandable in another. Plants that restore health—if not youth and life—are all around us, readily available for our use. Magic wands suggest the psychological power of one person over another, the instrument itself functioning primarily as a way of supporting belief, as a vector that focuses attention. Additional insight is provided by the Armenian story of the weaver who built a swing that moved by itself, planted a field of corn and a willow that swayed without wind, and invented a self-propelled loom.[6] Such marvels call to mind "the wizard of Menlo Park" and Benjamin Franklin and all clever inventors who, relying on natural principles, build mechanical devices that seem magical to those who do not understand them.

Finally, and most important, is the fact that magic looks like magic because some distortion of the normal categories of measurement has occurred. We accept as perfectly natural the transformation of sunlight into plant fiber in the course of several weeks or months, and into coal and diamond over the course of millions of years. We do not yet have a way to make the transformation from sunlight to usable fuel much more quickly, and even though modern science has undertaken to find ways to hasten the process, such a speed-up would have a truly magical appearance to many. Yet the time that Aladdin's mother spends waiting at court for a hearing—spread out as it is in the story—does secure her son's desire as surely as if she had been a person with the presence or *baraka* to apply stronger pressure over a shorter period of time. We also accept as natural the power of ice or a growing plant to split a rock, and the concentrated power in high explosives is within the range of our sense of possibility. The concentration of power implied by the formula $E = Mc^2$ is, on the other hand, something from another dimension, something we cannot be comfortable with. Yet it functions in our world. Moreover, the celebrated Einsteinian formula tends to blur the distinction between matter and energy—two categories normally kept separate in our world but not in the bright-shadow world. Magic can also be seen as a structural phenonenon in which normal categories, demarcations, boundaries are disregarded (things may be speeded up, spread out, fused, or concentrated) in a way to which modern sciences has made us somewhat accustomed. The point is that the bright-shadow world is not a realm that lies wholly apart, separate from ours. Instead, the two worlds exist in an oblique or tangential relationship to each other, each slightly skewed when studied from the perspective of the other. Certain forms of power available in the bright-shadow world, mistakenly known as "magic," are thus not entirely out of our reach.

The Will

This point about the availability of magic power also relates to the will, a faculty accorded extraordinary importance in traditional narrative. Certainly there is no form of powerlessness more devastating than the loss of will: when this happens, as in melancholia, one is incapable of reaching out for whatever tiny resources may be at hand. Conversely, under many conditions there is almost nothing that proves more empowering than the act of really wanting something. This point has been richly illustrated by the cases of Morgiana, Ma'ruf, and Aladdin, and it is underscored by Richard Burton's comment on the dynamics of *Thousand and One Nights* as a whole:

> Amongst Eastern peoples, and especially adepts, the will of man is not a mere term for a mental or cerebral operation, it takes the rank of a substance; it becomes a mighty motive power . . . which . . . will perform a prime part in the Kinetics of the century to come. (*1001*, Suppl. IV, 426).

Burton's optimistic prophecy remains unfulfilled, and when we think about will, we are most likely to think of willful individuals (given too much to their own ways), or of students who choose to attempt what they are really unable to do, or of certain concepts linked mainly with "primitive" societies.

For example, we find some trace of Burton's concept of will in the Sudanese concept of *Wagdu*, a force that "is not of stone, not of wood, not of earth; . . . Wagdu is the strength which lives in the hearts of men and is sometimes visible because eyes see her and ears can hear the clash of swords and the ring of shields." Frobenius reports that although at times Wagdu disappears from the earth, even for hundreds of years, its return is eagerly awaited, so that true believers may once again enjoy the fruits of power, exactly as Black Elk does in North America.[7] To forsake violent forms of power, to espouse subtler psychological and spiritual forces like the *will*, like *wagdu*, is to move back to the world of the bright shadow.

In willing, the actor summons up and seeks to dominate (i.e., direct) certain vectors, which appear critical to a situation, so as to carry out the purposes he has in mind. At work, says Harding, is "an active wanting that can stand the impact of reality and has power to release [a person] . . . so that he can put forth his greatest effort and to sustain him through all difficulties and frustrations until he attains his wish."[8] Involved in an actor's control of the important vectors in a situation may be threat, the assertion that "I will dominate you," readiness to take whatever moves the situation may demand, an awareness of the dynamic structure of a situation (who else in the situation has power, where the cracks and crevices are), luck, the capacity to assert mental pressure, bravado. The actor has under his or her control whatever physical or psychological factors may exist in the environment that are relevant to the actor's needs. The vectors are lively and responsive.

Burton was correct when he identified will or desire as critical elements in the power structure of the bright-shadow world, for will is indeed a reflection of the enormous importance of subjective factors in every power situation. As Robert Assagioli observes, "The discovery of the will in oneself, and even more the realization that the self and the will are intimately connected, may come as a revelation which can change, often radically, a man's self-awareness and his whole attitude toward himself, other people, and the world" (9). Assagioli's position is supported by Otto Rank, who defines will as "the power which consciously and positively, yes, even creatively, forms both the self and the environment."[9] As Rank sees it, the goal of psychotherapy is to transform the negative will experience (based, he says, on the individual's early and humiliating realization that he is different from others) "into positive and eventually creative expression" (19); in short, to help a patient to will again, to will confidently and without a sense of guilt.[10]

Where will is lacking, observes Assagioli, such qualities as "aggressiveness and violence; fear; depression and despondency, greed and all forms of selfish desire" may dominate the individual."[11] Conversely, keen, positive desires, strongly felt, indicate that one is alive, unenchanted. To will means to choose to summon up, even in the darkest situations, whatever resources one has, however slight they are, from the most distant parts of one's network, so as to begin to construct or reconstruct one's situation, recognizing that usually there are some factors in one's network that can be applied to the situation. This is an act that requires considerable energy, and there may not be at a given moment much to call upon. Then the will is not sufficient. Or opposing forces may be so overwhelming that one must eventually succumb.

Many incidents from popular narrative illustrate effectively what can be achieved when the will is introduced into a situation and an individual takes responsibility for his or her own well-being. From *Thousand and One Nights* again, there comes the story of Ishak of Mosul, sitting in despair in his tent in the winter rain and mud. His servants bring him food for which he has no heart, all he desires being a woman from the tribe of al-Mahdi whose singing he loves. A sound is heard at the tent door, and there she is (VII, 136). In the *Pentamerone* Basile tells the story of Peruonto and his family, shipwrecked at sea, floating on a cask, apparently beyond help. Suddenly Lady Vastolla comes to herself and asks the big question: "Why should we make exit of life inside this hogshead? Why not wish for this vessel to become a splendid ship, so that we may escape from this peril and arrive in good port?"[12] The wish in some sense creates the reality. In various *Jataka* tales drought is attributed to the anger of a hermit; a little dog is reminded that all it needs to escape from a tight spot is to gnaw through a rope; and victory in battle is attributed to resolute resistance (II, 171; III, 5). And in an Italian story, "Pome and Peel," a young man when threatened observes boldly, "Doomed whether I speak or keep silent, I choose to speak" (Calvino, 98).

Lady Vastolla *chooses* to reimage the situation in which she and her family find themselves. In mentally turning the hogshead into a splendid ship, she identifies certain roles she and her husband may play if they will become actors, apparently persuading him to put aside his despair by an act of will and to add his physical strength to her sheer determination to save her children. She assembles the vectors necessary to turn a dark situation into a hopeful one. The structural role of the will is to create a situation (however imaginary) in which existing physical powers can be brought into play. The dog in the *Jataka* story apparently has never before tried chewing rope and for a time is so distressed at its situation that it cannot see the bone-rope analogy. Once this clue emerges and the dog grasps a way out, its will to escape returns, becomes relevant. In the Calvino story the young man's will to assert himself is a product of the realization that in a lose-lose situation action is nobler than inaction. And what of poor Ishak, in whose situation we have all been at some time or another? Does he choose to remember, relive, some spot of joy at this desolate time and not simply to go over and over again his present misery? Or perhaps he goes out and finds the woman he desires. It is also probable that certain of the networks of which he is a part—perhaps the tribal structure of his world—provide connections across which desires can be transferred. In any case, the structural role of the will in this story is to impel some action that relieves the situation.

Nowhere is the force of will more apparent than in stories like that of Moses in the bulrushes, in which a young child, who has scarcely even begun to achieve individuation, is abandoned to forest or water and survives, in part at least, because it refuses to give up, to die, to be diverted from its destiny. Stories of the "White Parrot" type, which are Spanish, Iranian, and ultimately Indian, form part of this widespread group.[13] They describe the problems of two children who are born (each with a beautiful star on the forehead) while their father is away, fighting for his kingdom. When the wicked palace butler reports to the father that the children are black, the father orders them thrown into the river, their mother into prison. As actors they virtually cease to be. But a fisherman, making a determination of his will, saves and raises them, and eventually their father hears about them, realizes who they are, and hires an old witch to destroy them once and for all, accepting the butler's story. The father cannot accept them as actors in his world. The will of the children to survive is to be tested in a situation where all the vectors are negative. The witch (who may be seen as representing all harsh physical forces in the environment) first persuades the girl that a fountain of silvery water is needed for their house, and the boy reluctantly goes after it. By alertness and courage (which he has plenty of, once he gets into the game) he is able to secure the water, despite the lion that has been set to guard it); so his sister has her fountain. The witch creates another vector, persuading the girl that she must have a twig from a very special tree, guarded by a snake, and again the brave lad is successful. The frustrated witch's third effort to destroy the young boy is the most serious of all: the lad must fetch a parrot from a round stone in a beautiful garden, but if he touches the bird too soon, it will fly away and he will be turned to stone. A problem in patience and timing—two resources which a young lad may not have.

Many vectors of great delicacy dart through this situation. Indeed, as a result of his eagerness, the boy experiences petrification. "Frozen" at a particular stage of development, he is finally rescued by his resourceful sister, who dares/wills to go looking for him herself and who demonstrates, in reaching for the bird, the sense of timing and sensitivity to situations that very early develops in some young women. Despite the odds against them (one malevolent adult and one ignorant adult), brother and sister organize numerous wildly divergent vectors—the aid of the fisherman, their own courage and resourcefulness, the ability to return to a task repeatedly—which together create a quite productive network. The boy projects his will three times into the situation, effectively but not conclusively, because he is as yet uncertain about his moves; the sister, with greater self-assurance and greater finesse, uses her will to resolve the issue once and for all. It is not difficult to see how such a narrative, with its beautifully climactic structure, could bend the personality of young listeners in some very productive ways, show them how to turn despair into success.

It is also a point of faith in the material we are examining that under certain conditions it is possible to reject a reality that seems unacceptable and to will (image) a more favorable position. This is what the infant Moses does—and the same point might be made about the infant Oedipus. In another story a man kept as a slave is dismissed with the blunt statement from his master, "Thou wast not my slave." And a hashish eater awakened from an erotic dream complains about not being allowed to sleep till "he had put it in." It is probably unwise—certainly unrealistic—to suggest that such incidents mean that anyone can have anything he/she wants badly enough. Every teacher knows students whose abilities are too slight to enable them to achieve their goals.[14] Certain actors—or certain actors at certain stages of development—cannot assemble the vectors of certain networks. However, the effect of centering or focusing attention and bringing the imagination into play can be powerful indeed when will and desire are the emotions being focused.

Exerting the will is possible only in contexts for which the actor has some feeling, a sense of his/her resources. Otherwise the will can project one into situations of grave danger. In *Thousand and One Nights* Greedy Kasim finds his way into a treasure room where his brother Ali Baba discovered enormous riches. But Kasim cannot remember the words (i.e., assemble the vectors) that will enable him to escape. On the other hand, the rogue is by his very nature one who has few material resources but a great ability to impose his will on situations, restructure reality to suit himself, and face critical situations without blanching. So if one is seriously interested in life-enhancement, some balancing is essential when the will is being brought into play—between the need to reach out aggressively in self-trust and the need to be realistic in one's wishes and avoid being taken in. One must be aware of the psychic energy one possesses at a given moment, for as Assagioli notes, "the discovery of the will in oneself, and even the realization that the self and the will are intimately connected, may come as a revelation which can change, radically, a man's self-awareness and his whole attitude toward himself, other people, and the world." (9)

Concentration has become an important theme in our culture. One hears sports coaches calling on their players for greater intensity and blaming losses on a failure of concentration. All teachers of spiritual disciplines—meditation, for example—speak of the need to focus attention as sharply as possible. Paolo Soleri, the architect, finds a solution to the urban sprawl of our age in mammouth "archologies" capable of holding millions of people so that even larger spaces will be left open for recreation. Biological life occurs, he argues, when life-substance achieves a certain thickness, when the networks reach a certain level of complexity.[15] Students of perception and creativity plead for the development of a capacity to carry out the task of psychological centering.[16] J. C. Pearce asserts that any move against "the certainties and energies of 'the world' calls for an equally sure conviction and a concentration on balance of mind. To center all the forces on the restructuring of an ordinary event in a non-ordinary way calls for exceptional organization of self."[17] When the power generated by such focusing is seen as an actual component of our world, the powers delineated in fantasies and popular tales begin to look less mysterious than they once did, and the world of the bright shadow takes on a reality that confirms what some childlike adults have known all along.

8 Moral Ties

Here we consider the positive side of issues having to do with morality in the bright-shadow world, evil (as enchantment) having been treated in chapter 5. A working definition? The theory of multiple worlds or realms of being suggests that morality consists of those actions that support and are supported by a particular world or network. When we speak of the bright-shadow world, we confront a network dominated by an existent force called "Goodness" (my term is purposely naive), which struggles against various Malevolent forces. The Goodness treated in traditional narrative about the bright-shadow world is something filtered out of the Judaism, Christianity, Islam, and Hinduism that engendered these stories. In them, the goodness of a person is a matter of his/her commitment to Goodness, the sum total of all those forces in a network that seek the implementation of what is life-enhancing. Responsibility for goodness/Goodness in the bright-shadow world seems curiously (but not exclusively) to fall upon the shoulders of young women.

Every great culture is oriented to a peculiar moral network and thus to its own understanding of goodness/Goodness, but this fact less and less often implies that all members of a network find satisfaction in it. The morality of the bright-shadow world is close enough to the dominant morality of the Western world, however, to permit its use as an instructional tool by that great system (fairytales and folktales and religious parables and legends are indeed used to teach morality, and many do seem to reflect borderline ties with various religious traditions), but these similarities may hide some basic distinctions between our world and the bright-shadow world. For example, the goodness of these stories does not seem to fit any of the types described by von Wright in his *The Varieties of Goodness*. It is not really instrumental goodness (a good knife), or technical goodness (good at something), or utilitarian goodness (a good plan). Nor does it fit, even, into von Wright's understanding of goodness as a virtue, for it is something more than a series of praiseworthy qualities (the "bag of virtues" approach). It has to do with an active, sensitive commitment to a network of creative forces presumed to be operating in the universe.[1] The most serious "sins" in the bright-shadow world are a loss of will and ability to control one's own life, meanness and bad-spiritedness, forgetting one's goals. By the same token, the dominant virtues are personal and domestic—gratitude, kindness, generosity, loyalty, persistence, personal dedication to certain issues. It is of such virtues, which from our modern perspective may be of less than overwhelming importance, that the goodness of the bright-shadow world is forged.

Any consideration of moral philosophy and moral psychology today inevitably leads one to the work of Lawrence Kohlberg; it is particularly relevant to the material I am dealing with here because its focus is on education and because it relates to moral growth and development. Kohlberg opposes the "bag of virtues" approach,[2] along with indoctrination (it does not work) and values clarification (a cop-out), and instead he identifies the achievement of "justice" as the goal or commitment of "moral people"—of whom Martin Luther King was a supreme example.

Kohlberg also marks out a series of developmental stages through which individuals pass as they grow in moral stature, and these stages clarify his own moral thinking: (1) the stage of punishment and obedience; (2) the stage of reciprocity—satisfying one's own needs and occasionally those of others; (3) the stage of good behavior, being nice; (4) the stage of orientation toward rules and authority; (5) the social contract stage; and (6) orientation toward universal ethical principles or principles of justice, such as the Golden Rule and the moral imperative. Of all these stages we find traces in traditional narrative, though it is also quite clear that traditional narrative does not recapitulate this list. What is missing from Kohlberg is the sense of other dimensions of reality that nurtures the bright-shadow sense of morality (*Philosophy of Moral Development*, I, 17–19).

The moral position espoused by Bruno Bettelheim provides yet another point of contrast. Bettelheim's views are important because, as we know, he has found fairytales a useful tool in the moral instruction of children and because he is a major influence on contemporary child-rearing practices. I have already suggested that Bettelheim's views are grounded in modern thinking and that he does not give much place to postmodern views, which in many ways I find closer to the position of traditional narrative. In *The Uses of Enchantment* Bettelheim argues that fairytales can show children the path to autonomous personhood or independence, values we of the twentieth-century enthusiastically espouse. Among Bettleheim's moral themes are the importance of a sense of the meaningfulness of one's experience (3), the use of one's cultural heritage as a means of growth (4), coming to grips with inner conflict (10), forming productive personal relations (11), recognizing anxieties (15), and learning to be oneself with another (279). Bettelheim stresses the role of the unconscious as a foundation for the intellect. He emphasizes the importance of extending one's interests beyond an immediate family, the power of hope, and the development of inner resources. It is, of course, hard to quarrel with any of this.

For Bettelheim, it is clear, becoming a mature, productive adult, able to function in the twentieth-century, is the key issue, and I have no intent to condemn such a stance except for its implication that the modern rational world IS and that everyone must dedicate his/her energies to it—*there being no other networks to inhabit*.[3] Bettelheim has neglected one of the important thrusts of traditional narrative, though one that can scarcely be fitted into the scheme to which he is committed. He stresses the need to normalize experience rather than to enhance it, and he implies that morality is the sum total of all the positive decisions we make about our behavior rather than a commitment to working with, being the instrument of, existent (though all too rarely recognized) forces operating in our world. The blind malignity of the Russian Baba Yaga and the wicked wazirs of *Thousand and One Nights* suggests the presence of an active force that is more than simply neglect, ignorance, or unsociability (I am, of course, sure that no one needed to tell Bettelheim about evil!). Similarly, the activities of Saktideva, Black Elk, and Psyche reflect positive drives to support, share, and sustain certain forms of goodness which they hold to be real and important.

The tension between modern moralities and those that might be linked with the bright-shadow world is reflected in a personal incident. Some years ago my daughter and I were traveling by train from Madrid to Paris on the last weekend of the summer vacation season. Our journey to the Spanish border presented no problems, but between San Sebastian and our destination the train was so crowded with returning vacationers that we could find no seats—not even a place to stand in the aisles. So we camped out all night in the vestibule of a coach. The conductors could not get through the cars to take tickets, and ours were still unpunched when we reached Paris, nine hours later. I contemplated turning them back as unused.

Several days later we reached our final destination by air, and it was discovered that one of my suitcases was missing. When, after a week's search, the luggage was recovered, I found the tickets, right at the top of my suitcase, and I had no difficulty reading the unwritten warning attached to them: turn these in if you dare, and we'll see what other troubles we can send your way!

My daughter argued that such an interpretation was the grossest kind of superstition, completely out of place in our enlightened world. I was less sure, open to the possibility that moral forces we had little knowledge of might be at work. I destroyed the tickets, unhappy with the eerie feeling that came over me whenever I thought about trying to turn them back. At work was a sense of the interconnectedness of all things and a conviction that one immoral act on my part could expose me to all kinds of reprisals from the universe. And, more positively, that I had some obligation to support, even in this trivial matter, certain forces of honesty and fairness I believed to be operating in my network, forces that an action of mine could strengthen or weaken, even though these forces certainly transcended any action I might take.

With such questions in mind, we can say that bright-shadow morality has the following structural elements.

1. The primary actors are those who have internalized a specific moral code or those who are undergoing indoctrination (through participation in some great quest, series of tasks, or testing program) either willingly or protestingly. And those figures, too, who rebel, defy, or remain indifferent because some other vision moves them, through ignorance, lack of imagination, or a sense of independence. And sometimes those who are puzzled or uncertain about how to act, but are aware of dimensions of reality beyond what is immediately apparent.

2. Among the important moral vectors are social pressures, rewards and punishments, conscience, various ambivalences, a range of feelings from strong desire to strong dislike, rebellion and acceptance, the determination to control or get one's way, a naive commitment to the good, and above all a strong sense of other dimensions of reality and a determination to respond to the influence of other worlds.

3. Power sources include community, consciousness at every level, promises of reward and threats of punishment, the spiritual realm to which ultimately every moral act is related, one's awareness of responsibility to the network.

4. The physical context includes various limitations placed on good and bad behavior; property, position, or other resources held by the principal actors or by others; deserts, rivers, long roads, and other

factors that hinder or aid the achievement of certain goals; and time constraints.

5. Characteristic denouements are the completion of a quest, the rescue of a land from famine, the reunion of man and wife after long separation, recognition of the value of the third son or daughter, and the completion of a task through the help of kindly animals.

In this context, "life-enhancing" must refer to all the ways in which some act or commitment reverberates through a network and creates situations with implications far richer than the physical/social factors that brought them into being.

The Participatory Consciousness

So we postulate a moral world requiring the very nicest balancing of objective and subjective factors, a world where the individual must be aware of certain hard moral facts, but a world as well where subjective input can make a difference. Indeed, the actors who stand out in the bright-shadow world are those who have attempted some shaping of the psychic content, have themselves forced things to fit, whose egos have become involved.[4] As Little Diamond says in *At the Back of the North Wind* during an especially difficult time, "I can't give in to this. I've been to the back of the north wind. Things go right there, and so I must try to get things to go right here. I've got to fight the miserable things" (150–51; Kohlberg's Stages 4 and 6).

Consider a case from *Thousand and One Nights*: al-Abbas counsels Ma'mun to put his uncle to death, and the uncle himself admits that the advice is good. "But thou," he adds to his nephew (who has declined the deed), "hast done after thine own nature and hast put away what I feared with what I hoped" (*1001*, IV, 112). The nephew has ceased to see the issue as a problem in objective statecraft and has brought back to this very important Middle Eastern relationship a personal, subjective factor, one always important in this area of the world. The actor becomes more than a ruler; he is a *person* whose responsibility is not to dominate relationships but to sustain and support them (Kohlberg's Stage 5).

The same point is made in a story told both by the Sufis and the Grimm Brothers about a king who learns that he will recover from an illness only if he samples the blood of all the children in his realm. For a time he seriously considers this option and all that it entails, only to conclude that his own recovery is not worth the death of a single child. This rejection of the dominant role for himself is a psychological vector of enormous significance, especially for one accustomed to all the ego-enhancement that kings require, and as he projects it, his health improves dramatically.[5] He discovers that he does not belong solely to a network of statecraft and royal power; that as king, he is also involved with his people. When he makes common cause with them, when he becomes a participant in their concerns and affections, he regains his health. He has tapped into one of the great power sources of bright-shadow life and has become, like a gnome in the Northern European tale "The Underground Workers," "one of those beings to whom is given the care of the world" (*Ehstnische Märchen*, 230; Kohlberg's Stage 6).

The rashness and impulsiveness which so often mark the behavior of folk and fairytale heroes is more often than not a result of the sudden, zestful—even violent—entry of the participating ego into a situation. A younger brother rejects hills of gold and silver in favor of something better: they do not move me, he asserts, speaking as a totally independent actor, and as a result, he encounters such marvels as the familiar tablecloth always covered with food, a knapsack from which a troop of men can be summoned, and a horn that will smash any fortification. All because he responded to his own sense that something was not quite right for him and took a chance on the unknown, the undefined.

In a Sufi tale Mojud repeatedly carries out the insane commands of a man dressed in "shimmering green"—takes off his clothes, leaps into a stream, works as a farmer, walks to Samarkand, and eventually develops wonderful talents—because he is always ready to participate in the moment, systematically *excluding purpose and direction* from his life (*Tales of the Dervishes*, 155). Our tendency would be to see a very weak actor/ego here, an absence of significant inner moral control, of purpose and goal. But traditional narrative tends to support a commitment of the self to emergent possibilities, to a network that is still being constructed, and to condemn a miserly holding onto the self and the roles society assigns to it.

Much the same point emerges from the story of Ma'ruf the Cobbler, which we have already surveyed. The primary motivation of all the great events of that tale is the misery of Ma'ruf, as husband to Fatima "the Dung." But he cannot make his own ego a participant in the situation because of her absolute domination of him/it. She is like an enormously strong defensive line in football that will not allow a quarterback to establish himself as an effective player. Then comes a break—power offered by the jinn (we may see it as the sudden discovery of a crack into which he can project his own ego)—and without any hesitation he is off to a distant city. At first he is shocked by his boyhood friend's deceitful scheme, but seeing how the game works, he gives it his own individual twist, and soon he is dominating, outdoing his friend (who tries unsuccessfully to remind him that the network in which he is participating so joyously is purely one of their own devising). But a man's willingness to work at a network may be part of its reality, and Ma'ruf draws the powerful ego of his new wife, Dunya, into his scheme too, and quickly she becomes an extension of his own ego, deeply, personally involved. By her own cleverness she thwarts malevolent forces and draws more and more power into her own hands. She has a marvelous sense of the vectors operating in the situation. So debts are repaid, evil is defeated, and the kingdom is stabilized. A joyous affirmation of the power of an actor to gain his ends by wit, courage, and personal involvement (Kohlberg's Stage 2).

The Pragmatic Element

Where morality is seen as an effort to preserve the network rather than to apply certain imposed and perhaps poorly understood rules, pragmatic concerns often (and happily) overwhelm idealism. The good I do may benefit me (as well as the universe), preserving my well-being or status, helping me to gain desired ends, even as I advance the cause of others. Moral stances should be useful, but there is also the possibility that the pragmatic approach may flower into something more. Consider the case of King Kalinga, whose story makes up *Jataka* tale 276 (II, 251).

Kalinga is deeply troubled by the devastation that has overtaken his land; the fields lie wasted, the cattle are dying, and even royal acts of piety have done nothing to alleviate the situation. Overwhelmed by a sense of guilt and inadequacy, Kalinga examines the lives of others in a much-blessed neighboring country and finds that they suffer from a similar sense of guilt. The king denies that he is virtuous, since once he accidentally killed a fish. His mother, the queen, confesses that she has favored the wife of her eldest son over the wife of the youngest. The royal viceroy recounts the discomfort he has caused his servants. A royal chaplain admits coveting the royal chariot. The royal driver once killed a crab while pursuing his duties.

The dispenser of the public rice cheated a seller out of a single grain. And a starving woman reached out her hand toward a sum of money left in her care. Yet despite all these "wrongdoings," the nearby kingdom prospers and assurances are made that in no case was any "sin" intended. All the actors seem reasonably relaxed and accepting of their own natures, the vectors at play in their lives. Kalinga internalizes what he has learned from his envoys and happily watches the rain begin to fall (Kohlberg's Stage 3).

It is easy to dismiss as irrelevant the (to us) trivial lapses in morality to which the people in the neighboring kingdom admit and to forget that the grain of rice held back and the killing of the fish are seen as serious breaches of morality in the cultural context presented by the story. Kalinga is aware—far too aware—of the seriousness of such acts but puzzled that the other kingdom continues to be blessed. His awareness, in fact, amounts to naivete: he is a puritan, a precisionist, who has gained nothing by his morality since obviously it has not helped him make contact with the powers inherent in the network within which he lives. In fact, his obsession with guilt may actually hinder the working of positive forces. The neighboring ruler clearly has learned to be much more relaxed about his moral behavior, has grasped the dynamics of his network, has tested the waters and reached some useful conclusions about the way power operates. Lapses, "sins," he has come to regard as the inevitable result of the physical facts that constitute the world, and he has realized that they do not seriously impede the operation of spiritual or natural forces.[6] The well-being of his kingdom seems to be linked to this understanding. Good sense carries the day, some balancing of subjective and objective factors that will actually work in a given situation. When Kalinga grasps these truths, he appears to adopt a more pragmatic attitude about good and evil, and the problems of his kingdom disappear.

Yet more abstractly: during a time when the physical context of life has shriveled up, two actors (who represent many other actors) are exposed to various tiny vectors, which are perceived by one actor to be of primary moral significance, involving fundamental questions of right and wrong. The other actor perceives that in the total moral scheme of things these tiny vectors need not be considered—indeed, to consider them would prove debilitating. In fact, life-enhancement is closely tied to accurate perception of the insignificance of these vectors. As a result of taking these vectors too seriously, the first actor loses contact with power sources (i.e., his ability as a king to tap into resources that will benefit his kingdom), and he is overwhelmed by physical disaster. The other actor, untroubled, maintains his contact with power.

Maintaining the Balance

A question of fundamental importance to pragmatic individuals is just how far they can push their affairs, when they will risk overloading the system by demanding too much, so that the whole structure breaks down and they lose everything. Many of these stories seem to illustrate Kohlberg's fifth stage. This sense of balance or right-ness, which traditional narrative turns into a moral issue, provides the germ of the modern ecological movement. And it is reminiscent of "Buddhist economics," which E. F. Schumacher has characterized as "amazingly small means leading to extraordinarily satisfactory results."[7] It also recalls the Balinese emphasis, which, Morris Berman suggests,

> is on balance—no variable is deliberately maximized—and the ethics of the situation is "karmic," that is, it obeys a law of nonlinear cause and effect, especially with respect to the environment. As Bateson puts it, "lack of systemic wisdom is always punished." If you fight the ecology of a system, you lose—especially when you "win."[8]

So the general position in traditional narrative is that an actor should never push too hard; to do so is to permit the entry into the system of those malevolent vectors that are always waiting in the wings and do not have human interests at heart. These forces will destroy all sense of fairness and altruism, along with those instruments that only function when employed with wisdom and moderation. Then naked egoism will rage unchecked.

Illustration of this truth can be drawn from many sources. In an Armenian tale, "The Flight of Chance," luck abandons the house of a peasant whose daughter misuses her father's resources, returning when the girl is ejected. In the version of "Hansel and Gretel" published in the 1819 edition of *Kinder- und Hausmärchen*, the Grimm Brothers (by now the old folktale is very much their own creation) have Hansel suggest that he and his sister ride together on a duck's back across a river separating them from home. "No," answers the wiser sister; "that will be too heavy for the little duck, it shall take us over one after the other."[9] In "A Tale of the Tontlawald" the heroine is warned not to eat the thirteenth dish, which contains hidden blessings, and she seems to accept this interdiction and grasp its rationale:

> We must not touch them, else it will be the end of our happy life. Alas, men would be on better terms with this world if they did not, in their greed, claim all gifts for themselves, without leaving something in thanks to the heavenly giver of blessings. Greed is man's greatest fault (*Ehstnische Märchen*, 31).

"On better terms with this world." What a splendid way to put it!

The theme is common in the *Jataka* tales as well. In story 72 a vile wretch, a kind of South Asian Kurtz, who first takes the ivory tusks of an elephant and then the stumps as a means of paying his debts, is swallowed up in a yawning chasm in the earth when he demands the roots as well (I, 176). In other stories the death of a tortoise that clung too persistently to its home and its ego is noted, and the hearers are warned not to say, "I have sight, I have hearing, I have smell, I have taste, I have touch, I have a son, I have a daughter, I have numbers of men and maids for my service, I have precious gold" (II, 56). And a warning is given to travelers who find metal and gems in a fountain but are discontented because they think there may be more (II, 206). In all cases the principal role of the actor is to go easy, to consciously limit his grasping for power, to ensure that a proportionate share of limited vectors is available for others. Experience is enhanced by restraint rather than by greed.

A certain sensitivity to the problem of legitimate enjoyment and unacceptable greed is reflected, too, in tales about making appropriate choices, choices that enable one to share a privilege or physical resource with others, choices that also reveal something important about the person making them, his/her place in the moral equation. The vectors that one allows into one's sphere of activity reveal much of importance about oneself. Here Kohlberg's fifth stage shades over into the sixth—the "Universal Ethical Principle Orientation"—except that in traditional narrative we are dealing with existent powers, not merely principles. A sensitivity to this issue is manifested in the modern attitude toward the budget-making process in any complex institution: budgets reflect priorities, which in turn reflect choices and goals. The situation requires balancing the demands of one's ego with practical considerations and a sense of the significant forces operating in the universe, even on a crowded train between San Sebastian and Paris.[10] In a Sicilian tale it is suggested that if two halves of an apple are offered to someone, a true friend will never take the larger half,[11] perhaps not even letting the friend choose first, but reaching out instead for the smaller piece. In "The Two Caskets" some well-informed and well-intentioned cats coach a girl to choose the least attractive of several boxes.[12] Covan's two brothers ask their parents for large, unblessed cakes before they set out on quests that prove failures, while Covan, the successful heir, chooses the small, blessed cake, which he never fails to share with those along his way.[13] In *Gesta Romanorum* a wretched carpenter, trying to recover some stolen gold, chooses the heaviest of three boxes and finds it full of earth.[14]

All of this has to do ultimately with a certain stance the actor adopts that involves nondestructive movement across the great networks of the world, where the power lies, power that can very easily be used up. This stance, with all its subtleties, is made quite clear in popular narrative: a carefree, devil-may-care attitude (with regard to one's own needs) is better than a calculating, egoistic, overly acquisitive stance (Stage 2). Self-interest is not categorically condemned, if it is sustained in a spirit of joyous, Ma'rufian abandon among others who are also promoting themselves. In such a case the number of operative vectors is actually multiplied. Ma'ruf is extremely greedy, but he does well and is not condemned—his manipulations are directed against others who are even greedier than he. Among high-minded equals, self-effacement is probably a better stance: one will get one's chance when the time is right. The balance, admittedly, is hard to work out, and it is suggested that humans never do entirely control a process: the real direction is given by the situation or the inner form of the material; the best that we can do is to be alert to possibilities so as to facilitate or bend the process and to be aware of limitations so as not to destroy the process we are trying to use.[15]

Fair play (Stage 2 morality) is an important feature of this sense of balance. This is a common motif in traditional narrative, and it is readily learned by many children who hear fairytales and folktales. Robert H. Frank suggests that when we are behaving fairly we are being guided by something other than self-interest. We may find his discussion of fairness in *Passions within Reason* rather heavily dominated by economic issues, but it is worth reading, nonetheless.[16] In bright-shadow terminology "fair play" means not taking more than one is entitled to, not going out of turn, not trying to win at all costs, not cheating, acknowledging the worth of other players in the game. The various leagues we establish are designed to ensure that individuals of various ability levels will compete together, and the handicap system is an attempt to make individuals of various abilities competitive. Ultimately adults in both the bright-shadow world and the real world learn that life is not fair, but even when they come to this sobering realization, those who are morally responsible continue to act fairly in their personal relationships. This may reflect their view that they do have an obligation to support essential Goodness—or the rather more existentialist conviction that the only Goodness is the goodness they themselves create. Generally speaking, this is school-boy, not sophisticated, morality, but after all, battles and moral victo-ries are not won in libraries and think-tanks but on the playing fields of Rutgers and OSU.[17]

The Great Virtues

An important by-product of the openness to experience traditional narratives project is the high value they place upon gratitude, kind-ness, generosity, and courtesy—all marks of an honest and open nature, all linked in various ways to the hierarchical, supernaturally oriented world that is the context of fairytale and folktale. These virtues are seen as much more than pleasant qualities that grease the wheels of life—they are the positive forces, the great vectors, that keep the networks functioning. How else but by a spirit of kindness can a world without credit cards and government subsidies be held together? How else can community be sustained? It is the way they fit together and contribute to a marvelous unity that makes them more than a "bag of virtues." We are dealing, quite clearly, with fifth-stage morality. The spirit at work here is neatly suggested in the Grimm Brothers' tale "The Two Travelers," where it is noted that "mountain and valley do not meet, but certainly human beings do, especially good and bad" (Magoun and Krappe, 385). Popular narrative worries a lot about these meetings.

The great national literatures offer many models of the generous and kindly individual. Widely disseminated are stories of the shoe-maker and his wife who make clothes for friendly elves and are hand-somely rewarded or of the poor who entertain a Jesus rejected by the rich (Stith Thompson, 342; Magoun and Krappe, 312). Ovid tells the story of Baucis and Philemon, who entertain the gods cordially (with-out recognizing them as such) and as a reward are given a pitcher always brimming with milk. Even in death they are permitted to be together, as huge oak trees, boughs intertwined (*Metamorphoses*, VIII). And from the Middle East comes a rich set of traditions about Hatim Tai, a sixth-century Arab chieftain who from his youth was noted for his extraordinary generosity. Near his legendary tomb were huge pots in which meals for the faithful were cooked; when after his death the camels of pilgrims visiting the shrine were slaughtered for food, his sons replaced the dead animals with living ones. Hatim Tai was a poet who left many verses in praise of generosity, a hero who appears in many Arab texts, even the central figure of a Punjab romance.[18]

The theme of kindness appears most dramatically in stories about kindness to animals, since, I suppose, animals represent in most striking form a certain helplessness that challenges and motivates those who have a sense of the sacredness of the natural world. Potent communities develop where people and animals live together in harmony and mutual awareness, and these communities can be seen as elements of the networks that make up the bright-shadow world. Moreover, this topic stimulates reflection on the interplay between idealism and pragmatism traditional stories delight in: kindness to animals, especially to small animals, offers very little by way of practical reward, though it may be richly rewarded in folktales and fairytales. For almost inevitably, it seems, the kindly person finds himself in a position where his only means of escape is through the help some animal—often the tiniest—can provide, so that an earlier moment of sensitivity to its needs pays off handsomely. The dominant actor becomes the sufferer, the sufferer (inferior actor) becomes the aid-bringer (the source of helping vectors). It is both significant and curious that on this point Mu'tazilite or rational Islamic theology is quite explicit: compensation for unmerited pain on this earth, the Mu'tazilites insist, is due not only to true believers and innocent children but also to animals. "An animal must receive compensation in another life for the suffering that the selfishness and cruelty of mankind has inflicted on it in this world. Otherwise God would not be just. A transcendental protection of animals, as it were."[19] M. Esther Harding takes another but equally interesting position when she asserts in *Psychic Energy* that animals have the bearing and dignity of completely integrated individuals. They are fully themselves. To respect animals is to respect the quality of wholeness in all living beings.[20] Fifth-stage morality shades over into something even higher, and the context of life becomes all-important: the choices an actor makes about his context determine that actor's fate. This is very much in the spirit of postmodernism.

The kindness-to-animals theme takes various forms in our material. The familiar story of Androcles and the lion, which goes back to classical Latin literature, is repeated in the *Gesta Romanorum*, where is found also the story of the rescue of the lion, the monkey, and the

serpent from a pit—and their gratitude (181, 213–14). Sometimes the
issue is one of mutual aid, as in "The Golden Bird" or "The Bird Grip"
story that has already been surveyed. A helpful fox patiently gives
the young seeker advice about how to secure the objects he needs,
continuing to help him however often the boy forgets his instructions
because only this lad can free him from enchantment. Uraschimataro,
a Japanese fisherman, throws back into the sea a turtle, and later this
same creature saves the fisherman from certain death in a ship-
wreck.[21] A fisherman's son has thrown fish back into the water and
has treated his cat, dog, and mouse with care. For him they team up
to recover a precious ring that someone holds in his mouth while he
sleeps. The mouse forces the sleeper to sneeze away the ring, and the
dog runs off with it; when the dog drops the ring into the sea, the fish
recovers it.[22]

In tales like "Psyche and Eros" tiny insects sort out a pile of
seeds a helpless woman has been commanded to arrange before
morning. In a Hungarian story the lad Ferko is starving. To him a
harsh brother will give no food—unless Ferko will let that brother
blind him. The blinding is indeed carried out, but Ferko is aided by
various animals he has assisted—a wolf whose damaged paw he has
treated, a mouse with a broken foot, etc. A striking contrast between
the behavior of animal and human actors!

In still another type of tale, the helpful animal is a snake, even
the king of the snakes, who behaves with the interests of human
beings at heart. In Swahili Hassebu (Joseph) stories and in *Ocean of the
Streams of Story* this august figure permits himself to be sacrificed for
the well-being of mortals.[23] In "The Charmed Ring" a merchant's son
who saved a snake from death is directed by the snake to his father's
palace, where he requests and is given various wonder-working implements (*Indian Fairy Tales*, 91). And Cosquin observes that in certain
Indian versions, the husband of Psyche is identified as *"le roi des
serpents."*[24] The biblical serpent is initially depicted as a beautiful creature that walks upright, the embodiment of many virtues. And it is
possible to read into the Genesis account of the temptation the idea
that the serpent was actually taking the part of ignorant man against a
God who sought to keep the blessings of knowledge to himself.[25]

The tradition of dressed animals is also related to this theme of
kindness to animals, though we know its history almost entirely
through the art of children's book illustration. C. S. Lewis in *Surprised
by Joy* notes his own interest, as a child, in drawing pictures of such
creatures—"the anthropomorphized beasts of nursery literature"
(6)—but I know of no other reference by writers or illustrators them-

selves. This phenomenon can be observed in such diverse volumes as Gustave Doré's illustrations for Perrault's *French Fairy Tales*, Beatrix Potter's *Tales of Peter Rabbit* (1901), Ernest Shepard's illustrations for Kenneth Grahame's *Wind in the Willows*, Patrick Baynes's illustrations for Lewis's Narnia books, various books by Maurice Sendak from the 1950s and 1960s, Arthur Frost's illustrations for Harris's *Uncle Remus* (1892), Randy Monk's illustrations for Joseph Gaer's retellings of the *Jataka* tales (1955), and the illustrations of Charles Bennett and Ernest Griset for *Aesop's Fables* (1866, 1869).

In other cases—Hugh Lofting's *The Story of Dr. Dolittle* (1922), for example—the animals, while not clothed, are humanized by their poses and gestures. Ernest Shepard's illustrations for the Pooh books make it clear that the animals in Christopher Robin's nursery are only toys, and as far as I have been able to determine, Shepard's, Tenniel's famous illustrations to *Alice in Wonderland*, and Jean de Brunhoff's for *Babar* are the only cases in which dressed animals and humans appear in the same drawings. This technique intensifies the horror-fantasy element in *Alice* and the warm good humor of *Babar*.[26]

An ecological dimension to this material merits note as well— the conviction that one is kind to animals out of respect for the entire natural network and a desire to ensure its well-being. Here, surely, there is ample opportunity for human beings to exercise creative talents. Dasent's story "The Two Step-Sisters" offers a common version of this theme: a lassie avoids damaging a hedge by stepping over it and relieves a cow by milking her, a sheep by shearing it, and an apple tree by plucking its fruit. In return the girl is shown how to carry water in a sieve by plugging up its holes with ashes (114). And according to *Ocean of the Streams of Story*, the king of Benares was once so impressed by the beauty of swans flying in white clouds that he caused tanks to be built to provide all living creatures with security from injury (I, 12).

An important complement to this theme of kindness to animals is the body of stories describing the devastating punishments meted out to those who practice cruelty. The theme occurs in the German tradition, in South Asian literature, in American Indian tales, and I am sure elsewhere as well. The Grimm Brothers' "The Dog and the Sparrow" is particularly harrowing: a dog that has befriended a bird lies down in the street and is run over and killed by a brutish wagon driver. The sparrow succeeds in destroying the man's horses and, by hammering away at the terrifying refrain "not poor enough yet," lures the man into butchering his own wife with an axe.[27] In *Jataka* 222 a hunter shoots two baby monkeys and their mother despite their pleas for life, and the earth yawns at his feet and he falls into the flames of Hell. In 438 a wretch kills and eats two lizards, a learned partridge, a calf, and a cow. He is torn to shreds by a lion and hurled into a pit. In 516 a man who splits open the head of a sleeping monkey spends seven years as a leper and is reborn in hell. And in 520 a vigorous protest is entered against killing a calf for leather for a sword sheath. In all of these cases a being who was presumed to be a very weak actor on the world's stage is suddenly identified as the center of many lines of force that protect it or (if that is not possible because of certain physical facts) avenge its death vigorously.

Cosquin argues that much of the material about kindness to animals can be traced back to Buddhist sources in Central Asia, and the amount of this material in the *Jataka* tales and in other South Asian sources is impressive. However, the peevish Hartland denies that all kindness-to-animal stories are Buddhist (a claim Cosquin never made): "Scholars . . . have told us that wherever a grateful beast thrusts her muzzle into the story, that story must come from India, and must have arisen since the rise of Buddhism." Many such stories, he argues, appear to originate in areas geographically remote from India. But there can be no doubt that this is a motif of great importance in Buddhist texts, a consonance between Buddhist themes and views we have been observing.[28]

The issues involved in working out a statement about comparative morality (our world's and the bright-shadow world's) are truly mind-boggling. The vastly different scope of the two worlds creates problems, especially when the moral issues are subtle. And there have been, certainly, very different reasons for telling and listening to fairytales: is the hearer a young Asian prince seeking wisdom about the ways of the world? or a modern child being helped to maturity by parents? or a public-school teacher agonizing over what he/she should be trying to teach about moral behavior? or an adult, of any time period, being alerted and sensitized to fresh dimensions of experience? The kindness-to-animals issue probably looks different in a high-minded, hierarchical world than it does to us, and seeking adventure in a world of boxes within boxes is not quite the same as seeking adventure in a world of scientific "facts." Moreover, our world has essentially rejected any supernatural basis for morality (though many of us maintain such a position privately), but such a position is often affirmed in the material we have before us. And as if all this did not make the issue difficult enough, we find even within the bright-shadow world itself great divergence of opinion about all kinds of issues—the place of pragmatism and idealism in the moral life, for example. Ma'ruf and Aladdin would surely have agreed with my daughter and attempted to return the uncollected railway tickets! But they would have rejected travel by train in the first place—as too slow, too earthbound.

"Simple" and "naive" are words that come to mind when we reflect on the morality of the bright-shadow world: issues are rarely complex or agonizing, and inhabitants of that world seem willing to risk and make commitments without always knowing what they are getting into. Pragmatism proves a strong counterforce to idealism. This gives the actions of folk heroes both charm and a certain breathless quality. Our world, by contrast, teaches us to keep things under control, close to the vest. The poker face is symbolic. Psychologically the characters of the bright-shadow world do not appear to live very deeply (though as von Franz has made clear, their actions may be of great psychological interest). And if these characters rarely push to Maslovian heights, their life-choices do bring Erikson to mind: they choose to trust themselves; they develop a sense of autonomy; they show initiative and industry; etc. That world is not dominated by mind, as ours is (knowledge remaining essentially unorganized), and it lacks the sense of unbearable paradox characteristic of so many modern systems. The story of Kalinga, just surveyed, sidesteps moral issues that a modern ethicist would feel compelled to consider seriously or neglect completely.

The siting of the bright-shadow world between opposites is also important for any consideration of contrasts. To us that world appears as a halfway place (either—depending on our sophistication—not the real world or just one of countless possible worlds), though to its inhabitants (i.e., those who have adopted its values) it is the focal point of all reality, ours being one of many worlds set in an oblique relationship to it. Speaking in the broadest possible terms, we can suggest that in the bright-shadow world intentions, acts, and results, both good and evil, create situations subject to an infinite number of permutations, certain elements being critical at one time, other factors coming into play at other times. Pragmatism and idealism find a synthesis here, as do aristocratic elements and concern for the common man, and the input of both hemispheres of the brain.

The objective reality of moral forces is recognized (far more than it is among us), yet a place is also made for the shaping of situations by individuals with their own agendas. Despite the relatively small psychological scale of the bright-shadow world, it is a place of many possibilities. And while the elimination of malevolent and illusory forces is seen as important, even greater stress is placed on preserving the moral balance (especially where the ego is involved), keeping the ecological system going, maintaining the networks that distribute power to the whole moral process, and, according to von Franz, struggling with that drive to destructiveness which is part of all of us. "It is that spirit of 'no life no love,'" which, she says, "has always been associated with the essence of evil."[29] The most serious moral condemnation is reserved for the egoist who rolls through life unchecked, paying no attention to the effect of his actions on the world around him. The power of such an individual is often traced to the fact that those who might rein him in are themselves victims of illusion or enchantment. These ineffectual individuals, too, are severely condemned.

Since the enhancement of experience is very much a moral issue, this material is rich in examples of moves to higher positions, and many kinds of small acts are seen as reverberating through great networks. Ordinary words and gestures can evoke spiritual forces. Appeals to the better nature of certain individuals can be more potent than legalities. The lives of others may be more important than one's own ego. Solutions to certain moral dilemmas lie in passing beyond objective and subjective considerations. A situation may be transformed by those who enter fully into it. Self-interest can legitimately be combined with the interests of others. It may be necessary to relax moral standards in order to achieve moral goals, to move from the comparative certainty of Kohlberg's Stage 3 to the terrors of Stage 6. Not a move to another context but some altering of the context in which one finds himself, by the introduction of new vectors and the discovery of new power sources, seems to be called for.

9   Personal Identity

"An ever-increasing awareness has made the *problem of identity* the most pressing psychological problem of our time."[1] So writes Reza Arasteh, an Iranian-American analyst with ties to both the East and the West. In the last few decades many adults have gone to incredible lengths to "find themselves." Others have felt their identities threatened by the work they do or the commitments they must—or cannot—make. The aggressive behavior around us stimulates our own aggression. We compete; we link ourselves with certain kinds of achievement; we feel that our identity is threatened by anomie or, if we do not like ourselves, we attempt concealment; we lament that only part of ourselves shows or that we are too fully identified by the wrong things—Social Security numbers, driver's licenses, test scores, credit cards, houses, jobs, and automobiles. We are, to the fairies of MacDonald's *Phantastes*, the "thick people" (17), trapped in a set of murky identity problems from which traditional narratives seem to offer some ways of escape. The many children's games that focus on problems of identity (Follow the Leader, Tag) forge a subtle but important link between the modern world and the bright-shadow world, preparing children for adult issues, building on many themes from fairytales and folktales.

Much of what actors in the bright-shadow world do is related to identity questions: they choose (and may be diverted from) certain goals they have accepted as their own; they forget names; they descend into and emerge from obscurity and are recognized by other people as people too; and if they are strong, they escape enchantment and go on quests that further enhance their sense of selfhood, enabling them to transcend earlier stages of limited awareness. Many figures in traditional narrative never come anywhere near achieving personhood, however: they remain simply older brothers, scullery maids, nameless wicked wazirs, greedy merchants, or loungers about. Thus much of this material supports Heinz Lichtenstein's suggestion that there is a "high degree of uncertainty about the chance of an infant developing into a human individual," Jourard's observation that it is "difficult, but possible, to reinvent one's identity," and Bottigheimer's position that by the mistreatment they face, especially the demand that they be silent, women in fairytales constantly find their identities threatened.[2]

From the rich variety of activities described here important patterns of achievement, integration, and experience-enhancement emerge. The actors in stories where the question of identity is important may have a strong sense of identity, need to develop such a sense, or for one reason or another abandon or never take up the quest for it. The physical context is the set of elements that direct the actor into certain kinds of activities or against which he struggles; the environment provides resources or diverts him from the project. The vectors in identity stories are negative or positive contacts with various physical and social factors, the actor's awareness of the reactions he generates in friends/rivals, and his own communications with his inner being. The power sources—his own psychic strength to carry out a project that will take time; the resources provided by other individuals; the praise or criticism of friends and associates (including animals); and a vigorous drive to self-exploration or self-achievement that seems innate in certain people—are whatever is needed to provide the initial impulse and to generate the power. In identity stories, to put it briefly, the actor begins to tap power sources deep within himself/herself and projects vectors of his/her own making into the physical context. If he/she is successful, a 'self' is found.

Modern psychologists have not been quiet on this topic, and from their work have come many theories about what identity is and how it develops. No one point of view, however, seems most applicable to an understanding of the issue as it is presented in popular narrative. Erik Erikson suggests that the human sense of identity grows out of the way an individual handles certain critical choice points in his/her life, opting (when making appropriate choices) to be a trusting, autonomous, generative, industrious, social person, a person of integrity and initiative. Heinz Lichtenstein traces our sense of identity to the experiences of difference and similarity each of us must face—even at the earliest stages of life. "The *sense* of identity, or awareness of identity," Lichtenstein observes, "involves comparison and contrast—with some emphasis on basic likeness, but with special attention to obvious unlikenesses" (*Dilemma of Human Identity*, 57–58). Self-image, he argues, is "perhaps vitalized" and certainly maintained by "the continual redefinement which accompanies comparison and contrast with others" (58).[3] And Norman Holland suggests that our identity is the sentence each of us is trying to live out, the single novel which the novelist writes all his life, the total lifestyle to which all the details of life contribute. Identity, he asserts, is "a basic trend that regulates mental functioning."[4]

For Jung and his followers, the elements that go into creating an identity are subsumed under the term "individuation," a process of "pulling together all those fragmented and chaotic bits and pieces of unconscious personality, into an integrated whole."[5] More specifically, "individuation" refers to a determined effort on the part of the individual to integrate the conscious or rational parts of the personality with the shadowy or unconscious elements so that "all the possibilities immanent in the individual" might be realized (Singer, 140). *Individuation* and *life-enhancing* thus come to mean very much the same thing, and both are involved in the process of transformation, a process that, as Jacobi notes, can be of greater or lesser intensity, depending on the individual.[6] While no fairytale about identity illustrates all of these approaches to the issue, certain narratives do stand out for the extraordinary richness with which they treat this theme. Two of them now, before we get into some of the details of the process.

For Black Elk, the identity issue began with that transforming vision experienced when he was nine. At this time he was taken ill and felt himself summoned to his grandfathers, gathered on an immense plain in the sky. At each point of the compass he saw great heroes, and soon they were dancing around him. There is something of the biblical Joseph's sense of identity in the grandeur of all of this, as well as the sense of "being different" to which Lichtenstein calls attention. Eriksonian choices are implied in the boy's acceptance of all this attention, which evidently would demand some kind of response from himself. At a celestial council the young boy was introduced to the powers of the world and given his name, Eagle Wing Stretches. The lad was also promised power of his own and given a red stick— the living center of his nation—which eventually he caused to blossom. After he was granted the powers of earth and heaven and sky, he found himself to be the "chief of all the heavens" (Neihardt, 31) and received tribute from many people. On a great bay horse he bore the arms given him by his ancestors, and he saw "the shapes of all things in the spirit, and the shape of all shapes as they must live together like one being" (43). Powerful vectors swirled all around him; he was living at the very center of the Jungian archetypes. After this tremendous affirmation of selfhood, Black Elk awoke and was welcomed back to life by his parents. For some time the young man drew a sense of identity from this experience, although the power of the vision seemed to fade as he became depressed over the decline of his people—he worried about his own powers of generativity; he was convinced that the vision and the identity actually belonged to someone else. It is clear from our perspective that the the power available to Black Elk was not sufficient to sustain and work out the cognition.

Being sanctified, empowered, commissioned, placed at the center of things, rendered special—these are the identity themes that come into play here and link Black Elk to the analysts whose work we have just surveyed. Throughout the remainder of his narrative, the vision and its possible meanings dominate Black Elk's consciousness. He is told by his father that there is some special task for him to carry out, and his parents acknowledge, accept, and affirm his role without any of the uneasiness felt by Jacob about Joseph's extravagant claims (Gen. 37:5–11). Once the sight of a spotted eagle stirs in Black Elk the queer feeling that he is back again in the world of his vision. On another occasion, given a coat of war paint, he recalls his vision and experiences levitation. In moments of weakness (as when he encounters white soldiers) thoughts of his vision strengthen him, and he makes the right moves. He derives strength, too, from a voice in the clouds. At sixteen he confesses that he does not know how to do what his grandfathers desire, but when a few years later his vision is reenacted by the members of his tribe, he senses the absolute reality of the other world, and this releases his own powers. He comes to regard himself as one who has seen into the heart of reality, an individual of initiative, autonomy, and integrity. If these qualities have ever existed they are displayed here!

In terms of our five-part rubric, certain things stand out—the continuity of Black Elk's sense of identity as an actor from the time of his vision to the end of his life, and the fact that he both dreams about the event and actually lives through it. The grandfathers constitute a power bloc to which he returns time and again—when he can absorb these awesome figures into his own personality. The physical context is the ever-shrinking hold his people have on the territory they have long roamed. The principal vectors are messages coming to him from the world of the spirit, his own highly ambivalent feelings of inadequacy and strength, and his continuing exchanges with his people. The denouement, however, is tragic, reflecting the frustration and failure which are such common themes of American Indian life.

A kind of response to Black Elk and his romantic experience of gaining identity through imagined contact with his ancestors is to be found in *I . . . Rigoberta Menchú. An Indian Woman in Guatemala.* The

struggle for survival and identity described here is far more demanding than Black Elk's because, in part anyway, Menchú does not have
in mind any return to long-gone tribal patterns but instead "wants to
play an active part in history," in the regeneration of her people. Hers
is a thoroughly contemporary story, concerned not with the blessing
of her grandfathers but with having enough to eat and with the establishment of a political order in her town that will contribute to the
well-being of her people. She too speaks for the enhancement of
experience, but in a way that brings out basic distinctions between
traditional narrative and contemporary third-world views.[7]

The story of Maqdad, from the great North African Hilal tribe, is
not unlike that of Black Elk. It is retold by C. G. Campbell in *Tales from
the Arab Tribes,* and we do not have the means of determining the
measure of fact and fiction in the version we have.[8] While still a lad,
Maqdad challenges a merchant to compare purses with him, the individual with the larger purse to get both. Of course Maqdad loses, but
in the process he gains recognition from the merchant—credibility as
an individual human being, if you like. Later he meets Zoro, who, he
learns, is afraid of almost no one because his death will come only at
the hands of an individual named Maqdad. Unhesitatingly, in a stunning display of "self-cognizance" (Lichtenstein, 61), Maqdad makes
his identity known: "Verily, my name is Maqdad." Later the young
man, following precisely the same pattern as Black Elk, meets his
ancestors and is taught all the techniques of fighting. So keenly aware
of his power is he that instead of slaying a number of enemies who do
not see him, he challenges them all to a fair fight: "Come at me one at
a time," he says," and if you slay me . . . you may escape from here"
(84). Cleverly he traps each one, letting the first entangle his feet in
vines, diverting another by waving a cloth, putting another off balance. He is a clever, witty warrior, a master of the arts of deception,
and a man of tremendous self-esteem. Eventually he compels even
the shah of Persia to acknowledge him and admit that "the pedigree
of the simplest Arab tribesman is better than that of the noblest
prince, and courage in battle is better than wide domains." This is a
stunning act of self-affirmation.

Maqdad's sense of himself as the leading actor in his story dominates this tale; he is a figure of great spontaneity and enormous
power, proud of his close ties to his tribe. The negotiations into which
he enters with his opponents are important vectors, surpassed only
by the admission that he elicits from the shah of Persia, which appears to satisfy him, at last, on the point of identity. Like Black Elk,
Maqdad finds in another's acknowledgment of himself an important

factor in his own identity. His power lies in his physical strength and in his lofty morality, characterized by his sense of fair play in dealing with his opponents. Yet when he challenges the merchant over the size of his purse, he has no power source at all except his own arrogance: he creates his own dynamic here, out of absolutely nothing. Maqdad lives in a riskier world than ours, more deeply committed to the past and to a sense of community, more responsive to wit and roguery than ours is. But the rewards (in terms of self-esteem) seem to transcend the rewards our system provides.

Threats to Identity

Many threats to a strong sense of personality are described in traditional narrative. There may be no one with whom to contrast oneself—or the contrasts may be too strong to handle. The unconscious may appear too threatening to deal with—or its existence may go unnoticed. The life-pattern may be so discontinuous as to make no story line at all clear. At critical choice points, insight and self-confidence may be missing. For Lichtenstein and other personality psychologists, symbiosis (a too-close linkage with some other life), "a ceasing-to-be, a dissolution of their reality as persons" (Lichtenstein, 8), the regression to some earlier stage of development (13), the loss of separateness (16) are real threats. We have already encountered this process in terms of the tragedy of enchantment; students of myth refer to this phenomenon as "engulfment." The term embraces not only the drownings or near-drownings of Odysseus and the hosts of Pharoah in the Red Sea. It may also be applied to the utter defeat of the Egyptians by Yahweh through the instrumentality of Moses and to the entrapment of Odysseus in the wiles of Calypso. You suffer loss of identity when you go on a quest without knowing what you are seeking, or when your mate refuses to recognize you, or you experience the ignominy of being a third child. Ma'ruf nearly loses his identity forever in the terrible shadow of his angry first wife, and he becomes a complete human being only when he is able to fuse his identity with Dunya's—which itself is an unusual pattern, though she is loving and loyal, as well as quite alert to the needs of a husband she truly loves. He finds himself in her support and affection.

In a famous Middle Eastern myth, Ishtar, the Babylonian goddess of beauty and sexuality, descends into the netherworld and is stripped of every form of the beauty from which she has gained her own sense of personhood. Life seems to be taking its revenge. And in the Persian *Tuti-nama* a king dreams that all his treasures are about to forsake him—wealth, strength, reason: his very being is undercut, his foundations shaken.[9] Such cases, even though their sources are fictional, suggest that other observers have noted what Robert Ornstein asserts—that "the everyday assumption of stability, whether about personality or about biology, does not seem to withstand a . . . rigorous empirical analysis."[10] Nevertheless, Odysseus' rebirth begins with the command of the gods to leave Ogygia, and it is completed by his wife's faithfulness. The king in *Tuti-Nama* stubbornly refuses to part with his good deeds. Out of the destruction of the forces of Pharoah Moses will rise to leadership, and as Ishtar returns to the upper world the elements of her personality she treasures are restored as well.[11]

Establishing an Identity

In the early years of the feminist movement we heard much of the idea that fairytales provided very poor role-models for girls, and Little Red Riding Hood, Sleeping Beauty, Snow White, and Cinderella were singled out as particularly striking (and unacceptable) models of female behavior. The possibility of such individuals ever achieving a sense of identity was questioned. More recently, however, other female behavior patterns in traditional tales have been noted (as have the frequently degrading roles assigned to males). In these stories women dare to play violent jokes on men, make terrifying demands of potential husbands, break out of enchantment by daring acts, go off in search of loved ones, push witches into ovens, defy interdictions, devise schemes for circumventing fate, and just happen to have in their apron pockets slippers that match.[12]

All of these ancient affirmations of wholeness and personhood find their modern counterpart in Arasteh's description of a personality type often found in the third world:

> Ordinary people who are active and experience their life in their simple community are not split. Although they live in a state of a minimum degree of awareness, they are integrated, witty, and related to real life situations. Their system of thinking has not yet become a barrier to their well-being. They are not in conflict with concepts and logic. They live intuitively, not instinctively, as is generally believed. They look at the world in a Gestalt sense and see configurations of things. Active and industrious,

these people follow harmonious principles and live creatively. (*Final Integration*, 121)

Sometimes the establishment of identity is as simple as this brief sequence from *Jataka:* "The eyes of ogres are red and do not wink. They cast no shadow and are free from fear. This is no ogre; it is a man."[13] More often, however, it is based on very complex processes.

Storytelling

One of the most basic of all techniques for establishing an identity is the act of storytelling itself, quite literally sitting down in front of a group in a coffee house on a winter evening in an isolated village, aware that you are responsible for the evening's entertainment, conscious that you have a hundred stories at your command and that through these stories you are the carrier of your culture. Confidence and a sense of the dramatic are required if one is to successfully play this role, assume this identity, and the storyteller will bring out certain sentiments or behaviors which his or her listeners may adopt as parts of their own personalities. Moreover, narrators can make their listeners feel significant as they recite their tales—they have the emotions of their audience under control, and as they discover what works, they gain their own sense of identity as artists. As they learn to function at several different levels of reality, their sense of their own experience is enhanced. And if the narrator is strong enough inwardly, he or she can use narrative skills to bargain for protection or even for life, as Odysseus (in the palace of Alcinous) and Scheherazade do. The storyteller is an actor who through the marvelous vectors and abundant power at his or her command can reshape contexts for listeners.

Walter Benjamin goes even further when he asserts that a story is "something that seemed inalienable to us, the securest among our possessions (*Illuminations*, 83)." Storytellers can carry their materials with them wherever they go, and while they have mind and tongue (how personal!), their power to narrate cannot be taken from them. Moreover, says Benjamin, storytellers draw strength from their "orientation toward practical interests" (*Illuminations*, 86)—they flourish when such crafts as pottery-making and weaving flourish, and like craftsmen they develop enormous pride in their skill. What is more, the story is born in confident, public utterance, contrasting thus with the novel, which is generated by the perplexed, solitary individual (*Illuminations*, 87). Thus it can be said that the story conveys more than information: "It sinks the thing into the life of the storyteller" because the story—and the storyteller—grow out of a great tradition, sustained by memory.[14]

And the postmoderns, with their powerful feeling for language games and narratives go even further. Lyotard speaks of "the preeminence of the narrative form in the formulation of traditional knowledge" (*The Postmodern Condition*, 19). Traditional knowledge determines "what one must say in order to be heard, what one must listen to in order to speak, and what role one must play . . . to be the object of a narrative" (21). And individuals, it could be said, are "only that which actualizes the narrative": they become people by telling and listening to stories (23). This position becomes increasingly important with the fading of various metanarratives that have formerly controlled human behavior.

Establishing a Role

In the course of an earlier discussion of similarity and difference (chapter 4), I identified roles as one of the axes along which individuals in the bright-shadow world develop and affirm their identities, and in the pages since then we have encountered many examples of strong role-playing but comparatively few cases of intense individuality. We can, in fact, unearth a significant paradox here—that in popular narrative one of the approved ways of gaining an identity is to allow oneself to be absorbed into a recognized and socially acceptable role that itself threatens one's sense of individuality.[15] Deutsch and Krauss survey this sometimes puzzling material in their *Theories in Social Psychology*, generally putting a positive interpretation on role-playing. To operate within a role, they observe, means that one is fulfilling certain expectations (175), and this can be a potent source of the sense of identity. Roles involve interactions with others (176), and through this process you gain some sense of how others respond to you, and this helps you fill in your own blanks. The possibility—so characteristic of our age—of deviating from one's role is both the result and the cause of strong personhood (177). And role rejections may bring out an individual's own basic traits, for one's own personality can be a "source of role conflict" (181). In short, "in the process of interaction with his social environment a person not only takes on characteristics as a consequence of the roles he enacts, he also begins to experience a sense of self. He begins to recognize that others react to him, and he begins to react to his own actions and personal qualities as he expects others to react" (181). One of the functions of the novel is to make explicit such reactions; in the popular narrative we can observe them, but rarely are we let into the mind of the character as he or she reacts. This material is particularly relevant to a study of the rogue—an individual who is always performing, always watching himself and his audience—but it also has its life-enhancing side, the sudden realization of the strength one gains as an individual when one subsumes one's own activities within a larger pattern. Again the paradox!

Identity through Boasting

To establish their identities, figures in popular narrative engage in shameless self-promotion, personal public relations that would embarrass even the most enthusiastic modern promoter (Cf. "Lord Peter," S. Thompson, 226 ff.). Their boasting serves a number of purposes—it arouses the curiosity and perhaps even the anxiety of opponents; it stirs up the courage of the boaster (a self-conscious expression of belief in oneself); it is yet another reflection of the belief of many prescientific individuals that the world is made by words, that reality is what a forceful person asserts it to be. Moreover, boasting is a useful heuristic device on the basis of which some functional version of the truth can ultimately be erected.

The "Fly Killer" or "Little Tailor" type of self-aggrandizement is well represented in the Russian tale of Foma Berennkiov, the wretched, one-eyed son of a poor father, who kills innumerable flies and decides that a life of slaughter is just the thing for him. On a post, for all to see, he inscribes an account of his deed, and soon all the great Russian heroes are seeking his help. One opponent, noting that Foma has but a single eye, decides that he might do even better if he put out both his own eyes. Foma decapitates him. On another occasion, all that Foma has to do to put his enemies to flight is to cry "Help!" Equally self-confident and resourceful is Valiant Vicky, the brave weaver. He kills a mosquito with the shuttle of his loom and immediately adopts the name Prince Victor. By luck and treachery he builds up an enormous reputation as a hero, killing both a lion and a tiger, and he describes his victory over a huge army as "a mere trifle."[16] By some trick, through certain vectors available to him, the actor persuades his associates to reimage his identity.

But fly-killing is not the only impressive trick available to would-be heroes. Referring to huge tanks as "finger-basins," (Dasent, 38), tearing up rocks, and pretending to squeeze liquid from stones are other tricks by which heroes convince the naive (and themselves as well) that their powers are greater than their size. In "Le Conte du Pusillanime" a lazy man pretends to squeeze water from a stone (actually he is squeezing an egg against it) and thereby so impresses certain criminals that they invite him to join their band. But he will not do any work, being content to boast of his strength. The robbers then determine to eliminate him, and he substitutes a log for his own sleeping body, on which they rain blows. Next day he complains of flea bites. When they pour boiling water over him, he complains of sweating.[17] In discovering his power to deceive others the tiny actor sheds his own sense of insignificance in the face of overwhelming evidence about how foolish everyone else is.[18]

Openness to New Realities

Another familiar story touching on the problem of identity in a much more profound manner is "Beauty and the Beast," a made-up tale but one composed of ancient elements, in some way related to the story of Psyche and Eros.[19] It appears to suggest that individuals can gain an identity by making daring and risky commitments, in which, perhaps, concern for the well-being of others is more important than concern for themselves. A merchant who has just suffered heavy losses finds himself abandoned by his former friends. As a result, most of his children experience problems of their own, only the youngest managing to hold herself together. In fact, as she grows more and more supportive of her father, she also grows more and more beautiful. Seeking to improve his condition, the poor man makes a bitter winter journey, loses his way, and at length comes upon a seemingly deserted castle, where he falls asleep amidst various delights. But the place lies under the control of the Beast, who demands that one of the merchant's daughters be brought to him. The beautiful youngest girl agrees to return with her father despite her fears, and with the encouragement of the Beast sends gifts back home to her sisters. She is opening herself up to all kinds of life-enhancing vectors. At night she dreams of a prince who comforts her and seeks in return only gratitude, loyalty, and trust. While she is at the castle, the young woman reflects long and seriously on her own nature, exploring her inner world carefully, and twice she refuses the Beast's offer of marriage. A visit to her childhood home proves exceedingly dull, and so she is motivated to keep her promise to return to the castle. But she has delayed so long that the Beast has died in sorrow and loneliness. However, her own grief and her willingness to venture into a new dimension of her own life break the enchantment, and the Beast revives as a handsome young prince.

The identity issues are clear enough. The youngest daughter and her father become persons by exerting themselves against all that life thrusts upon them, whereas the other sisters wring their hands in distress and lose whatever possibilities might open up for them. They reject roles as actors and become simply the frustrating physical setting which the third sister must put up with. She, by contrast, is involved in rich vectors—her negotiations with her father and the Beast—and these open up power sources for her, most notably, her capacity for love. She rapidly becomes a true actor, as does the Beast, who has been enduring incredible frustrations.[20]

Willing an Identity

Will, the determination to survive, to be recognized, is a critical factor in the struggles toward identity of most of the heroic figures of traditional narrative, and no case is richer in instances than that of Odysseus. Homer seems to have been exquisitely sensitive to this issue, for he provides a remarkably full account of the various ways by which Odysseus established his identity or persuaded those he met on his way home from Troy that he was indeed the warrior he claimed to be. His youthful determination to be in the forefront of the boar hunt, where he received his characteristic thigh wound. His eagerness to undertake the most dangerous missions during the siege of Troy. His determination to escape from the cave of Polyphemus (and then to go back for his hat). His capacity to keep himself alive during seventeen storm-wracked days at sea. His decision to leave Calypso. His defiance of Circe. And his plotting to regain his throne once he returns to Ithaca. Through many metamorphoses, the essential nature of the actor remains constant because that is what he wills.[21] The traveler's thigh-wound is enough to convince Eurycleia, the old nurse, of his identity, and by taking note of it she also affirms the significance of the moment when the youth who is now the aging hero brought down his first boar and established himself as a man. Telemachus finds his father in the man who brilliantly, deviously, plots his revenge in the great hall and snatches away the bow his son is about to string: the father is not yet willing to hand over his authority. And when the sceptical Penelope suggests moving a bed Odysseus had built into a tree many years before, she touches on her husband's pride as the maker of the home: she recognizes him not through a physical fact, or through the sense of command he exudes, but through a sensitivity she saw in him once which she again evokes. His anger at the suggestion convinces her, and she chooses to give him his name again—"You are Odysseus, the Sower of Wrath." But when all is said and done, neither the nurse nor the son nor the patient wife really knows, possesses irrefutable proof, and this, too, is very much in the spirit of the bright-shadow world, where identities do tend to shift about and where identification is, finally, a matter of someone's willing it.

Much the same point can be made about the response of Aladdin's mother to the claim of the Moroccan that he is the lad's uncle.

She has appropriate doubts, "but as soon as she heard his promise of opening a merchant's store for her son and setting him up with stuffs and capital and so forth, the woman decided and determined in her mind that this Maghrabi was in very sooth her husband's brother, seeing that no stranger would do such goodly deed by her son" (*1001*, Suppl. III, 62). "Determined in her mind" is critical here: she wills the identity. The reasoning is specious, but the decision is productive. Here, as in so many cases of the hero figures from the Old Testament, the personality is maintained and asserted by sheer ego strength, and very little else.

Interplay of Conscious and Unconscious Factors

Another great factor in the sense of identity achieved by bright-shadow world figures is the development and maintenance of consciousness, wakefulness, alertness, awareness. All of these conditions point to a state that transcends the normal condition of most human beings, who in this material are often pictured as dull, sleepy, and inattentive.[22] In discussing enchantment, I have already touched on many of the important challenges to consciousness. These threats include certain aspects of the sexual experience, being caught up in various mechanical processes, sleep and forgetfulness of course, and being diverted from one's goal. But it is not enough to suppress/control the power of the unconsciousness, for this state can also be fruitfully linked with sleep and sexuality, with dreaming and creative goallessness: the positive factors here must be allowed to do their part. Certainly the Jungians, in particular Neumann and von Franz, have done much with the interplay of conscious and unconscious forces in the human personality and, as we have noted, have traced the roots of individuation to the interplay of these seemingly opposing forces. Von Franz has stressed the creative power of the unconscious and has warned of the dire consequences to the individual of any neglect of this aspect of the personality. Between consciousness and the unconscious there must be a constant flow of materials if experience is to be properly enriched.

An important spokesperson for the importance of unconscious factors in the development of the personality has been Robert Ornstein. He has linked this concept to the two-hemisphere theory of the brain, the view that the left brain has to do with modes of consciousness that are intellectual, time-oriented, analytical, verbal, causal and argumentative, whereas the right brain stimulates behavior that is sensuous, timeless, gestaltist, spatial, synchronous, and experiential.[23] Ornstein has thereby affirmed the continuing importance of a very large area of the human mind not under the control of the waking consciousness, concerned with what is intuitive, mysterious, timeless, nocturnal, feminine. And he has done so in the context of a book on the personality, which he affirms is "something we must of necessity construct or *create* in order to survive in the world. . . . If this consciousness is a personal construction, then each person can alter his or her consciousness simply by *changing the manner of construction.*"[24]

The importance traditional narrative places on the consciousness/unconsciousness issue is reflected in many motifs that have to do with some individual's moving toward or regaining a significantly high level of consciousness:

> Waking up
> Emerging from misty, foggy places into clear light
> Bestirring oneself to productive action
> Being given or remembering one's name
> Being selected as one from many
> Going on and returning from a journey
> Receiving a revelation
> Grasping the true nature of something one had misread
> Discovering an appropriate metaphor, some hidden but
>   significant resemblance
> Experiencing a change of form
> Seeing oneself through the eyes of others
> Moving to a positive new relationship
> Transcending physical limitations
> Experiencing strangeness
> Experiencing synchronicity
> Performing an act of will

The traditional tale expresses faith in the value of these experiences, all significant factors in life-enhancement. But all too often in traditional narrative an actor fails to wake up, to break through the surrounding mist, remains with the lotus eaters or the herd, forgets about the journey or remains bound by physical limitations, misses the critical analogies. And thus, of course, ceases to be an actor.

Identity through Social Involvement

That identity is a social issue, to be gained through participation in a social network—whether in the primitive world, the bright-shadow world, or the modern world—seems to be accepted by all observers.[25] Popular narrative offers many accounts of some lonely and embittered monster or hideous old woman being destroyed by the isolated life he/she leads. The Homeric Polyphemus and the Russian Baba Yaga come to mind immediately. By contrast, rich lives are linked to socially rich environments, which both enhance and absorb them. The biblical Joseph functions within a courtly context; Moses against the challenging background of intricate political intrigue; Ma'ruf within a group of wealthy and appreciative merchants and, like Aladdin, at court. Saktideva's identity and destiny are bound up with the lives of several sisters whom he encounters at every turn and at several different levels of existence. No one has put the issue more sharply than Harry Haller, who observes at the masked ball in *Steppenwolf* that his "personality was dissolved in the intoxication of the festivity like salt in water" and that "all of us had a part in one another."[26] The paradox that continues to dog us is well stated by Lichtenstein, who observes, following Jacobson and Grinker, that "identification is a concept designed to make understandable how the 'inside subject' gradually becomes capable of relating to what is 'outside'." Lichtenstein argues that both as an infant and as an adult "man cannot ever experience his identity except in terms of an organic instrumentality within the variations of a symbiotically structured *Umwelt*."[27] Thus in popular narrative, actors are never separated from other actors or from physical contexts of resources and limitations; the operative vectors are contacts, points of negotiation and frustration into which we enter, and power is the force of all the other psyches or identities in the community, supporting or threatening the central actor, providing the material with which one can make an estimate of one's own personality by comparing it with the personalities of others. In overcoming or yielding up the self, one finds a new and richer self.

Dorothy Lee speaks to this important issue in describing the sense of identity she has observed among the Tikopia, a Polynesian people:

> [It was] radically different from mine; I found a social definition of the self. I found that here I could not speak of man's relations with his universe, but rather of a universal interrelatedness, because man was not the focus from which relations flowed. . . . I found a named and recognized medium of social continuity, implemented in social acts, not in words.[28]

Freya Stark makes a similar point about human beings in general, but out of her long experience in the Middle East:

The portion we see of human beings is very small: their forms and faces, voices and words, their ages and race perhaps: beyond these, like an immense dark continent of which their obvious self is but a jutting headland, lies all that has made them—generations vanishing into the barbarous night; accidents and impacts not only on themselves but upon their forebears; the cry of the conqueror, the sighing of slaves. Even the chemical variation of substances—airs, foods and waters—are all gathered to that point of light which is the person we know.[29]

Wendy O'Flaherty finds similar concepts in Indian dream material from many centuries: "The self is by no means so clearly limited to the individual as it is for us. That is, the individual feels himself to be a physical as well as mental part of other people, to partake in what McKim Marriott has called the 'coded substance' of other members of his family and his caste."[30] O'Flaherty quotes a passage from Salman Rushdie that sounds very much like Stark: "I am the sum total of everything that went before me, of all I have been seen done, of everything done-to-me" (224); and she cites many passages from Hindu literature suggesting that the "I" does not exist and that solipsism (I alone am real) is the source of many errors about the person that we make (224). And Ronald Berman echoes this theme when he suggests that "contemporary 'primitive' cultures . . . have much softer ego-structures than we do, and are characterized by a more communal and heterogeneous way of life, far less anxiety and madness, and much gentler subject/object distinctions" (*Reenchantment*, 170).

The concept of the person as embedded in the social order rather than in the individual ego, so that the boundary between self and world becomes tenuous or nonexistent, is treated by a number of social psychologists in the stimulating symposium *The Category of the Person*.[31] The focal point of this collection is an essay by Marcel Mauss, "A Category of the Human Mind: The Notion of Person; the Notion of Self," originally published in 1938. In this essay, which has been widely discussed during the last four decades, Mauss surveys the succession of forms the concept of person has assumed throughout history. Of special interest to us is the fact that among the Zuñi tribes of North America the role of the person is to act out "the prefigured totality of the life of the clan" (5); as N. J. Allen puts it, "the *personnage* is a member of a bounded tribal society" (31). Among the Zuñis significant movement took place between the person and the social group, rather than between the person and the inner self. In China, says Mauss, "birth-order, rank and the interplay of the social classes settle the names and life style of the individual" (14). "Modern individualism . . . is an exceptional phenomenon," Louis Dumont writes in the same volume (93), taking its roots in early Christianity, the product of Christ's teaching that "man is an *individual-in-relation-to-God*" (96).

Berman follows much the same line of argument when he argues that "the ego, which we take for granted as a given of normal human life, is . . . a product of the capitalist, or industrial, epoch. The quality of ego-strength, which modern society regards as a yardstick of mental health, is a mode of being-in-the-world which is fully 'natural' only since the Renaissance" (*Reenchantment*, 159). If this is true, the image of the personality in the bright-shadow world, as formed by the conjunction of elements from the society, does indeed reflect a notion of personality that has been—and is still—widely held. In that case, young Tiidu, whose life is transformed when he begins to take the world around him into account; and Saktideva, who says, "I must give myself wholly to this challenge thrown out to me"; and Ma'ruf, who gains his identity through the jinn, the power of the ring, his friend in Baghdad, and his wife Dunya—all these people, and many more who never once thought about "finding themselves" because they were never out of an osmotic relation with their environments, may have much to say to us.

These two diagrams illustrate the two opposing concepts of self-identity we have just been looking at—the individual according to Lee, Stark, and Mauss, and the person hinted at in Dumont's comments on modern individualism then picked up by Berman:

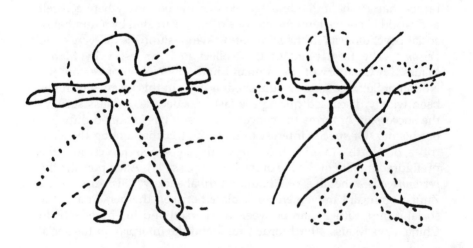

In the left-hand diagram, the outer world, the environment, represented by the dashes, is filmy, diffuse, shifting, and there is forceful movement out from the ego toward the environment and in toward the ego from the environment. The edges of the person are sharp and clear. Such is our view of the person. In the right hand diagram, which is a representation of a more traditional view of identity, the person, represented by the broken lines, becomes insubstantial as he/she comes up against the environment, the various segments of which are boldly outlined. Identify them as you will—work, political ideas, financial resources, natural forces. Their relationship with the person is osmotic, and the ego is too weak to create a personal identity separate from its context. Carlos Castaneda speaks of "luminous" or "tentacle-like fibres" moving out from the individual into this outer world.[32] Frank Waters notes that the Pueblo so powerfully identified their lives with the community that "they showed no sense of individuality, and seemed at once impersonal and anonymous" (*The Man Who Killed the Deer*, 139). David Griffin finds in "eliminative postmodernism" the view that the self is constituted primarily by the relationships in which it finds itself.[33] Many modern women report having suffered through something like this self-image, which is a result of modern training they are generally unable to turn to any creative use.[34]

According to the older scheme (on the right), the actor is highly vulnerable, exposed to the environment with little protection but also enriched by it, participating in it fully, and contributing to it. In the modern scheme (left), the actor/individual stands over and against, even in opposition to, the world, not as a participant but as a would-be governor or controller. That sense of the tendency of the human actor to break apart (as suggested by the right-hand diagram) is reinforced by the many stories in which the body is seen as a set of detachable parts, which can at will be separated and then put back together again, and the personality itself as really several personalities.[35] The Greek hero Perseus can gain access to Medusa and her head only by seizing the single eye shared by the gray sisters and passed between them. In an awesome moment he interposes his hand, seizes the eye, and refuses to surrender it until he gets the directions he needs. Current all across Central Asia (and elsewhere) is the story of the monkey and the tortoise: the tortoise invites the monkey to its home and halfway there observes that his wife is sick and her cure depends upon the heart of a monkey. Unfortunately, I left mine at home, observes the monkey; had I known of this need of your wife's, I would have brought it with me.[36] And the Grimm

Brothers recount the story of a cat's theft of body parts an army surgeon has stored for the operations of the following day. For the human parts eaten by the cat various parts of animals are substituted, along with parts of a thief's body. Corresponding personality changes occur, of course, in those who receive the parts (Magoun and Krappe, 425). The life-enhancing suggestion here is that individuals need to become a little freer with their personalities, a little more willing to branch out from what they assume is their basic nature.

Hidden and Lost Identities

This topic has a number of important ramifications, some of which were dealt with in chapter 6 under the heading of enchantment. Here we deal with identity problems arising from substitutions and displacements, various efforts to escape from one's identity or to reconstruct it or to deceive someone about one's own or someone else's. The many children's games that involve identifying—most notably Hide and Go Seek—seem to be preparation for or sensitization to this serious adult problem. All are cases where it is impossible to identify the actor or for the actor to experience identification—yet another manifestation of the actor's tenuousness. I have already cited stories of the "White Parrot" type, in which a wicked wazir conceals or sends away two children who have been born with some special mark on their foreheads and substitutes animals for them. His intent is to force the king, their absent father, to condemn/punish his virtuous queen. This kind of substitution ultimately requires the king (who is indifferent or imperceptive or preoccupied) to reassemble certain long-neglected parts of his world, which will enable him once again to be a wise and trusting person (von Franz, *Individuation*, pages 1–58). In another type of story a letter that reads "Kill the bearer" is altered to read "Marry the bearer to the princess." Such treachery always works against its perpetrators or their agents—witness *Hamlet*, for example.[37]

In various forms of the Jephtha story a father promises that in exchange for military victory he will sacrifice to the gods the person who greets him upon his return from battle, and thus he rashly dooms his own daughter (Judges 11). Because the father (in some versions) cannot carry out the terrible commitment he has made, he substitutes another for the daughter. But the ruse fails, for when the substituted person is questioned, she answers inappropriately. Thus in "The White Wolf" the girl's answers to the wolf's questions reveal that she cannot possibly be a princess: when asked what her father would do with a forest in which they are standing, the girl says, "My father is a poor man so he would cut down the trees, and he would saw them into planks, and he would sell the planks, and we should never be poor again" (*Gray Fairy Book*, 170). The real princess indicates that her father would turn the forest into a park where he and the courtiers would enjoy themselves. Diversion is of course the key, shifting the attention of the individual whose identity you suspect away from the implications of the question to its content. Generally the drive toward self-identity is too strong to permit the actor to be deceptive about what really matters.

In another variation of this theme a young girl is pushed aside—usually from her rightful place as bride—by another, ugly woman. Frequently the girl, who may be a princess, is on a journey and is bumped from her horse by evil attendants, attired in rags, and forced to walk. When the entourage arrives at its destination—the palace of the groom-to-be—the deposed princess is given menial tasks. In "The Goosegirl" the situation is resolved when the old king finally begins to listen to inexplicable warnings from certain animals and encourages the girl to tell her story to a stove.[38] Bettelheim devotes serious attention to this tale, concluding that the heroine "learned that it is much harder to be truly oneself, but that this alone will gain her true autonomy and change her fate" (143). In this chapter I am, of course, advancing the view that "true autonomy" may be neither possible nor particularly desirable.

In still other stories a wife must convince her husband, who is about to marry another woman, that her place has been unjustly usurped. This story is the basis of Shakespeare's *All's Well that Ends Well*, but the variants are worldwide. In one Indian version, a stepmother tries to substitute her own daughter as the bride, and in another a husband who is not moved by a signet ring he gave his wife is finally convinced when his infant, thrown up in the air by the wife, hangs there; the child is a Bodhisatta and a very desirable heir.

Another popular version of the displaced bride motif concerns a woman who must struggle for three successive nights to catch the attention of her drugged or otherwise stupefied husband, who has forgotten her and is about to marry someone else. The true wife can recover her husband only if she can compel him to listen to her story. This she does by persuading the substitute wife to let her sleep in her husband's bed for one night—and then a second and a third. The dramatic moment occurs when on the third night the woman intercepts the customary sleeping potion and opens her husband's eyes to the reality of his situation. Inherent in this motif (familiar from "East o' the Sun, West o' the Moon") are a number of important issues—

that humans are prone to enchantment by forgetting (a topic already discussed); that though the world is under some semblance of control, pieces do keep falling off, getting lost, disappearing; that the only hope of individuals in a situation like this is that someone will come along at the right time and make the critical connections; that virtue must be aided by artifice if it is to prevail.[39]

Reasserting Oneself

In almost every narrative we have surveyed in this chapter some effort must be made by a prominent actor to assure that identity is not lost in a complicated situation, or that it is recovered quickly if lost. Not all cases are as significant as that of Black Elk, but all do affirm, in one way or another, the importance of this experience within the bright-shadow world and, I believe, in our world as well. One could say that even if the identity is recovered, it is not the same identity as the one lost—it is always recovered with a sense of delight, freshness, and newness that raises experience to a higher level than before and makes losers/finders aware of themselves and of their awareness of themselves as they were not before. This is genuine enhancement of life-experience.

Traditional narrative offers accounts of many desperate actors who, when confronted with the possibility of forgetting someone or of being forgotten, resort to the obvious device of marking someone for later identification. Identity, as I suggested at the beginning of this chapter, means projecting certain highly personal vectors out into the world, and as these vectors grow weak, so does identity. Things are so fluid, so undefined, that people have to start putting tags on themselves and others. The many versions of the story of the faithful wife whose husband allows his friends to test her fidelity (one hides in a box and observes a mark on her breast when she is undressing) suggest how important identifications are in a world where identities and values are fluid and shifting. When one is dueling with a disguised opponent, it may be necessary to make a small wound in the opponent's skin for later spotting (El Shamy, 32). Morgiana resorts to something like this in "Ali Baba and the Forty Thieves." In other versions a jackal that has escaped from a panther by cutting off its own tail conceals itself later, while it and its friends are enjoying the panther's melon patch, by cutting off the tails of all its associates.[40] Shifty Lad notes that a tiny dot has been placed on his own cheek and adds similar dots to the faces of his friends. And in one of the most widely disseminated of all folktales a wife whose favors are sought by four distinguished local citizens asks each in turn to await her in a curious boxlike room lined with pitch. As each leaves, covered with the black stuff, he reveals to all who see him the extent of his lust.[41]

At other times the problem is to identify someone from a lineup, in which case the person to be picked will offer you a clue by which he/she can be recognized. The trick, of course, is to offer a clue that is obvious to the person making the identification but so natural in its context that the officials will not spot it. This is a true *case* (a situation that is a paradigm of many situations), with ramifications for problems of similarity and difference, perception, contextuality, and trans-contextuality. In the Sicilian tale "The Golden Lion," (*Sicilianische Märchen*, II, 73), a girl agrees to tie a sash around her waist on the eighth day of the contest. In "Le Prince Inespere" a bee tells a prince that the youngest girl, the girl he must pick, will have a ladybird on her eyebrow when the time comes for selection, and in other stories—and there are many—necklaces and sandal straps also prove useful.[42] These stories grip me, and I am not sure why. Is it the idea of the code that must be learned if one is to function effectively? Or the suggestion that the data we need is all around us—invisible to most, clear to a few who can see through the tiniest crack?

Emergence into Personhood

The case of the apparently simple-minded child, the beautiful but neglected stepdaughter, or the third child emerging from obscurity by asserting his/her identity, often by making some dramatic move toward maturity, also merits comment. In all these cases, life is being enhanced and a neglected actor is recognized, dramatically. Many familiar narratives imply that important childhood problems can be traced to adults who assume that differences between siblings or tardiness of development indicate mental inferiority. Otto Rank is closely linked with this issue. The element of shame may also be at work here, calling "into question, not only one's own adequacy and the validity of the codes of one's immediate society, but the meaning of the universe itself."[43] But if experiences of neglect and shaming are fully faced, they can inform the self and reveal one to oneself. It may also be suggested that some children are quite content not to become adult people at any particular time, whereas others will not be denied the chance to grow up or achieve personal identity as quickly as possible.

The motif of the emergence of the talented person from the undifferentiated mass finds its most famous expression in the biblical story of David saving the Hebrew army. The youngest son, not allowed to go to war with his brothers, not yet recognized as an actor, manages to reach the battle and perform some critical service (I Samuel 17:17). Sometimes the younger son, known contemptuously as "Boots" or "Dummling" simply outwits his brothers at some roguery or carries out a quest they cannot complete.[44]

No single description of personhood, self-identity, or maturity based on this material is possible, and even where descriptions resemble each other closely, differences appear. I conclude this section by contrasting four possibilities.

Bruno Bettelheim in *The Uses of Enchantment* provides, by implication anyway, a statement of the thinking of our twentieth-century secular world on the issue of maturity, which is close enough to the concept of identity to be usable here. For Bettelheim maturity means having the resources (tools, associates, mental abilities and attitudes) for whatever hard times may come. These resources may include imagination, certain aspirations, a sense of hope and security, and the capacity to handle dark situations—anxiety, pain, frustration—in a productive manner. Bettelheim suggests that a mature sense of identity also involves the capacity to enter into productive human relationships and to choose worthwhile models, all the time preserving enough independence for the lonely journey. He acknowledges the importance of being open to unexpected dimensions of reality and of having the wit to outmaneuver those who may threaten harm. Bettelheim holds up before us a strong individual capable of dealing effectively with a powerful, material world, a person who has become truly himself or herself (278). It is no surprise that he found in fairytales much to support his basic position.

Postmodernists, who have "deconstructed" the "complete human being" (Bettelheim, 279), see the self as just another product of the language games we play, a metanarrative like the metanarratives of democracy and progess-through-technology that we have accepted because they help us make sense of a world that really has no meaning. Postmodernists tend to find all masks for the self equally valid— even the most bizarre. Their stress on knowledge as the ultimate resource forces them to downplay the traditional view of education as *bildung* or self-development, and they see the individual as a constantly shifting entity most (or only) alive when he/she has become a functioning node in some greater network.

Quite a different point of view about identity comes from the

Jungians, tied specifically to the concept of individuation. F. W. Martin *(Experiment in Depth)* examines the ways individuals can enrich and deepen their lives by bringing in material from the unconscious. As we have seen, this is a (the) key element in the process of individuation, but not one that Bettelheim says much about. Martin stresses the importance of looking within to that spot called "the Deep Center," from which springs the capacity to find a way through life and enter into creative relationships. But this deep center may also enable one to separate oneself from the group and develop one's own uniqueness, no matter how deeply one may be buried in a horde of siblings. It may enable one, also, to tear off masks and reveal something of what lies beneath the surface. In this process, the individual will inevitably encounter his/her shadow, the darker part of the personality, and may thereby learn from mistakes and experience transformation to a higher level of being. It requires a constant struggle toward full consciousness and a willingness to live dangerously, drawing strength from the archetypes that inhabit the unconscious and accepting joyfully each new stage of life as it comes.

Much of this harmonizes with the view of maturity/identity characteristic of the bright-shadow world, though certain elements are lacking and emphases differ. Consider again the case of Saktideva, certainly one of that realm's great (if insufficiently known) heroes, an actor who becomes a mature, fully integrated personality at a much higher level than he had ever dreamed of, despite the many forms of chaos and disintegration he has to face. We see him first as a gambler and nonserious fellow, willing to take a stab at a question he encounters casually, the real answer to which he has no idea about. But then, for some reason never fully explained, he becomes serious; he makes a commitment, faces despair, deals with rebuffs, and pursues his goal even when there seem to be no roadside markers. He dies (after a fashion) and is reborn, and he is able to respond to lucky breaks and the wisdom of others along the way. He can understand the speech of animals because he is attuned to other dimensions, and he copes effectively with all sorts of people—hermits, pregnant women, fisher-kings, angry sons, merchants. He learns to do the next thing, no matter how ambiguous the directions are, and in true Brahman style lives on the margin between this world and the world of the spirit, handling the confusions of his spot well, not demanding greater certainty than the situation can provide.

Saktideva's story suggests that the raw materials for gaining an identity in the bright-shadow world, enhancing experience, are not nearly as well processed as the materials available (or that we believe are available) to us, in our real world, through psychoanalysis and kindred resources. Maturing, gaining an identity, are messy processes. Of course, the state of affairs facing *us* is the result of centuries of "development"—a long period of working out and debating psychological theories, sophisticated educational systems, and programs designed to help us along. Many of these resources, however, obscure the really fruitful paths that were opened to us when we were children by traditional narrative. Even though all that the bright-shadow world offers is the family or clan, certain rituals, and a very few models, none of them very well known, nevertheless its clues may be clearer and more realistic than what our world provides for us. The tools it makes available are limited to established rites of passage, a certain forcefulness of personality demonstrated by a few, some stories from the past, and the wit of a few tribal rogues. Its weakness is a certain reluctance to acknowledge the place of the unconscious in the process of gaining an identity. But this is understandable, given the weakness of the operative vectors and the constant threats, in generally unstimulating environments, of sleep and forgetfulness and engulfment rather than growth in the group. The one who risks all finds himself/herself balanced perilously between the terrors of sheer wilderness on one side and a rigid, paralyzing social structure on the other.

More positively, I would say that when we deal with twin issues of identity and the bright-shadow world we must take seriously the way other dimensions, other modes of consciousness, impinge on emerging human personalities. MacDonald hints at this idea toward the end of *Phantastes* when he muses:

> Self will come to life even in the slaying of self, but there is ever something deeper and stronger than it, which will emerge at last from the unknown abysses of the soul: will it be as a solemn gloom, burning with eyes? or a clear morning after the rain? or a smiling child, that finds itself nowhere, and everywhere? (166)

Some Jungians have penetrated as far as this, but in what he says MacDonald goes well beyond their central position.

Why certain individuals suddenly start to promote themselves is still a mystery. Self-identity hangs from sky hooks fashioned out of some inexplicable grasping for position in the scheme of things, the discovery that one enjoys using one's brain, a determination to avoid enchantment, the desire to supplant, skill in world-reading, openness and wit, and more often than not a sense of the beyond. Folktales are told and heard because all humans tend to slip back into the undifferentiated mass, but they are loved and remembered because of the sturdy individuals they sometimes hold up for our admiration, individuals whose capacity for growth is clearly linked to the very tenuousness of their essential natures.

10 The Experience of Knowing

I have observed that the most wonderful thing in the world is how people come to understand anything.
    —*George MacDonald,* At the Back of the North Wind.

My advice, in the midst of the seriousness, is to keep an eye out for the tinker shuffle, the flying of kites, and kindred sources of surprised amusement.
    —*Jerome Bruner,* On Knowing

In the bright-shadow world learning and understanding differ radically from most of the experiences we have with these processes. This we have noted in some detail in chapter 3, where the diffused alertness so characteristic of individuals in the bright-shadow world was discussed. The sense of wonder expressed so charmingly by Little Diamond at the start of this present chapter appropriately suggests the marvelous and certainly unexpected places to which learning even the tiniest bit of information may take someone, as well as the pleasure to be derived from the experience. In the world of the bright shadow hints and subtle gestures often count for more than hard data, drowsiness and forgetfulness can obscure clear thought (or serve as channels for inspiration), and the boundaries between individual and world—so basic to the objective/subjective orientation that has dominated the modern world—may prove maddeningly, or delightfully, uncertain. The kinds of facts typical of that dimension of experience seem to require somewhat different modes of apprehension than we normally employ, "a peculiar cognitive style," says Alfred Schutz, echoing what Claude Lévi-Strauss has to say about the skill with which preliterate people read their world, noting that "the passionate attention which they pay to it and their precise knowledge of it has often struck inquirers."[1] And at quite the other end of the historical spectrum, we find in postmodernism a keen interest in nonsensory perception, which is also reflected in traditional narrative and a rejection of "the grand narratives of legitimation" (Lyotard, 51) by which the modern world organized knowledge. As Paul Feyerabend says, knowledge is "an ever increasing *ocean of mutually incompatible (and perhaps even incommensurable) alternatives,* each single theory, each fairy tale, each myth . . . forcing the others into greater articulation and all of them contributing, via the process of competition, to the development of our consciousness" (*Against Method,* 30). We have now moved into the field of heuristics, the study of ways of promoting discovery, in which much important work is being done.

Spotting hints and significant resemblances, seeing patterns where others see only confusion, and letting subconscious forces play their part—this is what is required to navigate the problems cast up by the bright-shadow world and, perhaps, in the process to learn new things about *this* world and about oneself. Long before her consciousnesss admits it, Beauty knows who the Beast is, and it takes a clever passerby hardly any time at all to connect the ostrich in the town square with the missing jewel. Perhaps the most important point to be made, however, is that in the bright-shadow world knowledge is not organized, as it is in our world—there are no libraries, no journals, no university curricula, no think-tanks. Hence the storing of knowledge and its transmission are carried out completely informally, quite carelessly—by our standards. Nevertheless, through this important topic the bright-shadow world, like the postmodern world, challenges our understanding of *what it means to know* and introduces important life-enhancing elements to the process of world-reading in which we, like so many characters in fairytales and folktales, are engaged.

A typical bright-shadow-world problem in learning/knowing/ perceiving goes something like this: a youth and a maiden in flight change themselves into features of the landscape. Their dull-witted pursuer returns to his chief with the confession that he has seen nothing of his quarry, nothing, indeed, but an old man near a well and a ladle. "Dummkopf!" (or its equivalent) shouts the chief: those were the pair you were chasing! With just one image in mind, the pursuer paid no attention to other possibilities and missed his quarry completely.[2] But though the pursuer was dull, we are impressed by his chief's ability to spot relevant details on a large and very complex canvas, zeroing in on a tiny cluster and assessing its significance with great accuracy.[3] Do the well and the ladle suddenly strike him as particularly apt disguises because their appearance on that spot was so natural? Does he realize that had he been in flight he might have tried a similar metamorphosis? There is a leap of insight here, an immediate cognition without any basis in previous experience: the "of course" of insight dominates, not the "consequently" of logic. Knowing-experiences like this occur constantly in traditional narrative. What vectors seem to be at work?

Intuition

This is a broad category covering many kinds of knowing-experiences that cannot be pinned down to words and logic. "Intuitive" is a designation applied to someone who has a sense of being directed from within, often through the voice or vision of a loved one, a parent or other person involved in one's deepest being. Feyerabend suggests that this kind of learning starts in childhood (72), when nonsense is acceptable (270), and that it is a *"new observation language"* (79), that is, a way of knowing quite different from what has been taught in the modern world. The experience accords unusual significance to various signs, hints, and gestures that strike most people as having little or no significance. Intuitive people exhibit an unusual kind of confidence in difficult situations, since they expect some guidance from within at critical moments—and often do receive it! And they tend to grow passive in the presence of powerful rational vectors whose significance they may be unable to assess. Intuitive abilities are often linked to a powerful response to dreams, dancing, a capacity for communication with animals, the ability to make deductions from the tiniest hints provided by the behavior of other human beings.[4] Not a course of study one will find in any school! Actors in such cases can look deep within, and because they do, they see signs everywhere in their physical context.[5]

We begin with three spectacular and puzzling stories from South Asia, Central Asia, and Egypt. A tale from the Mongolian collection *Sagas from the Far East* poses the question of how a person communicates the fact that he/she has been murdered—when there is no one around but the murderer to report the truth. As he dies, a young prince says "Abaraschika" into the air. His villainous companion, the murderer, reports this word to the king, the dead man's father, suggesting that the utterance was meaningless. He gives the impression of wanting to be regarded as a faithful and reliable reporter of a deed he could not prevent. But the king is not so easily put off, feeling that the word must have some meaning—a meaning that is indeed revealed to him by a bird that witnessed the deed. The reporter is the murderer and himself transmits the information that damns him.[6]

The bird is not the key to the puzzle, I think, being merely a symbol of (the royal) intuitive powers, as birds often are. The king (we must assume) has long suspected the loyalty of his son's friend, so he is sensitized to the situation. Far more critical to the unraveling of the mystery are the prince's faith that an utterance he made *in extremis* would somehow get back to his father and be taken seriously, the murderer's mistake about how the information would be interpreted (how did this fellow manage to escape? is a question that should naturally occur to the king), and the father's brilliant deduction about what happened: "If my son had anything good to communicate he would have done it by words which his supposed friend could have carried to me." Perhaps we are to assume that the prince had a long-standing reputation for clarity of utterance, in which case the nonsense phrase was intended to suggest that something quite unclear was overwhelming him. And perhaps, too, the nonsensical element was meant to convey the dying prince's realization that a world in which a supposed friend was a murderer made no sense at all. In sum, a great many bits of information are available to the person who can fit them together intuitively, carried, ironically enough, by the very one they will condemn.

What can we say about a world where strategies like the son's—and thinking processes like the father's—lead to the truth? Certainly that it is closely knit: the two actors must know each other extremely well if the son's strategy is to work. And one must know that the other knows him or her well. We are dealing with a network where intelligence depends on keeping a lot of antennae up (we have noted this time and again) to catch whatever relevant bits of data float by—not a world like ours, where information has been processed and reprocessed and overprocessed for easy use by lazy human beings. And a world that is somewhat less complex than our world: the single anomaly (how did this fellow escape?) is quickly noted. Son and father and murderer whirl together in a grave but passionate dance, and as they dance the truth rises up for all who will look to see.

The Egyptian tale to which I referred has as its central actor a grammar-school teacher who supplemented his income by wandering about the village giving Qur'an readings. One day he noted that the door of a bedroom of a neighboring house was ajar, and he hurried away; next day he glanced at the door; the following day he looked in and saw a woman asleep on the bed; the fourth day he went in, gently put his hand on the woman—and fled. When he got home, his wife accused him of wrongdoing.

What did she know? How did she know it? Of course, the verb

"know" is itself part of the problem. The wife's explanation of her insight is that three days earlier the village water carrier had glanced at her; the next day he stared; then he spoke; finally he tried to touch her. Apparently the wife saw analogies between her husband and the water carrier striking enough to prompt her to speak out.[7]

What are the steps of this intricate negotiation? Certainly none that fits very well into any structure we have been trained in, any vectors we normally make use of. One important connection between Qur'an reader and water carrier is that both are concerned with orality—water is drunk, the Qur'an recited. Each is a "specialist" in extremely intimate material closely connected to the essence of personhood. Thus there is some reason for drawing an analogy—two men with similar interests may behave in similar ways. But this step requires the wife to make a leap from her own case to the case of the woman her husband noticed. The leap may be clarified by a concept drawn from the psychologist Mahler, who finds the source of infant identity in some "flowing-over" or "assimilatory mechanism" by which an infant draws psychic material from its mother and from this builds its own psyche (Lichtenstein, 75). The wife may have experienced some flowing-over from her husband's psyche, as husband and wife often do: she is aware of his sexuality. In any case, she works her way quite easily through this mysterious network: she is a true creature of the bright-shadow world. By contrast, we possesss only the most clumsy tools to talk about the relationship between the two events: does one cause, result from, or reflect the other? Are they similar, and if so, what is the point at which the similarities are really operative? Truly this is a world of shadows for those who seek rational understanding but a world of breathtaking leaps and marvelous, knowledge-related moves for those who can manage the experience.

The environment in which these special intuitive powers flourish is strikingly suggested by the third story to which I referred, a story from *Kalilah and Dimnah*, the great Arabic collection of animal tales. The central figure here is Bilar, one of a group of retainers to be granted special gifts by the king. Given the chance to select whatever gift he wants from the royal hoard, Bilar takes some beautiful objects to the mother of Gobar so that she can help him with his selection.

> When the mother of Gobar saw the golden diadem, she admired it and wished to take it. So she looked to Bilar round the corners of her eyes, (meaning) that he should indicate which of them was the best and most beautiful and excellent. He signified to her by a wink that the garment was better than the diadem. But

the king was looking at him when he winked. When she perceived that the king had seen Bilar wink to her concerning the
garments, she feared lest the king should conceive some miserable suspicion about her in connection with Bilar. So she passed
by the golden dress, and took the diadem. Bilar lived for forty
years after this time, and whenever he went in to the king, he
used to shut his eye, as the king had seen him shut it when he
winked to the mother of Gobar. But for the subtle intelligence of
this man, and the great wisdom of the woman in leaving the
dress and taking the diadem, and the wonderful knowledge of
this man in making a habit of winking his eyes all through these
years, two persons would have lost their lives, or been accused
and banished from the king's presence. (232)

What an awesome situation! What potent, uncontrollable vectors,
darting out from what terrifying power sources! The existing climate
of suspicion can render dangerous the slightest misstep by the ac-
tor/courtiers involved. All three principals are attuned to the prevail-
ing mood of suspicion, ready to pick up clues as to what the others
may be thinking. And all spot the significant clue, unrelated as it is to
the process at hand. Bilar and the mother of Gobar escape because the
king does not trust his own intuitions; he does not feel he can make
an issue of something as insignificant as a wink, even though he may
suspect its significance. The best he can do is to exact a high price
from the two allies: Bilar must maintain a certain role for forty years,
for the king may pounce if at any time he can convince himself that
the eye-twitching was not completely natural. So both the mother of
Gobar and Bilar must attend constantly to one of the tiniest and most
intimate gestures a human being can make, in the process rendering
this tiny gesture far more significant than it was originally. The situation will always be dangerous, for royalty does not like to be excluded
from secrets—and yet royal anxiety may be groundless.

To review, at more abstract levels:

1. A dying actor (1) directs a vector (sound) toward another actor
(2), to whom he is closely related. This sound-vector is enough to
incriminate another actor (3), the murderer, who actually transmits it
to Actor 2. Actor 3 downplays the significance of the vector. Actor 1
regards it as critical. How can a sound-vector be so important? Its
importance lies in the questions it raises: why was Actor 3 not a
power source in the time of difficulty? Why was Actor 1 feeling so
isolated and vulnerable when Actor 3 was there with him? These
questions lead the intuitive Actor 2 right to the truth.

2. The Qur'an reader's wife knows that vectors have been flowing out of his psyche into the psyche of another woman in the village because she herself has been the recipient of psychic material flowing toward her from the water carrier (and in the past, of course, from her husband). In neither case has there been any conscious effort to seduce or to allow oneself to be seduced; the fact is, simply, that power (sexual power) is present, operating at a far more basic level than received morality. The physical context, a small village, where everyone is close to everyone else, contributes to her deduction.

3. In the third story, an important vector passes between Actors 1 and 2, as Actor 3 watches. Unwittingly Actors 1 and 2 have become conspirators, devising another vectoral scheme to convince Actor 3 that the vector he saw was of no significance. The physical context requires that they sustain this new vector for the rest of their lives. Actor 3, very much in the position of Browning's Duke of Ferrara, cannot intervene without letting 1 and 2 know that he has been taking some minor issue far too seriously.

Intuition is linked to the capacity to turn inward and to respond to what one hears there, from an inner voice. Harding speaks of some "nonpersonal part of the psyche . . . not connected with . . . the I" that appears to be some other speaking within (18), sometimes taken for the voice of "that creative 'old man' who has fathered every invention man has ever made" (57). We are dealing here with a rare and precious consensus between the actor's inner being and certain vectors rising from within but closely linked to the outer physical context as well. Can this faculty be educated, brought along, developed? I think so—by encouraging individuals to take the time to listen to inner promptings, to perceive more intensely what lies around them, to connect various parts of their experience, and to put some confidence in their ability to make good guesses.[8]

The process of listening that Harding has described is nicely suggested in a conversation a Lapp fox has with himself at a difficult moment. Through it he moves from doubt to certainty.

> Taking one of his back feet between his two front
>   paws, he said quietly,
> What would you do, my feet, if I were betrayed?
> I would spring forth in haste!
> What would you do, mine ear, if I were betrayed?
> I would listen carefully.
> What would you do, my nose, if I were betrayed?
> I would catch the furthest scent!

What would you do, my tail, if I were betrayed?
I would steer the straightest course!
Let us be off! Let us be off![9]

Presumably the fox was convinced by this canvass of his own inner resources that he had the ability to go ahead. The power of these resources, as he surveyed them, is neatly suggested by the device of giving each its own voice, as if each were a power source quite separate from the fox himself.

A similar point is made in a story Calvino prints, called "Invisible Grandfather," about a young girl without parents who gets good advice from the voice of her dead grandfather, speaking out of the fireplace (103). The hearth, all by itself, seems to evoke certain deep memories of her grandfather's approach to problems. The old man's voice and mind are "trapped" by the girl's memories of him and "ignited" by the sight of the fireplace. The Grimm Brothers' story about the Goose-Girl (Magoun and Krappe, 324) runs along the same lines. In all cases the actor discovers within himself/herself another, wiser actor who for some reason—perhaps because he or she is not exposed to the hurly-burly of life—can make the principal actor see clearly the vectors actually operating in the situation.

The intuitive powers of Calvino's young woman can also be traced to the tight structure of family, home, and beloved furnishings in which she lived, to the physical context of her life. All knowledge develops within networks, contexts, and this is as true in our world as it is in the world of the bright shadow. The actor is nothing apart from his or her physical context.[10] About to yield to Zuleika, Joseph sees his father's warning face looming up before him. Jane Eyre sees her mother's when she is about to surrender to Rochester. And Castaneda notes, "I became aware that the tenuous pink light and the buzzing were very steady. I had a moment of intense bewilderment and then a thought crossed my mind, a thought that had nothing to do with the scene I was witnessing, nor with the purpose I had in mind for being there. I remembered something my mother had told me once when I was a child. The thought was distracting and very inappropriate . . . . and then I clearly heard my mother's voice calling me."[11]

Understanding Animal Speech

Another important manifestation of the state of intimacy that seems to lie close to the heart of the intuitive process has to do, once again, with man's relation to the animal world—the ties of the two-leggeds to the four-leggeds, as Black Elk puts it—seen this time as the ability of human beings to understand the speech of animals. Here vectors deriving from lesser actors, embedded in the physical context, are discovered to be of immense value to the principal actors. Are the latter sensitive enough to their environment to grasp these vectors? This gift is an indicator of unusual perspicacity, a sign of profound openness to spiritual realities hidden to most mortals, and proof of active participation in one's world.[12]

Thus in "The Princess and the Crocodile Hunters" it is observed that ultimate wisdom is to know the names of the stars, how to add all the numbers in the world, and how to speak the language of animals. Being close in spirit to the animal world—empathetic—is essential (Amina Shah, 94). In "The White Snake" a taste of snake meat (again the mouth is involved) enables a boy to gain wisdom, understand animal speech and the problems of animals, and call on help at a desperate time (Magoun and Krappe, 67 ff.). Black Elk's power of interpreting animal speech was noted and respected by all who knew him, one particularly dramatic moment occurring on a cold winter night when a coyote began to howl. Black Elk says, "It was not making words, but it said something plainer than words": there were bison on the next ridge, but also hostile men (Neihardt, 151). This stress on the participatory ego—an important factor in understanding animal speech—is reflected, too, in the observations of Prince Anados, as he travels through fairy land, in MacDonald's *Phantastes:*

> I was brought into far more complete relationship with the things around me. The human forms appeared much more dense and defined, more tangibly visible, if I may say so. I seemed to know better which direction to choose when any doubt arose. I began to feel in some degree what the birds meant in their songs, though I could not express it in words, any more than you can some landscapes.[13]

In a Sufi tale with Kafkaesque overtones, Saif-Baba asks some animals to explain to him

> why it is that a mere cat and a tiny sparrow can tell me things which I, with the miraculous benefits which I have received, cannot see?"
>
> "That is simple," they both said together. "It is that you have become so accustomed to looking at things in only one way that your shortcomings are visible even to the most ordinary mind."

This worried Saif-Baba. "So I could have found the Door of the Third Piece of Advice long ago, if I had been properly attuned to it?" he asked.

"Yes," said the dog, joining the discussion. "The door has opened a dozen times in the past years, but you did not see it. We did, but because we are animals, we could not tell you."

"Then how can you tell me now?"

"You can understand our speech because you yourself have lately become more human. But you have only one more chance, for age is overcoming you." (*Tales of the Dervishes*, 174)

Note the links between the inability of the human to see the door and the inability of the animals to speak to him, and between both of these factors and the inhumanity of the man. Saif-Baba's growing sensitivity (it is noted that he has become "more human") seems to involve an increasing respect for the natural world, a sense of the need to preserve the man/nature balance, an awareness of the sacredness of things. Perhaps, too, the idea of animals speaking is so bizarre (even to a medieval South Asian) that those who are spiritually unprepared for it will simply be baffled, confused, angered. Whatever networks of traditional, rational understanding have been constructed will be undercut, and new ones will not be forged to replace them.

Finally it should be noted that communication with animals seems to resemble the phenomenon of speaking in tongues or charismatic speech, which may appear mere senseless babbling to those not attuned to it but which can be converted by those with sharply focused sensibilities (such as Saif-Baba demonstrated) into an oracular message strikingly relevant to the concerns of a particular person.[14] Of his vision, Black Elk says, "I remembered . . . words that went with [certain pictures]; for nothing I have ever seen with my eyes was so clear and bright as what my vision showed me; and no words that I ever heard with my ears were like the words I heard. I did not have to remember these things; they have remembered themselves" (49). The experience of transcendence could not be described more clearly.

Dancing

For actors oriented to rhythm and movement and to a kaleidoscopic external setting, dancing is another important instrument of knowledge in the world of the bright shadow. Dancing and storytelling are a common cultural pair. In dancing, actors yield control of their lives to certain powerful rhythmic vectors over which they have very little control. I have already noted, in chapter 6, the links between this activity and enchantment. More positively, dancing provides insight and knowledge that penetrate every aspect of the personality; it is more physical, more emotional, than any other way of knowing, "somthing to be experienced through intimate contact, rather than to be received through telling" (Neihardt, xv). "Trance-dancing" is a form of meditation practiced by (among others) American Indians and the Sufis of Islam, by which consciousness is focused on some spot deep within the personality. The great Turkish mystic Rumi prized dancing even more highly than storytelling as a means of gaining access to esoteric knowledge. His *Mathnawi*, to which many references have already been made in these pages, is a treatise on the hidden knowledge to be gained by exploring various suprarational states of consciousness. The dance liturgy or *sema*, which he developed, was practiced by his followers, the Mevlevi dervishes, on many occasions—even at funerals.[15]

In *Turning On*, an account of several consciousness-raising groups she visited in the 1960s, Rasa Gustaitis describes the way Fritz Perls, the celebrated Gestalt analyst, would actually "speak to" a partner while dancing with her. In *Zorba the Greek* Kazantzakis recounts the way his hero, Alexis, in Russia alone and knowing nothing of the language, communicated even complex ideas to his friends by dancing. G. I. Gurdjieff, in *Meetings with Remarkable Men*, analyzes the complex dances of the Caucasus region of Southwest Asia, right down to the "alphabet of postures" that enables the dancing monks to read gestures as neatly as most of us read words.[16] And George MacDonald, in *Phantastes*, not only describes a particular dance but tries to break through its hypnotic power and explain what is going on:

> I seemed to hear something like the distant sound of multitudes of dancers, and felt as if it was the unheard music, moving their rhythmic motion, that within me blossomed in verse and song. I felt, too, that could I but see the dance, I should, from the harmony of complicated movements, not of the dancers in relation to each other merely, but of each dancer individually in the manifested plastic power that moved the consenting harmonious form, understand the whole of the music on the billows of which they floated and swung. (107)

Inwardness, plasticity (i.e., ability to be shaped), analogic flow, the sense of networks, the capacity to experience high moments, the haziness of boundaries between the individual and the group, and an extremely specific message—of such critical elements of the bright-shadow world is this experience made![17] The possibility of communicating by rhythms alone (a legitimate extension of dancing) may bring to mind the insane dwarf, Oscar Matzerath, of Gunter Grass's *Tin Drum*. With his red and white drum, Oscar says, he searches the timber port for his missing grandfather (38); after his mama's death he depends on it constantly, for "it always gave the right answer" (174); and he is able to communicate with, even control, large audiences, providing therapy with his instrument (534–35). Oscar also knows by smell, and, he claims, by the soles of his feet. Edward Dillard offers an explanation of this phenomenon: "If all that exists has its own patterns of pulsations, and Oscar has an ear for them, then he can conjure up things and events by beating out a rhythm that forces individuals . . . to oscillate and dance . . . to the tune of his frenzied drumming."[18]

Dreaming

About dreaming as a means of knowing there is an enormous literature today; indeed, it would be hard to identify a spiritual/psychological/physiological/anthropological phenomenon that has attracted as much interest in the past century. Interest has focused on both the meaning of the dream content and the kind of reality that can be ascribed to it, and investigation has gone on in sleep laboratories, on the couches of analysts, and through the examination of myths and fairytales. Erving Goffman summarizes modern thinking succinctly: "Presumably the dreamer cannot put into his dream anything that is not in some sense already in him; he must make do with traces stored up from the past" (*Frame Analysis*, 113). Traditional thinking, however, is open to broader possibilities.

Denizens of the bright-shadow world are never hesitant to function on the basis of the information they have received through dreams and to encourage others to dream in order to make contact with their own innermost natures. Not to dream, as not to dance, is to be seriously out of touch with the most fundamental realities. Like the Chinese philosopher Chuangtzu before him, Rumi, one of our foremost authorities on the bright-shadow world, enjoys playing with the idea that our world is only a sleeper's dream, an idea that frightens us (because it suggests insubstantiality) but would make little difference in the bright-shadow world (where the illusion of substantiality has never taken hold anyway). A sleeper's dream, of course, and why not? Rumi encourages those who enjoy their dreams to learn from them too, since no one is ever hurt in a dream (*Mathnawi*, II, 97), a position affirmed in *At the Back of the North Wind* (20, 154). Through dreaming, an actor discovers that he/she has actually become two actors, operating in two different worlds, between which important vectors pass. If the actor is essentially a rational person, he/she will quickly identify one world—waking life—as the only reality. An intuitive person will rejoice in the ability to move between the two worlds—and in the freedom to grant either of them priority at certain times.

In certain societies the dream becomes an enormously important element in the construction of reality. Wendy O'Flaherty has documented the role and significance of dreaming in traditional India, where, according to Roger Caillois, the dream was regarded as "a consciously willed effort that will be realized provided only that it is pursued sufficiently long and with sufficient vigor."[19] My problem, no doubt, with Rumi, with whom I have been trying to converse in dreams for a long time! From Kilton Stewart we have a report of perhaps the world's most thoroughly dream-oriented people, the Senoi of the Malay Archipelago, who make the reporting of dreams the substance of daily breakfast-time conversations and work hard at helping children shape appropriate interpretations of their dreams. The Senoi are taught to utilize all the forces that the dream universe brings to them so "dreaming can and does become the deepest type of creative thought."[20]

Thus we may understand why Owen O'Mulready has only one desire—to have a dream, "for he had never had one"[21]—and why fairytale figures are not at all reluctant to take seriously the advice given in dreams. In *Thousand and One Nights* a wazir gives a painter highly detailed instructions about painting a picture from one of his dreams. A fowler is to be setting up his nets, and a bird is to fall into one of them. The other birds are frightened and fly off, though the mate of the trapped bird comes back and frees it. Waking from sleep the fowler observes that the birds have escaped, repairs the net, and puts fresh grain around it. This time two pigeons come by, the female is trapped, and the husband makes no effort to save her. The fowler kills the female, and a raven attacks and kills the disloyal mate. "I would have you pourtray [sic] me the presentment of this dream," the wazir instructs the painter, "even as I have related it to you, in the liveliest colours . . . and dwell especially on the fowler and the falcon" (VII, 233). I assume that the wazir recognizes the relevance of this dream to his own situation. By an act of will, the wazir forces two contexts into one reality and freezes certain vectors for later use. Is he the fowler, dealing harshly with those beneath him, or does he play falcon to king/fowler? In this case the painting becomes a kind of mandala, through which the wazir may learn to reflect on productive relationships. Whatever the truth, the message belongs to that gray area of personal identification so characteristic of the bright-shadow world. But what a productive experience to be able to bring back the whole thing and then have it painted out in detail, for reference at whatever future time it is needed!

And we can hardly neglect the delicious story about the man in Cairo who laughs at a dream of treasure buried in a house in Baghdad. His friend, a Baghdadi, recognizes that his own house is being described, returns home, and digs up the treasure (*1001*, IV, 289). The actor has discovered in his own inner being material that fits exactly material from the very extremity of his context, and neither he nor we grasp what the linking vectors are; they belong to another level of consciousness.[22]

How is the connection forged between waking life and the dream experience? Telepathy? The dredging up of old images that had been forgotten? The demand of a dream that it be lived out? A certain consonance between what a person dreams and what the person is? Mahlerian overflow? Some insight is provided in the *Mahasupina-Jataka* (#77), where a series of dreams are reported to a wise man and accurately interpreted by him. In this case the dream-interpreter seems to have spotted a single theme running through all of them, thereby gaining a clue to the real-life context to which these dreams were speaking. He confirms and expands his hypothesis by asking the king who has dreamed to come to him and by observation gains an understanding of the direction the royal unconsciousness has been taking.[23] From here on, it is just a matter of following the issue out to some conclusion—as the dreamer himself cannot. The point of the story about the Baghdad treasure trove seems to lie primarily in the power of one man to recognize the relevance of what he is hearing—or to force extraordinary personal relevance upon material someone else is treating very casually.[24]

Scenario-Building

Another information-gathering technique familiar to those who regularly employ intuition and pay attention to their dreams involves constructing scenarios based on available data, then following out these constructs to all their possible conclusions. Here the actor is both dramatist and actor in a drama. In the story, the actor creates a drama and then watches himself/herself acting in it. As many physical contexts as may be needed are created, and the actor takes his/her place in them sequentially until the information needed appears. The power source is imagination, and the vectors are the various forces that play upon the actor in the drama until the revelation that is sought occurs. While these conclusions will not have the force of hard facts, they are often firm enough to provide the basis for some action.

There is a celebrated case at the end of Dickens's *Bleak House;* Mr. Bucket, the detective, desperate to track down Lady Dedlock before she destroys herself, rises high above London (in his mind, of course) and examines every likely spot in the great city until he gets a firm setting on the direction his quarry has taken. Anados, in MacDonald's *Phantastes,* confesses that he has used the same technique: "Sometimes I acted within myself a whole drama, during one of these perambulations; sometimes walked deliberately through the whole epic of a tale; sometimes ventured to sing a song, though with a shrinking fear of I know not what" (106).

But the most interesting application of this technique is to be found in a contemporary Egyptian play by Tewfik al-Hakim, *The Tree Climber.* In this absurdist drama, which has its roots deep in Egyptian folklore, the intuitive, charismatic type is a dervish who is called in for help with a disappearance and possible murder. The dervish's standard technique is to imagine himself on a train and to report what he sees outside the windows. He suggests that the husband has killed or will kill his wife, and when the husband objects—Why was I not told?—the dervish replies, "The train had not brought me to where I could see further than I had seen."[25] The very denial of knowledge affirms its possibility, nevertheless. This phenomenon has been discussed by many students of the imaging process, the observations of Stephen Kosslyn being particularly pertinent. Kosslyn notes that many scientists report playing mentally with images, "twisting and turning them in various ways" to see what emerges.[26] Images can be "examined and classified" very much as material objects can be studied perceptually, Kosslyn notes (90), and separate images can be "glued together" by the mind (98). A familiar memory device, of course, is to visualize a room or other scene and locate in it the things to be remembered.[27] This way of learning and knowing is essentially an imaginative extension of world-reading, discussed in chapters 3 and 4, and what al-Jahiz's traveler did as he thought about where the jewel had gone was to make a little drama, putting into it an actor whose role had not (until he came along) been taken into account— the ostrich. At this point, knowledge blossomed. Always there is the possibility of an imaginative extension of data in hand—vectors—

into areas where little as yet is known but where certain extensions of data consciously held into the realms of the unconscious may provide useful information.

Reading Hints

The capacity to pick up hints is critical in the knowledge system of the bright-shadow world, where, as I have already suggested, knowledge is very poorly organized. At the very least, hinting teases us into attention. A more obvious gesture by Bilar and the mother of Gobar might have completely eluded the attention of the king, and the capacity to separate the tiny but important clue from a mass of irrelevancies is often what separates the hero from the crowd (Harding, 32). DeBono speaks of the ability of one kind of memory to amplify the tiniest differences between patterns and make something special of them (*Mechanism,* 63, 92). Hint-reading has always been important, moreover, to those in search of spiritual truth, which often seems to hide in material reality. Thus in the *Mathnawi* Rumi observes that

> since God has called the (external) sign (aspect) informative, the eye of the gnostic has remained turned towards the sign.
> Color and scent are significant like a bell: the neigh of a horse makes (one) acquainted with the horse.
> The sound made by any thing conveys the knowledge of it. . . . The colour of the face indicates the state of the heart. (I, 70-1)

And later he adds:

> The spirit has beheld the wine in the grape, the spirit has beheld thing (entity) in nothing (nonentity). . . . In hot July they (the Pirs) [spiritual teachers] see December; in the sunbeams they see the shade.
> In the heart of the grape they have seen the wine. (I, 231)

So Rumi, in his own distinctive way, calls attention to another important knowing faculty—the capacity to pick out from a panorama certain features, even very small ones, that convey critical information. The actor who can read hints is acutely tuned to every vector in a situation, and the vectors themselves are abundant, some meaningful in a situation, some not. The physical context is extremely rich in details but lacks overall structure. Power sources are perception, wit, and the ability to make combinations. The material relating to this point is abundant, suggestive, and often highly amusing.

Often it is some insistent detail that is the clue to a problem. Eurycleia feels the scar on the thigh of the beggar she is bathing and knows immediately that she has Odysseus before her. (No doubt many other factors, largely unidentifiable, prepared her for this realization—a fact that scarcely diminishes the wonder of it.) In a Lapp tale Andras Baive has no trouble tracking an opponent even though he runs through a bewildering series of metamorphoses—stone, music, wreckage—because in each new metamorphosis some distinctive characteristic of the individual who is being pursued can be detected by a keen eye (*Lapplandische Märchen*, 155 ff.). In "Soria Moria Castle" an old woman recognizes Halvor by the way he stirs ashes in the hearth (Dasent, 403). In a popular Middle Eastern story a girl realizes that her lute teacher is aboard the ship on which she travels when she picks up a lute to play it: only her teacher could tune it this way.[28]

At a critical moment in "The King of the Waterfalls," the queen rides a horse with what is apparently a wooden saddle, except that at certain points gold sparkles from beneath its rude surface. A farmer's daughter goes for a a walk with a strange dark man, and when he combs his beard she notes beneath it a tangle of green seaweed (Briggs, *Personnel*, 158). And underneath the shriveled skin of an old hag, an Indian prince finds glowing the most beautiful face he has ever seen (*Old Deccan Days*, 153). Others feel prickles or find pins sticking in their jackets, become aware that they are not, as they had thought, alone, see something in the darkness, or detect some faint perfume which brings to their minds some other reality. In all these numinous experiences, stubborn physical facts nearly overwhelm vectors that have traveled far from their power sources and grown very faint.

Behavior is another important kind of detail. In fact, learning about people by studying their responses is one of the oldest tricks of preanalytic psychology. A familiar case is Portia's analysis of her lovers in terms of the chest each chooses. The quiz to which Lear subjects his daughters, to determine their love for him, might also be cited here, except that the testgiver himself is not in control of the situation. In *Ocean of the Streams of Story* Padmavati perceives that Vasavadatta is a person of quality by "her shape, her delicate softness, the graceful manner in which she sat down, and ate" (I, 110), and in the same collection a king realizes that an individual is innocent of charges because when the accused is threatened with a dungeon, "the colour of his face did not change, and he seemed without fear" (I, 357). In such cases, only an actor prepared to look between the cracks, beneath the surface, at the tiniest detail can learn what someone had indeed best learn.

The language of gestures can be very eloquent and very complex, and the most surprising things can be passed along by the movement of an eye or finger, the toss of a head, the intake of breath. But there is even more in this material—a whole grammar of gestures that is presumed legible to all who are in on the secret. The vectors launched by one actor can be read by another, if both are functioning within the same context or set of assumptions. Otherwise communication will be thwarted.[29] This seems to be a topic that appeals to every frame of mind, every point of view, and it is treated in a wide range of stories from many countries. Two examples will serve.

In a Bedouin story, "The Folly of Jealousy," a beautiful girl puts a finger on her eyes, teeth, and navel, revealing thus that her name is "Ain" (eye); that her father is a king; that his strength (in his teeth) is second only to his daughter's beauty; that his kingdom is "Surri" (navel); and that over his palace is a pomegranate tree (*Tales from the Arab Tribes*, 27). In a similar tale from Armenia, "Le Tisserand Intelligent," an ambassador does not utter a word in the presence of a king, merely tracing a circle on the floor with a black rod. The clever weaver who claims to be able to interpret these signs enters into a discussion with the ambassador through signs of his own. In one circle he sees a threat of encirclement by the neighboring king, and he responds by placing knuckle bones on the floor: to defeat you would be child's play for us. The envoy then scatters millet seeds about: our soldiers are numerous. The weaver responds by setting a rooster to eat up the seeds, etc. When both trains of thought are moving in the same direction, this process can be quite dazzling—like the old comic routine in which neither partner allows the other to finish a sentence. (See *The Olive Fairy Book*.)

But that the technique can break down badly is suggested charmingly in another Middle Eastern story, "The Peasant, the King and the Sheikh." Can the foreigner pose a riddle that the wise men of the kingdom cannot solve? The foreigner gestures toward the learned men, but of his meaning they have no idea. So they take an indirect approach, calling in a loutish boy with horny hands and a patched shirt. When the visitor points with his finger at the peasant, the peasant raises two fingers. When the visitor puts his hand up, the peasant puts his hand on the floor. The visitor takes a hen out of a box and throws it at the peasant, who takes an egg out of his shirt and throws it at the visitor. Immediately, surprisingly, the latter says, "You are my teacher." Later it is discovered that each was putting a very different interpretation on the gesture, the peasant thinking that the visitor was putting him down contemptuously, the visitor thinking that they were discussing theological issues. Each was playing his own game in his own context (Amina Shah, 13).

Modern, rational-world scepticism is reflected by the comment of the "capable administrator," Kamensky, in Rebecca West's *Birds Fell Down:*

> But I may have become a little mad as the years went on. Seeing connections, you know, between things in fact unconnected. Like the old woman you find in every village, who comes on a branch blown down from a tree by a gale and thinks it has been laid there by the butcher as a sign to the baker that the day has come to fulfil the plot they have long had in the hatching, and there will be arsenic in the next loaf she buys.[30]

A place for criticism there surely is. But sometimes the traditional modes uncover truth that rational thought cannot open up, simply because there is no control over the lines or vectors along which two minds will diverge, and sometimes, too, reality can be made to conform to the interpretation a strong-minded individual puts upon signs that come to him or her. To some degree, what is there depends on what one is willing to see.

The use of "sky hooks" is still another aspect of hint-reading that can help along the knowing process. I mean launching a concept with no—or virtually no—means of support, creating out of the very weakest kind of data a knowledge-structure of considerable strength. As Gregory Bateson has observed, an explanation of some phenomenon may enable discussion of it to begin, even though this particular explanation is eventually shown to be incorrect. As an illustration Bateson points to the Buddhist rejection of the concept of the self, even while it is employed as a means of getting psychological discussion started (*Mind and Nature,* 95, 149). Few questers in traditional narrative start off with anything more than the sketchiest idea about what lies ahead of them.

Deducing

Deducing is not as tricky as hint-reading, for there is not one actor who actually knows what the truth is. The dominant actor must develop the whole thing, sometimes making amazing mental leaps. The Bedouin gather valuable information about camels by a study of the prints they leave on the ground. For example, Sheikh Mizeil is able to pick up from footprints much about the nature of the person who made them (*Tales from the Arab Tribes*, 190), and eye movements in humans may prove far more eloquent than those who make them ever imagine. In *Ocean of the Streams of Story* there is an account of a cook who is unable to control the quivering of his eye when he serves the king poisoned soup; noting this, an advisor to the intended victim urges great caution and feeds the cook the soup (I, 461). In "The Three Clever Men and the Demons" a heavy cauldron missing from the kitchen is traced to the river by deep footprints, and the detective licks the skin of several sleeping men who are suspected of the theft until he finds one whose skin is free of salt: he has been in water up to his neck with the cauldron and is indeed the culprit (*Old Deccan Days*, 205–6). In a *Jataka* tale the following series of brilliant deductions is made about a Brahman:

> There must be a snake who has gone into that sack, and entering he must have gone in from the smell of the meal when the brahmin at his breakfast had eaten some meal and gone to drink water without fastening the sack's mouth: the brahmin coming back after drinking water must have gone on after fastening and taking up the sack without seeing that the snake had entered: if he stays on the road, he will say at evening when he rests, "I will eat some meal," and opening the sack will put in his hand: then the snake will bite him in the hand and destroy his life: this will be the cause of his death if he stays on the road: but if he goes home the sack will come into his wife's hand: she will say, "I will look at the ware within," and opening the sack put in her hand, then the snake will bite her and destroy her life, and this will be the cause of her death if he goes home today. This he knew by his knowledge of expedients. Then this came into his mind, "The snake must be a black snake, brave and fearless; when the sack strikes against the brahmin's broadside, he shows no motion or quivering; he shows no sign of his being there amidst such an assembly: therefore he must be a black snake, brave and fearless:" from his knowledge of expedients he knew this as if he was seeing with a divine eye. (III, 212–3)

Having accepted the premise about expedients and their importance, the clever observer can read the situation just as clearly as Mr. Bucket the detective can read his image of London, or the dervish in the al-Hakim play can unfold the future from his imaginary seat on the imaginary train. For the uninitiated, truly a "divine eye" at work, and for nearly everyone, a very plausible tale.

In *Thousand and One Nights* the hiding place of a treasure is deduced from the behavior of a gardener who seizes and beats a person for venturing too close to it in an innocent search for water. Clearly the gardener had something to hide. Elsewhere it is observed that a cake was kneaded by a menstruating woman (she was weak and kneaded it poorly); that a kid was suckled by a bitch (the meat near the bone was hard); that the sultan was a bastard of low birth (he did not sit at meals with his guests and gave them presents of food rather than money) and his wife a gypsy (she had black, bushy eyebrows). In the *Mathnawi* there is an account of a physician who makes a brilliant diagnosis of the problem of a young woman who has been forced to marry someone she does not love by feeling her pulse as he mentions a series of names, including that of the man she loves (I, 12). And in *Thousand and One Nights* a clever man deduces that there is a serpent under some bricks—he observes dampness on two tiles, and when he hears a dog bark, he concludes that the dog is near a well, because the bark was followed by an echo. There is a certain thrill to stories of this type, in which a daring intellectual leap more often than not lands squarely on the truth!

Oblique Speech

This category embraces situations where information is passed indirectly—perhaps through the mouth of a third actor ignorant of the import of words he/she is uttering—yet clearly enough to be grasped by the person for whom it is intended. In an Arab story a man tells a girl who has a butterfly tattooed on her navel that he has seen her naked—something he knows will embarrass her—by mentioning butterflies in slightly unusual contexts (*Tales from the Arab Tribes*, 110 ff.). She can receive the message because it is neatly buffered by the butterflies! Boccaccio is fond of this kind of tale, which contributes so much to and is so largely a product of the furtive, distinctly amoral atmosphere he strives for. In one of his narratives a woman devises a clever way to use her priest-confessor to inform her lover what his next steps should be. She complains to the priest about what her lover has been doing, and when the priest chides the man for his lustful behavior, the man realizes that actually he is being instructed by his friend. The priest also serves as a psychological buffer for the woman, who can be more frank about her tastes with him than with her lover: when she tells them to the priest, they are the lover's sin; when she tells them to her lover, they are her sin.[31] The success of the communication depends on the fact that two persons are "on the same wave length" and alert to even the merest possibility of communication. The classic model has two people separated in a strange city. Does each have enough sensitivity to the other's typical thought patterns to make a fair guess about the most likely meeting place? Can each discern the critical synapses of even the most tenuous network? Those who do, belong in the world of the bright shadow.[32]

Another form of obliquity often noted in this material has to do with overhearing the conversation of others. In this case a vector is presumed to have special importance by an actor who realizes that it is relevant to but not meant for him or her. It may even be that he has been purposely excluded. In stories of the "White Parrot" type, children learn about their origin by eavesdropping on a conversation between two birds or, in one case, by listening to two beds, once boys, talking to each other (*Roumanian Fairy Tales*, 36). Calvino prints stories about a princess who overhears four witches discussing an ointment that will cure the king; about a young man named Peel who hears fairies talking about a wizard's horses and learns that he can save Prince Pome by cutting off the head of the white one; and about a young man who learns (as he hides under an ogre's bed) how to unclog a fountain so that it will once again spout gold (*Italian Folktales*, 95 ff.). And in *Tuti-Nama* a son who has resolved to cut off his father's head hears a musician talking to his daughter, urging her not to disappoint his guests by refusing to dance any longer. The son realizes that he must not expose himself to reprehensible talk by spilling his father's blood (274).

In this case the son makes a connection between two very diverse issues, the common tie being the harm that children can do their parents. He is able to do this because at the moment his own psyche is highly sensitized to the parent/child issue, and his mind will seize whatever it can that is relevant to the problem. Knowledge is transferred because the one who must know is part of an extensive network of meanings, and it is transferred, characteristically, at a higher level of significance. The blind wretch Ferko, crouching beneath the gallows, is quite ready to hear how to regain his sight, and Saktideva, marooned on an island, listens eagerly when birds talk about flying to the very place he must visit. Rapunzel has been singing the song with her name in it for a long time, and the names of Rumpelstiltskin, Tom Tit Tot, and Tittle Ture are available to anyone who needs them—for they hang out there, in the air, right now.

Communication across Distance

Much that has already been said about networking and telepathy leads us to one final aspect of the knowing process as it is described in traditional narrative. I have in mind the way knowledge is passed across the bright-shadow world with no identifiable means of transmission. In one *Jataka* tale, communication takes place when two distant brothers merely think about each other (III, 277), and in another, the tie that binds is a flowery wreath dropped into the water (IV, 144). More "normally," however, warning is given by water that becomes turgid or bloody, or when a wife drinks milk that tastes like blood, or when her marriage necklace snaps in half. A bell rings when a husband is in trouble; a knife rusts or drips blood; a seal ring pinches; red lotuses fade; blood flows from a gash in a tree; a watermelon bleeds when pierced with a knife; the arm of a friend sails through the air; a left eye winks; a silver spoon tarnishes. Often the object through which the signal passes is some kind of life-token, its decay being in some way the cause as well as the sign of trouble. Such cases constitute a phenomenon of considerable interest to postmodern thinkers and hint at a spiritual or psychological skill once far more common than it is today.[33]

Knowledge is intimately related to being, and the more intensely, the more completely, one knows oneself, the more open one will be to the data that lies all around. And the more significance a person can see in the information that comes to him or her, the greater will be his or her store. Much information, we have seen, is available to anyone who attends to details and can devise meanings and niches for these details and shape significant connections for even the wildest array of data. This is a point on which Feyerabend is most insistent. And conversely we moderns are beginning to suspect that a lot of the data we have so patiently collected is not really germane to the issues facing us. In the bright-shadow world material is less well defined, worked out, than it is in our modern world: the vectors from which actors gain knowledge are more various, not as well controlled as in our world, so that under certain conditions anything can become anything else. So it is a world where knowing depends upon one's ability to think in metaphors, consider problems obliquely, exercise one's imagination, enter boldly into the most bizarre viewpoints.[34] All of this adds up to an experience of knowing that is radically different from what our world offers us, a way of knowing that often moves people far from their starting places, their normal assumptions, and thus promises to enrich their lives in all sorts of surprising ways.

11 Some Typical Bright-Shadow-World Problems

In the course of considering a number of themes common to traditional narrative, we have encountered various problems characteristic of the bright-shadow world, to some degree at least a result of its loose network structure and its chiaroscuro coloring. At first glance, many of these problems seem childish, irrelevant to adult concerns—how the hero gets into the palace, how the cat escapes the hunter, how the riddle is solved, how the real wife is identified. The peculiar quality of these problems is related in some way to the disorganized state of knowledge in the bright-shadow world, to the fragility of the bright-shadow personality, to the way morality combines subjective and objective elements. Foucault's preference for dealing with ideas by proliferation, juxtaposition, and disjunction tells us something important about him—and about the world we are dealing with in these pages (Shapiro, 77).

Thus it can be claimed that sometimes even the apparently silly difficulties encountered in fairytales have serious implications, hide complex structures, point toward significant enhancements of human experience. The hero slipping into a garden in such a way as not to disturb those present is all of us finding our way into some strange and threatening place and being there satisfactorily. When we understand how the cat escapes the hunter, we gain some sense of the way all living things are bound together and how the behavior of one affects all. Stories about the individual who finds something only after he or she has stopped looking for it point up the importance of enlisting the aid of the unconscious when the conscious mind fails. And to learn to exploit another's weaknesses—unpleasant as that sounds—is also to begin to understand human motivation and the range of responses of which human beings are capable.

This chapter undertakes to identify certain typical bright-shadow-world problems and describes techniques employed by bright-shadow people in solving them, techniques that can be characterized as tangential, lateral, indirect, techniques that challenge or circumvent accepted truths about how the mind works. All of these problems grow out of the efforts of individuals to identify unclear boundaries, define situations, and understand extremely diffuse and uncertain situations. In its own way this material asserts the stand of Feyerabend "against method," for the overriding "truth" that emerges is that no one need/should accept another's metanarrative, play another's word games. Every successful problem-solver is his/her own person, with his/her own script, operating in his/her own context, with his/her own power sources, managing his/her own vectors. Thus the orthodox and the literalist need not apply, but the witty and ingenious, the imaginative, those interested in tiny, seemingly irrelevant details, are welcome. A sense of the inner structure of a situation is more useful than analysis of its parts, and the ability to feel one's way may prove more productive than knowing exactly where one is going or what one will do upon arrival. Randomness and disorder have a certain value of their own. Thus popular narrative challenges much of the dominant thinking of our time about problem-solving, though its themes are increasingly being heard in important places today.

Choosing

Choosing is an important bright-shadow-world activity—increasingly unimportant in our world, I will make bold to say, where a superabundance of data often makes decision-making automatic, and where individuals are often quite well protected from the results of their choices. Not so in the bright-shadow world, where little information is available, most of that incomplete and ambiguous, and where there is no escape from choices once one has made them. The process is more difficult and has more serious ramifications. This theme is familiar through Shakespeare's most fairytalelike play, *The Merchant of Venice*, where three suitors for Portia's hand must select one of three caskets; the suitor making the "right" choice gets the woman. This motif is also the basis of the children's game of selecting the hand or fist that holds the stone/marble/candy/coin. The actor must select from several possibilities the power source critical to a given context, with very few—if any—vectors to guide deliberations.

Such games involve picking up whatever hints you can from a context about the correct choice, as well as using what you know about the wiliness-quotient of your opponent and his/her way of approaching problems. And one cannot hope to win at choosing unless one realizes that things may not be as they seem—though along what axis the deception and the truth may lie is never easy to determine. In the case of the two fists, for example, one must be aware of the possibility of several levels of deception on the part of the one who does the hiding—as two of Portia's suitors were not. (What will he assume that you assume that he assumes about his moves?) The winner of the casket contest, for example, will turn aside from the obvious glitter of two of them and be strangely drawn by some kind of challenge that the least attractive seems to hold out. And he/she will realize, too, that there is no point to a game if the "correct" answer is palpably obvious. And where a series of choices is to be made—as in the game of holding out one or two fingers—one needs to be aware of the development of certain rhythms. In some traditional narratives an animal helps the chooser to respond correctly (this may be interpreted as the operation of unconscious forces), and in other cases—again *The Merchant of Venice*—someone in the know offers clues to the correct option. (But in this case, the clues must be apparent to only one person, or it must be apparent to only one that clues are indeed being offered, or only one may be capable of picking them up.) Successful choosing may persuade the lucky person that he/she is somehow "favored" by the powers that be, or that he/she has unusual powers of insight, a very active unconscious or a keen sense of the operative rhythms of the situation. All are life-enhancing realizations—if they are kept in check.

Still other possibilities are raised in the East European story "The Magic Ring" (*Yellow Fairy Book*, 180). Offered a sack of sand or a sack of silver, Martin responds, "There must be some trick about this; I had better take the sand." He wisely shies away from one vector—the obvious choice, the rational choice—since if it is operative, there is no real point in the game. (Thus the fact of the game itself, something thrust upon you by another, is a significant vector to consider.) So this is a test of the actor's sense of significance, of ability to discriminate the meaningful power sources from the irrelevant. Is the actor tough-minded or timid? And of course at this point the possibility arises that the obvious choice is also the correct one, the deviser of the game counting on the clever person's avoiding that option. Much of the reasoning depends on whether the deviser of the game wants to prevent someone from winning or help someone win. Here is another critical vector. Goodwill and a capacity to read the world accurately at several levels at once are also important elements, and the contest usually comes out satisfactorily, though another factor enters here from the storyteller's point of view—the desirability of telling stories about successful people!

Making Subtle Contact

It is easy enough to slay dragons and kidnap helpless women, but far more difficult to touch individuals who tend to recoil from your touch, or to let yourself be seen by someone who may fear the sight of you, or to find again the lovely girl you saw once at the ball. The context is tenuous, the power potentially overwhelming, the vectors employed necessarily of the greatest delicacy. Teachers frequently encounter this challenge. There are a lot of private, very fragile people in traditional narratives, who, nevertheless, need to be heard from.[1] A model here is the prince's strategy for discovering Cinderella—by going throughout his kingdom, trying the tiny slipper on girl after girl. The natural approach, subtle buffering, the use of mirrors, reflections and insinuations seem to hold promise in such situations. Words of Lucretius come to mind: "Objects tucked away in the inner part of a house, however long and winding the approach to their hiding place, can . . . be brought to sight along devious routes by a series of mirrors. So the image is flashed from mirror to mirror."[2] One thinks of Ma'ruf, freshly arrived in a strange city, meeting a boyhood friend by chance, being introduced to a series of merchants, accepting their values, devising a scheme that accords with their thinking—and then developing a scheme of his own to overreach them. Such is the method of gentle contact, reaching deep within another person, but in such a way as to threaten him not at all.

Prince Anados, in MacDonald's *Phantastes*, cannot manage to get close to a dream-dancer without finding her rigid and cold. Premeditated surprise will not do it, for all the dancers are tipped off to his approach by their exquisite sensitivity to his bare intention. Even the delicate vectors his very gentle mind projects are too much for them. What he finally devises is "to allow my mind to be occupied with other thoughts, as I wandered around the centre-hall [so that there cannot be any extrasensory spill-over], and so wait there till the impulse to enter one of the others should happen to arise in me just at the moment when I was close to one of the crimson curtains." It works! Anados escapes from the power of his own mind to influence the behavior of others and so is able to come into contact with people who are behaving spontaneously (110)! Children use this technique intuitively in games that require the surprise selection of other players.

How does another prince, from yet another distant land, who must make his way into the garden of a palace, desperately needing information from the people there, make his presence known so that he will not arouse concern and be ejected immediately? Well, in the Persian story "What the Rose Did to the Cypress," Prince Almas-ruh-bakhsh moves randomly outside the garden for several days, and only when his presence has been accepted there as normal, when he himself has set aside goal-oriented behavior and fallen into a random mode, does he insinuate himself into the garden via a stream of "inflowing water."[3] Moreover, he lets himself be seen in the garden for the first time by his reflection in the water—indirectly. He further diffuses whatever threat his presence might generate by engaging in unusual but nonthreatening behavior—weeping and smiling, for example, subtly and gently inserting himself as a fully human being into situations, avoiding any form of introjective behavior. In short, the actor blends himself into the environment and refrains from projecting any but the gentlest vectors.

In an Indian tale, "The Faithful Prince," Bahramgur loses his wife and is warned against pursuing her to the Emerald Mountains. But wearing a cap of invisibility he passes through seven prisons to reach her, and instead of revealing himself directly, he remains invisible, eating from her dish as he sits beside her, till she realizes that he is there (*Wide Awake Stories*, 38).

Such narratives point to a set of attitudes and a technique quite different from those that dominate our thinking about human contact, where the practice is to confront what is next to you, projecting the most obvious lines of force, going directly to what you imagine to be the heart of the issue, boldly, unhesitatingly. But Anados uses something very much like chaos (we might call it a "subconscious lunge") to overcome the tendency of his own mind to plan and calculate. Prince Almas rids himself of all that is threatening in his nature—even his masculine essence—and of course in the process risks losing himself, if not his life. And Bahramgur projects even less of himself into the situation—nothing more than the sense of a certain way of sitting and eating. When his wife grows accustomed to that, he is able to transmit a sense of sharing, of being-with-her that is peculiar to himself. Perhaps only her love for him can reconstruct his own being out of such nearly-not-being.

Escaping Sets

Sets, groupings, or patterns are the most common means of organizing material in the bright-shadow world, a point discussed in chapter 4. A set is a particular grouping of vectors through which an actor organizes and interprets a context. But individuals can also become "set" in their ways, blind to nonset possibilities. Hence the problem of reasserting randomness and chance once again, creating situations where a significant amount of confusion may open up new conditions and possibilities. Edward deBono speaks about the importance of disrupting in various ways certain established patterns "so that the information can come together in new ways"—"exploratory rearrangement of what is known," he calls it (*Mechanism*, 237, 249).

In a Sudanese story, "A Discerning Old 'Faki'," a woman goes to a wise man to seek his help in recovering her husband's love. Bring me two hairs from a living lion's whiskers, the Faki says, and when she does, he observes that if she can carry out such a difficult task, she hardly needs his help in regaining her husband's affections.[4] In *Ocean of the Streams of Story* a monk is taught the art of contemplation by carrying around the city a pitcher full of water without spilling it (I, 237). In *Thousand and One Nights* a clever person heals a sick king by diverting his thoughts from his health to physical exertion: when the king learns to work up a good sweat his symptoms disappear. Giles tells the story of a man who became a great poet when he began to project himself through the masks of others, finding a freedom in their personae which his own rigid personality would not permit him.[5] And a schoolboy who has been warned by his uncle not to eat a dish of baklawa (because it is poisoned, the uncle says) leads his schoolfellows in eating it anyway. He covers up his deed by breaking the uncle's knife and gives this explanation: my pen broke; I tried to mend it with your knife; the knife broke; I was so distressed that I ate the baklawa in an attempt to commit suicide! Unfortunately, I could not die! The angry uncle, who has no trouble seeing through his nephew's scheme, forgives the lad, impressed by his cleverness (Nasr-ed-Din Khoja, 71–74).

The Sudanese woman must be helped to escape from the negative image she has of herself as a person without inner resources. The monk needs to put aside his self-image as a person who cannot concentrate. The king must learn to forget himself and to focus on purely physical realities. The poet needs a source of inspiration different from his own set personality. And in thinking about his situation the uncle must move from the second half of the equation, "clever rascal," to the first half, "my nephew." Each of the leading actors possesses a power source that can be tapped; each must be shown the devious, indeed difficult, path to it. (If it is not devious and difficult, the stories imply, the inherent worth of each individual is in some way diminished.)

In the Middle East (and indeed throughout the developing world) the market area of any city is the best place to cast one's net randomly. Suqs and bazaars and passajis may not appear as strange and confusing to lifelong residents as they do to newcomers, but such places never cease to lose their enriching power, their ability to call one out of whatever niche one finds oneself in, no matter how familiar they become. As David Chaffetz noted of the Afghans he observed in the 1970s,

> They stroll, they go [to the bazaar] for no other reason than to mingle in the living theatre and imbibe the spirit of the place. They know that every tangent, every movement of the *dasht* and *bagh* around the city, must resolve and flow, whirlpool-like, into the bazaar. They do not feel the need to spend their lives elsewhere but in the bazaar.[6]

Even though the set is familiar, it provides many resources for escaping familiarity and moving on to new things.

A similar effort to escape sets by forcing oneself to encounter novelty is reflected in an Irish folktale about the hero Covan. "Let them wander where they will," says Covan of some cows he has been given to herd, "and never seek to turn them from their way, for well they know the fields of good pasture. But take heed to follow always behind them, and suffer nothing that you see, and naught that you hear to draw you into leaving them."[7] Covan wants to do nothing that will inhibit the ability of the animals to do what is best for themselves, but he will be on guard against their foolish behavior—the tendency of randomness to deteriorate into chaos.

In another story already cited, a bored fox (whose set is a sense that life has nothing more of interest to offer him) lies down in the road and asks, "What would happen if I were to pretend to be dead?" As a result, he gets to play several profitable tricks on passersby, secures some nice fish from a fisherman's sled, lures a passing Lapp into buying a bag of bones, and appropriates a reindeer for his dinner (*Lapplandische Märchen*, 223 ff.). To recover his lamp in the story of Aladdin, the wicked Moor sets out to acquire all the lamps in the city: his set is privation, and he breaks it by overloading the system. And Gilguerillo, in "The White Slipper," realizes that love for the princess (his set) is futile and tries to "busy himself in other directions" (breaking the set). The payoff, as is normal in the bright-shadow world, comes when he least expects it: while he is immersed in a book (a new set) he finds information about a medicine that will cure the princess's father and enable him to gain her hand (the old set transformed and enriched by a new context).[8] In these cases vectors that are present in the situation but have not as yet been recognized are allowed to move about as freely and rapidly as possible until they make productive contact.

Boccaccio tells the story of a cook who produces for his master's dinner a crane with only one leg, the other having been eaten by the cook's girlfriend. When the master expresses surprise and disappointment (the set is unacceptable), the cook claims that cranes never have more than one leg (challenging the master's set). His master takes him to a field and shouts "Ho! Ho!" at the cranes there, all of which have two legs (the set reasserted). But if you had shouted "Ho! Ho!" last night, the cook observes, that crane also would have had two legs.[9] The story suggests a looser structure of cause and effect than we are accustomed to (how easily the cook breaks the set) and creates a lose-lose situation for the master, who is locked into one way of thinking. The cook's position is relatively safe, since it is impossible to go back to the original situation, where, it is implied, some judicious "ho ho's" might have cured the crane, reestablishing the master's set; moreover, there is no end to the disparities between the two situations in which the cook can take refuge. His power lies in the fact that he can always alter the set to create a situation the master cannot deal with.

Set manipulation is also illustrated in a story from the *Disciplina Clericalis* of Peter Alphonsus, where the principal actor is himself a storyteller and a master of patterns. Usually he narrates five tales every night to the king, at which point the latter falls asleep. But one night the sleepless king asks for yet another tale, and the narrator, exhausted, begins the endless story of a man who went to market, where he bought a thousand sheep, which he had difficulty getting across a river. Finally he found a narrow place and began to move them across, one at a time. Having reached this point in his story, the narrator falls asleep, confident that the shepherd would manage the thousand crossings, only to be awakened by the king, who wants to hear the end of the tale. I will complete it, said the narrator, when the merchant gets the last sheep across. The king is satisfied: he has to sympathize with the narrator's desire not to bore him, and to urge the narrator to get on with it would be to to break the set and go against the narrator's own best judgment as a teller of tales, his need to get the sheep safely across, and perhaps to have no story at all the next night. The narrator is playing with two sets, of course (the story and the real world), and he can move back and forth between them in reaction to the royal response and his own needs.[10]

Contemporary psychological thinkers have contributed to the

concept of set-breaking. Carlos Castaneda discusses the importance of halting the "internal dialogue"—the mind's ceaseless process of too-rapid image-formation (*Tales of Power*, 12, 13, 236, passim)—thus frustrating the brain's attempt to group or file things too quickly, before all the possibilities are noted. Robert Ornstein has noted the importance of peripheral vision, the sidewise glance, as a means of taking in possibilities that lie outside the set (which is presumed to lie directly athwart the vision). Ernest Schachtel talks about allocentric perception—the human ability to view an object as something "other" and to see it fully and completely despite the fact that it is of no immediate use to oneself. Paul Watzlawick urges changing the set (rather than determining etiology) as the best way to handle intricate problems. And Edward deBono's concept of vertical thinking is essentially set-thinking, thinking that is limited by the assumptions or ground rules that come with the problem. His answer to the problems created by sets is lateral thinking, thinking that tries to solve a problem by stepping outside the assumptions. If individuals feel that they are not getting credit for the work they have done, the solution may lie not in gaining recognition for them, but in helping them to realize that they do not really need it, to help them "switch-over" their thinking, to put themselves in a new context.[11]

Gilguerillo solves the problem of being in love with an uninterested woman by turning his attention to books—another set, a rich and abundant one. That set leads him right back to the one he had abandoned, but at a new level. Covan solves the problem of having to run this way and that after the animals in his charge by substituting for the traditional image of the herdsman's task quite another view of his role. Peter Alphonsus's narrator substitutes a real-life time scheme for a fictional scheme so that he can catch forty winks, and Boccaccio's cook turns responsibility for the damaged poultry over to the king. All are fundamental alterations by bright actors of established arrangements of vectors.

Entrapment

In a world where power is sometimes enfeebled and identities uncertain, it may be necessary to trap your rival in a position where he or she will be forced to accede to your wishes or to admit what you wish him or her to admit. This is the other side of the enchantment issue. Penelope, in the *Odyssey*, tricks her husband with a statement about their bed, suggesting a possibility he cannot, because of who he is, allow to stand unchallenged. In a familiar Middle Eastern story a tailor claims to be a prince, and when suspicious individuals hand him a bit of sewing to do, he is too proud of his craftsmanship to botch the job—as royalty would certainly have done (*Crimson Fairy Book,* 326). But how could a battered Odysseus or an ignorant tailor possibly know what he was being tested for? When attention is diverted, as it so often is in entrapment, the victim really does not know what is expected of him/her. Puzzled, he/she fails to separate the significant from the insignificant vectors in the context. The individual is a prime candidate for entrapment.

A banker and a farmer in an Indian tale make a wager about who can tell the wilder story. The banker devises a silly narrative about a bird swooping down and carrying away a hundred camels from a caravan, simply a tall tale, not a true case illuminating some basic structure of reality. And it is a story that has nothing to do with the farmer, does not touch him in any sensitive spot. The farmer, however, knowing exactly what vectors to project and where, reports that his father had a mare on the back of which grew huge amounts of wheat, which the banker's father borrowed but never paid for. Trapped, albeit by a story whose validity has never been checked, the banker pays for the wheat: it is his life's work to see that loans are paid off, and he has a sense of responsibility for his father's obligations that he cannot neglect. The farmer's story hits directly at the banker's fundamental sensitivities (never mind that it also reached out beyond the frame of the story), overrides the banker's desire to win the wager, and even blocks out what must have been his amused resentment over the fabrication about wheat growing on the back of an animal. And surely the banker cannot fail to appreciate the way the farmer creates money for himself so readily. In a sense the farmer loses the wager, for his story is not really as wild as the banker's, but the banker accepts it, at least at one level. Whatever loss of esteem the farmer may have incurred is more than made up for when the banker pays his father's obligations. In this story loss and satisfaction, frustration and fulfillment are almost miraculously combined—in a most effective trap (*Olive Fairy Book,* 64).

The most spectacular cases of entrapment, however, have to do with the recovery of real loans or deposits of money or goods for which the owner has no written receipt, no way to force the borrower, the holder of the goods, to admit his/her obligation. The issues may seem small, but the struggle is titanic, waged between the little fellow with no resources and the big-time slicker confident that no one can call him to account. Thus in a widely disseminated Sufi tale, in which the borrower categorically denies that there ever was a loan, the lender invites him into a coffee house and before a number of guests tricks him into denying that he borrowed one hundred dinars. I borrowed only twenty, the victim asserts, realizing immediately that he has been had.[12] The structure that will compel him to meet his obligations, a structure based on the technique of diversion, is erected in a split second and collapses after it has performed its function when the guests, who will now validate the lender's claim, leave the room.

What are the fundamental realities here, the vectors and the power sources the borrower can exploit? One is the human vulnerability to which the story calls attention, the vulnerability of individuals in a society that offered them far less protection than ours does against the reckless, the irresponsible, the dishonest. But an important source of power for the lender is personal influence and leverage, wisely and sparingly used, in such societies. In a preliterate society, where written documents, stamps of authorization, and notaries did not exist and where communal trust was really the only legitimizing factor, the one who lent money or left it in trust had little but the integrity of the borrower or holder and the power of the community (insofar as he/she could assemble it) to appeal to. But there is the possibility that the lender can erect a sturdy and functioning structure on virtually nothing at all, again, a sky hook. This is why diversionary tactics are so effective: it seems possible to trap the reluctant player in some mistake which will work on his/her self-esteem and cause him/her to make some small admission on which the lender can build to force restitution. Because so many relevant vectors exist, there are a thousand responses that your opponent can make to your apparently innocent question, a thousand implications which he/she cannot see quickly enough and against which he/she cannot protect himself/herself. You can switch from one set of assumptions to another faster than any opponent can follow your moves, identify your intentions. You are in control of multiple vectors, one of which is aimed directly at your opponent's heart.

A widespread variant, again making use of witnesses, is to be found in the story, already noted from *Ocean of the Streams of Story,* of a woman whose affection is sought by four distinguished men—a royal chaplain, the chief magistrate of the community, the prime minister, and a wealthy merchant from whom the woman wants to recover certain moneys. (The roles in various versions may be altered.) As each would-be seducer arrives, he is assigned a small compartment from which he can hear and see the others as they arrive, and where each is daubed with tar smeared on the walls. When the first three are in place, the merchant is lured into saying, "I told you that I would give you the money your husband deposited with me." The woman has trapped her witnesses too, for all are now smeared with tar, and she can "squeal" on any who proves reluctant to testify. The tar is a guarantee that they will be witnesses—and true ones, at that, for it is a symbol of the fact that each could be diverted from certain values he was thought by the community to support (I, 17 ff.).

Managing Conflicts

This issue takes us back to chapter 3 again, on world-reading, and to questions raised there by (among others) Eric Berne and Thomas Schelling. Conflict is an essential part of most fairytales and folktales. Conflict management involves helping two parties realize what they are fighting about, seeing that they fight fairly, encouraging them to consider each other's point of view and develop possible strategies that will turn lose-lose situations into win-win possibilities. Or, as Melvin Konner puts it, "How can two creatures capable in every sense of inflicting damage on one another avert such damage without running away?" (*The Tangled Wing*, 211).

All too many conflicts in popular narrative are settled brutally, by dragon-bashing, for example, or putting down the third son. The internal dynamics of such situations offer little of interest, and the possibilities of life-enhancement are minimal. Even if the proper person does win out in the end, a great deal of ugliness is encountered on the way, and nobody feels very good about the settlement. The hideous Gollum in Tolkien's *Lord of the Rings* illustrates the results of this process. There are a few cases, however, where some kind of negotiation is carried on to the benefit of all concerned. Where the boat is too small to carry everyone at once, or certain individuals deem it useful to cross together, a strategy of sharing or waiting is devised that will protect the places of all concerned. And where several members of a group each have one highly developed talent to offer, a way of enabling each to contribute effectively to the common purpose is worked out. The lines of force that run through these tales are of great structural interest, and the bargaining that goes on, both explicit and implicit, creates a rich layer of experience. A complex example of such conflict management is to be found in the tale of "The Cat, the Mouse, the Owl, the Ichneumon, and the Hunter" from *Ocean of the Streams of Story* (I, 296).

Relationships of hostility and dependency exist among the animals and between the animals and the hunter. The cat is at the very center of things, the principal object of the hunter's quest and the chief hunter of the other animals. Lots of strong vectors are directed at it, and it directs many other lines of force against the other animals. The owl is somewhat safe (but also quite isolated) at the top of the tree where it lives, as long as it does not make any silly mistakes, and the ichneumon (a small, mongooselike creature common in India) and the mouse reside together at the base. These two are of little interest to the hunter, whose presence tends to protect them from the cat. The hunter stands outside this tense little grouping, an external force generating certain actions among the animals, but no more than that—like an unseen planet noted only because of the pull it exerts on the other bodies. The cat threatens associates above and below, hunting by day, vulnerable to human attack, caring about no one but itself. It is the dominant actor, with a major power source in its control, yet still, curiously dependent on several weaker actors.

The owl, at the top of the tree in the vines, has a pretty good position: the cat is some worry, but it apparently will not or cannot climb the tree. The owl can fly and seems safe enough, except for the fact that it wants the mouse badly enough to be a threat to the tiny creature, although to get it, it must ally itself with the mouse's companion, the ichneumon. But the ichneumon is also a direct threat to the owl, and the mouse is relatively safe as long as it can play the two off against each other, picking up some tangential protection from the cat at the same time. The role of the ichneumon in the story is to force the mouse toward the cat, with whom the mouse can deal, since the hunter wants the cat and has managed to bind it with ropes. The cat, being bound, can function within a restricted area but cannot roam. Hence the artificial alliances on which the story is based.

The role of the mouse, the tiniest and weakest of the actors, builds as we move into the story. As has been noted, it enjoys a certain relationship with the cat, pushed toward its natural enemy by ichneumon and owl. They are too weak to attack the cat, so it is an effective shield for the mouse. And feeling affection for its protector, the mouse wants to help the cat, bound as it is by the hunter. Although the mouse is not foolhardy enough to trust the cat without the hunter's protection, it is willing to gnaw through the ropes binding the cat, being careful to finish its job just a split second before the hunter arrives. The mouse can escape, then, because the cat will have to attend to the hunter, if it itself is to escape. The mouse cannot act so quickly that she will be exposed to the owl and the ichneumon without having the cat's protection. And yet if it delays too long, it will fall prey to the cat. The denouement of the little drama is a real venture into the unknown, a fascinating examination of the effective use of gaps and loopholes.

Here is a classic conflict situation (though in our world we are rarely called upon to balance so many factors in a situation at once), a complex set of sympathies, aversions, alliances of convenience, and indifference, with a strong unifying factor at work and some good reasons to limit whatever violence is contemplated or expressed. A marvelous ecosystem and a closely bound matrix, though composed of very cynical individuals: personal benefit is the only basis for altruism. The group is large enough to generate real conflict, and there emerges that terrible situation where two essentially hostile figures exist in a mutual dependency-threat relationship. The moment to which the story brings us is the instant at which the mouse finishes gnawing through the rope restraining the cat and then makes its own escape. The mouse must be sure that the cat understands the plan, for a dead mouse and a still-bound cat are unacceptable. In short, the mouse tells the cat how it plans to trick it. It manages the conflict effectively.

Metaphor-Making

Metaphor-making is central to a world where so much is based on analogy and similarity, where little dramas that enlarge the framework or context sometimes help resolve various kinds of problems, especially in the areas of communication and persuasion. An individual is forced to take more seriously than he or she had intended an image which he/himself, she/herself has devised. The analogy element is critical, and the power of this technique lies in the fact (noted by Minsky) that one may not know how to make use of it.[13] For example, in *Kalilah and Dimnah,* A leaves with B a supply of iron for safekeeping. B appropriates the iron for himself and when A seeks its return says that rats ate it. A hides B's son, claiming that eagles carried him off. B observes that eagles cannot carry off a child—and quickly grasps the implications of his own image (59–60).

Variations are numerous. For example, the Grimm Brothers tell a story about a man who is trying to recover a foal taken wrongfully by a man who claims that the animal is an offspring of his ox. The owner of the foal fishes in the middle of a road, and when the king comes by and seeks an explanation, the man replies, "I can fish on a dry spot just as well as two oxen can have a foal" (349). A Hungarian folktale tells the story of a man who has found a cache of money, about which his wife also knows. She will surely tell the neighbors, so the husband does all kinds of crazy things, including fishing in a field. When the wife tells the neighbors about this—and about the gold—they conclude she is crazy on both scores. And in a Central Asian tale,

"How Ananda the Wood-Carver and Ananda the Painter Strove To-gether," one artist seeks to get rid of his troublesome rival by sending him, via a burning funeral pyre, to work on a temple in heaven. But the man cleverly escapes the pyre, pretends to have returned from his heavenly tasks, and says that a painter is needed there. That poor man has no recourse (if he is to save face and preserve the so-cial/cultural network in which he lives) but to die on the pyre himself: he must move into the metaphor with which he had hoped to trap another. In such cases one actor forces upon his victim a context from which the victim cannot escape, since he/she suggested it in the first place.[14]

Finding Things

In traditional narratives objects, places, and people are always getting lost, or valuable things are being found, and we know enough about the loose structure of the bright-shadow world to understand why this should be so. Lost wives and beautiful girls with tiny feet are being searched out, as are magic lamps, the answers to riddles, and cures for a variety of royal afflictions. In the sometimes drowsy bright-shadow world very few people pay much attention to any-thing or file things away carefully. Much of the lore of children also centers on this topic, particularly the various rituals that must accom-pany the discovery of four-leaf clovers or coins, feathers or horse-shoes.[15] In this brief section we consider a particular approach to finding things, by analogy, imitation, and modeling—techniques known to naive psychologists that are often surprisingly successful.

In "The Sultan and the Cobbler," an Egyptian tale, we have the story of a ruler who loves to wander about his city. One day he hears a riddle from a young man who claims to make four piastres a day: "I eat one piastre, I repay the second, I lend the third, and I throw the fourth into the river." The sultan, intrigued, demands that his wazir discover the meaning of these enigmatic words, and the wazir can recall only that his master heard them while wandering the streets. So this man, who has all his professional life been accustomed to acting vigorously, adopts a passive role and begins to wander too, hoping to encounter the vectors that will bring the solution to his problem. Listening carefully but casually, he hears merry singing from a cob-bler, spends a few minutes with the tradesman to cheer himself up (actually he is bringing under control his fear-induced purposiveness, which can only get in his way), and finds that he has found the very person who posed the riddle.[16]

The frightened wazir is, of course, following one of the oldest and most productive techniques for finding something, which is to repeat the process during which the loss occurred, this time subjecting it to careful scrutiny. For there is always the possibility that by observing the model one can learn what happened in real life. This technique is familiar through Bassanio's story, in *The Merchant of Venice:*

> In my schooldays, when I had lost one shaft,
> I shot his fellow of the selfsame flight
> The selfsame way with more advised watch,
> To find the other forth, and by adventuring both,
> I oft found both. I urge this childhood
>   proof. (I, i, 140–44)

What is particularly striking is the absolute sincerity with which the wealthy Venetian proposes this trick—a considered and highly rational appeal to the less-than-rational. Great ships and large fortunes are at stake, and Bassanio offers, persuasively enough, a childhood game.

The same serious view of the possibilities of this technique is to be found in "Ali Baba and the Forty Thieves" when a question arises about how to find where a man was taken blindfolded by captors. He is blindfolded again, allowed to relax (so that the data gleaned from his first experience and stored in the unconscious will not be blocked), and set to walking. Alert to remembered stimuli—the feel of the road, a peculiar smell, perhaps certain noises or a breeze—he is able to bring his friends to the same place once more (*1001*, Suppl IV, 383). And again in *Thousand and One Nights*, Caliph Haroun al-Rashid tosses a ring into the Tigris, but five months later he wants it back. He casts another ring into the same section of water, and divers quickly recover both rings! Perhaps only sultans have all the vectors of a context under such complete control! A model focuses, intensifies, reduces to the smallest possible scope the issues important to an individual at a particular time. In a curious way, the use of models affirms the rationality, the stability, of our world, yet any actor who attempts this technique must be very loose, very relaxed, if he or she is to hear what the world is telling him or her without being diverted by its more obvious sights and sounds.

Telling Someone Something

In the bright-shadow world, as in real life, it often becomes necessary to bring to the attention of some powerful person information that it may be difficult for him/her to hear. Unfortunately (history is full of dead messengers), bad news seldom elicits a mature, rational response. Some kind of buffering is needed, something to absorb the shock that will inevitably be felt by both the one who must be informed and the one who must bring the news. Storytelling, an indirect approach, can provide this buffer, a neutral, nonthreatening ground from which the serious issue may be contemplated.

From Rumi's *Mathnawi* comes the story of a king who desperately sought some profound spiritual experience. His subjects, tired of his inattention to matters of state, start tramping around one night on the roof of the palace. What are you doing up there? he asks. Looking for camels! How foolish! You won't find camels up there! Nor will you find God while sitting on your throne (*Mathnawi* II, 318). The model puts an entirely inappropriate actor into the context the king is occupying, thereby forcing the king to say the difficult things that must be said. In the widely disseminated "Lion's Track Tale" a husband seeks to divorce his wife on the grounds that the king (the lion) has been with her. "I saw the trail of a lion," the husband says, but the king coolly replies, "Return . . . to thy flower-garden and fear nothing, for the lion came not near it" (*1001*, VI, 131). In other versions of the story the king admits that the lion has entered the garden and touched the fruit but insists that it did not taste. The metaphor, which is adroitly picked up by the king, permits a great deal to be implied that cannot be said (out of fear of offending royal sensibilities—after all, we are discussing a lion in a garden) and creates the possibility of easier movement of thought than our more rigid and exact means of communicating permits. The husband is drawn into the situation and offered a well-buffered but quite acceptable version of a distressing situation. The real issue is effectively skirted, yet everything that must be said is indeed brought out.

Escaping Traps

This is the reverse side of the entrapment issue already discussed and a significant aspect of the earlier theme of set-breaking. Anecdotes that present this issue in the most graphic form possible are the story of two ring doves from *Kalilah and Dimnah* and the story of Antonio's escape from Shylock's clutches in *The Merchant of Venice*. The two birds, when caught in the hunter's net, do not thrash around wildly until they are hopelessly enmeshed. Rather, they fly off, carrying the net with them, to a place where they can extricate themselves quietly.[17] And Portia frees Antonio from Shylock's demand for a pound of flesh by insisting that Shylock take no more, no less than a pound and that no blood be shed. Reach for power sources that no one else has thought to tap; make use of vectors inherent in the situation even though at first glance they do not seem favorable. If there is a contract, take it absolutely literally; your opponent is no doubt intending to interpret loosely, even metaphorically, the parts that do not work in his or her favor.

In *Thousand and One Nights* (VI, 202 ff.) there is an interesting variant, its central figure a merchant who asks what product sells best in a certain city and learns that it is sandalwood. So he puts all his capital into this commodity and enters the city, having been warned that cheats there will try to devour his substance. When he tries to sell his fine wood, he is told that it is virtually worthless: people use it for fuel. (And he actually sees the man who told him this using such wood for cooking—that man is going to great lengths to support his own deceptive story.) But this same individual agrees to buy wood from the new arrival for a certain measure of *whatever the seller wishes*. Seller agrees, and buyer takes the wood. On the next day the by now badly confused sandalwood merchant is accused by a man with one eye of stealing his other eye and given till morning to settle this dispute. By this time the poor merchant has torn his sandal, and he must satisfy the demands of the shoemaker who repairs it. As if this were not enough, he loses at a game of Order and Consent and is told to drink the ocean. The townspeople have got the better of him, but in the process he has learned the great value of sandalwood.

To escape from such a slew of difficulties, the poor merchant visits a wise sheikh, who advises him to ask the wood-purchaser for a measure of fleas—half male and half female. Unable to discriminate so precisely, the rascally purchaser must return the wood. He is further instructed to make the blind man prove which of several eyes belongs to him by removing his remaining eye for comparison. He is told to ask the shoemaker (who claims to be discontent with everything, including his pay) if he is happy that the sultan's enemies have been defeated. And as for drinking the ocean, the poor man is instructed to agree to the task if his enemies will hold it up to his mouth.

The tormentors of the sandalwood merchant expect him to submit to their outrageous demands out of his own sense of fair play or because he is too weak to challenge them. It is the role of the sheikh to help the merchant see that if the village rogues are going to make outrageous demands upon him, expecting him to be a gentleman still, he had best abandon his own sense of justice. When the merchant challenges his enemies at their own game, their position collapses.

Actually there are two anecdotes here, loosely connected by the "whatever the seller wishes" stipulation. In the first of these a secondary actor tries to downgrade the value of some power source the primary actor feels is important. The secondary actor's purpose, of course, is to gain more of it, as cheaply as possible, for himself. And he carries out some elaborate ruses. In the second anecdote the primary actor, who is the target of many sharp and threatening vectors, is able (with the help of a sheikh) to uncover the reverse side of these vectors, their other meaning, their further significance, and hurl them back at his tormentors.

Answering Riddles

It is hardly surprising that a world that places such importance on alternate means of knowing, unorthodox problem-solving, and shifting, uncertain visions of reality should also be interested in riddles. Riddles, says Elli Maranda, question "the authority of social and cultural rules . . . playing with conceptual borderlines and crossing them for the intellectual pleasure of showing that things are not quite as stable as they appear."[18] Riddles are unique, too, in that they are devices for both hiding material from those who had best not know it and revealing it to those who should.

In riddling, a common object is identified by perfectly ordinary words that are not usually used with reference to it and represent an altered way of looking at it. The actor disguises a context by clever vectors that cast the familiar in the light of the strange. One set is defined by carefully chosen words, and the riddle-guesser must identify another set to which these words also apply. Something is perceived to resemble something else in a way that is both surprising and intriguing/satisfying (Opie, 74). If the context of the new set of words can be discovered, the riddle will be guessed, and the process opens up the all-important possibility of seeing something from another's point of view. But if the words used are sufficiently remote from the reality to which the riddler is pointing, and the point of view is sufficiently strange, it may be impossible to guess the riddle.

Riddles are often used in popular narrative to screen undesirables out of some kind of contest—often matrimonial—as in the case of Portia's three caskets. The one who guesses or interprets the riddle correctly gets the bride. Bassanio succeeds by taking seriously the implications of the three signs. In the case of Grimm's tale "The Clever Little Tailor," the princess—the "riddle princess," as Lüthi calls her (123)—arrogantly demands that all her suitors ask her a riddle. If she can guess it, the suitor dies; she will wed the one who is

able to baffle her, and we are delighted when the little tailor is successful, supposedly enhancing his life greatly at this point.

In another Grimm tale a suitor tells a riddle in which "one slew
none and yet slew twelve," about a poisoning case in which twelve
persons very peripherally involved in a situation died. Baffled, the
princess orders her maid into the suitor's bedroom at night to listen to
his dreams, but the man, suspecting that something like this may
happen, is spending the night elsewhere. On the second night the
suitor has to drive away another spy, and on the third night the
princess herself, in a "misty gray cloak," creeps into the suitor's room
and hears the answer from the suitor, who feigns sleep. When the
suitor is condemned to death the next day, he produces the gray
mantle, abandoned in his room, as if to prove . . . what? That the
princess was cheating? That she had become bored with her game
and wanted now to marry? That she could find the answer only by
entering deeply into his subconscious? (Magoun and Krappe, 93). No
doubt some little-explored level of her consciousness prompted her to
leave the mantle behind in the suitor's room, to signify the end of the
game.

Another way of solving the riddle problem is to make up an
answer and impose it upon your situation, claiming that it fits the
riddle and is therefore as good an answer as any. This is a matter of
exercising the will; the subordinate figure, the one who must guess
the riddle, takes over the dominant role, declaring the meaning of the
vectors. Thus in "The Secret-Keeping Little Boy and His Little
Sword," a young man working for the Magyars, who are being
threatened by the sultan, decides that his answers to such questions
as "Which stick grows near the root of the plant; which at the middle;
which at the top?" or "In what order were certain fools born?" are
probably as good as any answers the sultan may have. So he puts
them into an acceptably rational framework and imposes them on the
situation; the sultan has no recourse (if he is to appear a sensible
person who is above special pleading) but to accept the young man's
responses. A person who refuses to accept a suitable answer does not
really know what riddling is all about—he/she is simply asking
his/her victim to guess what is on his/her mind.[19]

Finally come those great stories in which the answer to the riddle involves nothing less than the total commitment of the answerer
to some kind of unimaginably difficult quest—such as the search of
Oedipus for the murderer of his father. In the quest of Saktideva for
the Golden City, the protagonist, to whom the riddle is posed, answers flippantly at first, his very manner revealing that he does not

grasp the seriousness of the question. The answer, which he finally gains, demands a journey of staggering length and enormous hardships, transforming his life, leading him across contexts to the spot where he can pose a question of his own to the princess, "What are you doing here?" *Enhancement* is scarcely strong enough to describe what the journey has done for his life.

What characteristics of the typical bright-shadow-world problem have emerged from the material in this chapter? Typical difficulties are those that can be resolved only by interdependence, by acting within a network, by enlisting the aid of others. Or the task may be to find what is lost, to identify—or realize that one must identify—someone, or to choose between options. In many situations one person is trying to "psych out" another at the same time he/she is being "psyched out." The possibility of facing an ironic situation must always be considered—but rarely is. A sense of helplessness at the start of an engagement is common, as is the dominance of a set of assumptions that limit one's vision of possibilities. The demands upon the principals are very heavy.

Are there characteristic internal structures? Apparently so. These would include very tight linkages between the actors, each influencing the other profoundly, though subtly; often this influence goes unnoticed for some time. Confrontive paths tend to give way to gentle, insinuating ways, the actor perhaps using elements from the physical situation to conceal himself/herself. The multiplicity of operative vectors—and some difficulty in spotting them—make it difficult to identify what the problem is, or if indeed there is a problem. Aid is usually—always—available if one can spot it in unlikely physical sources or unlikely actors. Among the most important vectors are goodwill, buffering, and attention (whether focused or diverted). Important power sources are the unconscious (though getting to it may be a problem), the will, and various kinds of confusion that one may induce in opponents. Random and free-floating elements are common. Consistency of behavior tends to be valued highly and expected, and one set of events may copy another set. Almost any situation may be altered by wit and will.

Finally, what potentialities for life-enhancement are implicit in these structural elements? We may note just a few. The achievement of reading a difficult situation correctly, in a way that furthers one's own goals and puts one in touch with some significant reality. The realization that one has as much right as anyone else to determine what is correct. The pleasure of joining with others from the same network in a great project. The chance to escape limiting assumptions. Discovering one's place in a network. The experience of plenitude or abundance. Achieving—if only for a time—some sense of identity. The management of conflict so that both parties can gain something. Discovery of the similarities between very different parts of life—and of the significance of others' points of view. The problem situations described in traditional narrative are few, but the possibilities for growth through them are numerous.

12 Nimble Riding—a Question of Style

I described in chapters 3 and 4 some of the basic structural principles of the bright-shadow world, the principles perceptive individuals can pick up if they set out to read the world productively—and not simply to read about it. We have followed these principles and their implications into issues lying at the heart of the bright-shadow world. We have described the inner structures of a number of experiences, and we have noted many forms of transcendence or life-enhancement that seem to be suggested by this material.

But as our examination of a variety of traditional narratives proceeded, we also watched important patterns or structures breaking up, networks threatened by chaos. Deconstruction lies at the heart of postmodernism, and it is a critical theme in traditional narrative as well. Certain individuals have found it impossible to establish themselves securely in the world or to persuade others to acknowledge their identities. Family ties have often proven fragile, constantly threatened by poverty and egoism (to name just a pair of negative influences). Passive responses, worthwhile in themselves, are often overwhelmed by the sheer power of material forces. Knowledge gained in various odd ways has sometimes proven unreliable, and communications between various parts of networks have proved tenuous indeed. In short, the elements we have made much of—actors, vectors, power sources, physical facts—often work against the positive actions undertaken in many stories, and the famous last line of so many tales—"And they lived happily ever after"—does not always promise much of substance after all.

Indeed, the bright-shadow world may be not legible but unreadable—if legibility implies metanarratives that all can accept—not orderly but chaotic; amoral rather than moral; precarious, not just unstable. The context shifts constantly because vectors diverge crazily and power sources are undependable. Actors, as we have seen in chapter 9, are easily assembled from pieces lying about and just as easily disassembled. It is in the light of such possibilities that a certain nimbleness of style emerges as a characteristic critical for survival, and something that I will call "nimble riding" as the most typical activity of the most typical actors. Let us suggest that in the final analysis traditional narrative exists to celebrate, teach, and encourage this kind of activity, which is both deadly serious and lightly parodic, and that it is both a way to protect one's flanks and a primary tool for the enhancement of experience. "Riding" implies a loose and easy kind of dominance—the horseback rider barely clinging to his mount, the surfer atop the wave crest for just an instant, the network dweller barely maintaining control over all the strands or vectors that come together in his or her consciousness. "Nimble" suggests all that is light-footed, -fingered, -hearted, lively, energetic, bouncy, mercurial, just-balanced, improvisational. Goffman will have it that all of us are engaged in acts of self-presentation and that in this process we engage in all kinds of fabrications (*Frame Analysis*, 83 ff.). I find the trampoline an apt symbol here, a means of rising above, however briefly, the physical forces that hold us to earth. Style often carries the day.

With nimble riding I associate clever little tailors, rogues and thieves, dragon slayers, third sons, loyal but rejected wives, and others who have only themselves to rely upon—and whatever tenuous support the network in which they live can provide them. The famous "Perseus" of Cellini comes to mind, dancing above the waves as he attacks his particular dragon, as does Browning's Bishop Blougram, who characteristically observes: "Our interest's on the dangerous edge of things. / The honest thief, the tender murderer, / The superstitious atheist." Such are the striking figures who do not require to be right, who can do without a clear sense of where they are going, who have no need to find themselves, who can summon sufficient willpower to survive all manner of culture shocks when they must. Nimbleness is well illustrated by the clever individual of one tale who, when presented with a problem and the barest hint of a solution says, "I know enough now and shall manage quite all right."[1]

At the center of so much lightfooted activity in the bright-shadow world, perhaps its most stylish citizen, stands the rogue, one of the key figures of traditional narrative. An alert and fully actuated individual, with a far keener sense of self than is possessed by those around him, the rogue moves easily between the bourgeois environment, which somehow nurtures him, and other worlds, which promise benefits. Both good and evil, the rogue is, as Stanley Diamond

suggests, "the *personification* of ambivalence,"[2] creating and destroying, giving and desiring, planting one foot in the primitive wilderness, the other in the civilized community. Jung saw him as a de-
scendent of Mercury, the alchemic figure who transmutes and
transforms, the psychopomp who leads souls between two worlds.
Civilization must suppress him, of course, though the folk have not
always, for as Jung observes, civilization cannot be ambivalent about
the human condition: it must structure itself carefully, and the trickster is the enemy of structure: he represents disorder; he threatens
boundaries—in the present instance, property, ego stability, and
prosperity.[3]

But the folk have also recognized the rogue's vitality and high
spirits. Consequently we delight in Clever Hans, Little Klaus, Nasr-
ed-Din Khoja, Robin Hood, Michael the Fox, and Goha, the wise fool
of Sudanese literature. But at the same time we wish not to become
their victims. Not all are exactly rogues, of course, but all participate
in some way in antinomian, boundary-breaking activity. All sit over
and above our everyday activity, like great brooding spiders, manipulating the order so profoundly cherished by denizens of the bright-
shadow world into the forms of chaos that lie just beneath the surface
of things. Nevertheless (and however), the rogue represents one of
several "preferred ways to be human" (Lichtenstein, 14) because he
makes such effective use of the essentially unbalanced nature of human beings.

What does the nimble-minded (and -footed) rogue suggest to us
about human experience? By watching this important actor, we may
learn first that the physical context of life can always be put to use in
unexpected ways, constantly, surprisingly transcended/rearranged
so that new possibilities emerge and old resources are ruthlessly exploited. One can never be sure of the place of "facts" in any structure.
Second, the vectors or lines of force that course through the system
are very prominent, darting unexpectedly and without warning from
level to level of reality. Deceptions and fabrications are important,
and metaphor and analogy play an important role, as do wit and
agility, both physical and psychological. Power (which to the uiniti-
ated seems in short supply) lies in a potent combination of wit and
human greed and stupidity; in reimaging situations that have grown
too familiar; in off-beat definitions; in the disruption of categories; in
sleight of hand and exploitation. The actors, who are characterized by
great wit and lightness of movement, pop up at the most unexpected
places in the structure. Often a figure who seems completely insignifi-

cant takes on the dominant role, humbling those thought to be powerful. Much of the actor's force lies in the actor's style.[4]

Resource Redistribution

This is a basic way to chaos, given that property is one of the
cornerstones of bourgeois stability and that attacks upon private
property are a fundamental reflection of refusal to accept the limiting
but stable values of the bourgeoisie. A network has resources, elements that can be put to use, and the nimble-minded tend to have
very few inhibitions about encouraging owners to share possessions
with them. This is said only half facetiously, for it has been observed
that "it is hard to even begin to gauge how much a complication of
possessions, the notions of 'my and mine,' stand between us and a
true, clear, liberated way of seeing the world."[5] As a matter of fact,
the amount of thievery that goes on in popular narrative, in myth and
legend, is truly amazing, and it determines the tone of much of this
material: nothing is safe unless it is nailed down, and though owners
of property suffer, it may be that civilization as a whole is advanced.
But at the same time it is made clear that even the poorest, most
wretched individual—Ma'ruf the Cobbler, for instance—can exert
his/her will creatively in a situation. The Bird Grip must be stolen if
the king is to see again, as must Aladdin's lantern and the giant's
sword. The central incident of the great Norse/Germanic myth is the
theft of the Rheingold. The great Greek epic—and I am tempted to
say High Greek civilization itself—begins with the theft of Helen by
Paris. The Indian epic *Ramayana* is dominated by events flowing from
Ravenna's theft of Sita, a fact that has major implications for Indian
women right down to modern times. Out of Jacob's theft of Esau's
birthright emerge the Hebrew people. The children's game of Musical
Chairs seems to offer some encouragement to thieflike activities—
with each turn there is one less chair, and survival depends on finding a chair before someone else gets to it. And Nasr-ed-Din Khoja
puts the best possible face on the situation when he observes, "Men
of learning and piety do not go out of their way to cheat people" (63).

Theft is placed in many different, positive lights in traditional
narrative. It is seen as a way of getting the resources of a network into
the hands of people who will make use of them, not simply store
them away. It is doubtful that Esau, a brutish chap, could have pulled
his people together into a nation. In the Gospels the pride in "much
goods" stored in "great barns" is vigorously condemned. Theft also
becomes a means of releasing pent-up psychological powers; a legitimate thrust against those who are too weak or stupid to protect what

is theirs; even an act of great elegance and refinement, to be appreciated as we might appreciate a musical performance. Witness this South Asian account of gambling as a profession:

> I decided to follow the path opened by Muladeva, past master of thievery. I entered a gambling dive and mixed with the gamesters. I noticed with great satisfaction how clever they were at all twenty-five varieties of the art which forms the basis of sound gambling: their almost indetectable tricks with the gaming boards; their sleight-of-hand; the oaths and insults which their tricks excited; the impulsiveness with which they put their lives at stake; the force and efficacy of their methods and systems for gaining the confidence of the players; how they flattered the strong and bullied the weak; the expert skill with which they picked partners and the variety of allurement with which they tempted them; how they argued differences of stakes; their generosity in distributing their gains; and finally the all-prevailing hum from which everywhere raucous voices emerged.[6]

The rescue of a princess in the French tale "The Miller's Four Sons" depicts the work of a thief at its most positive (S. Thompson, 296).

Typical of the kind of individual I have in mind is the Sudanese folk-hero Goha, who sometimes plumbs the depths of stupidity, sometimes rises to mastery of the most recondite arts of deceit. He fills both roles in a way that challenges every category with which we are familiar.[7] In a shop Goha tries on a pair of culottes, changes his mind, and selects a caftan instead, which he walks out with. When the merchant demands payment, Goha observes that he exchanged the culottes for it. At the start of his article on jokes and the cognitive unconscious Minsky cites a version of this story told by Freud, using it as the basis of his argument that certain "ineffective or destructive thought processes" must be repressed if thinking and problem-solving are to be effective. This joke, he appears to suggest, is an invitation to a dangerous area of reflection, where useful conclusions are probably impossible (Groner, Groner, and Bischof, 171). Postmodernism is not so timid.

In another story linked to Goha a poor man moistens his dry bread from the vapor of a rotisserie; the butcher demands payment, and the judge finally pays him by jingling coins in his hand. Goha has a large sheep, and his friend suggests eating it, since judgment day is coming. They do, and Goha realizes that he has been tricked. While his friend is swimming, he disposes of the man's clothes, for he will not need them: judgment day is coming. And when a wretched blasphemer demands bread of Goha because he is God's guest, Goha takes him to a mosque and suggests that he seek bread there, in God's house. Goha's repertoire of foolery is based on the technique of riding a single word or concept from one level of reality to another: in the clothing store he is the well-dressed sheikh, and the proprietor is so flattered to have him come in that he cannot bring himself to note that the culottes no more belong to Goha than the caftan. Goha simply alters his definition of ownership: not what he has paid for but what is on his back. The butcher is paid in kind: the man took a smell; the butcher gets back a sound. The sheepowner and the blasphemer have no imagination—they cannot see how easily their own tricks can be used against themselves. Every vector that is launched at him Goha reverses, sends back to its point of origin. So we can say that the networks of the bright-shadow world are easy to ride if one has a vehicle flexible enough, lively enough to navigate the cracks and crevices open to every clever person.

A certain virtuosity in moving about one's network is a characteristic common to the great rogues. All kinds of stops can be pulled out as one personally manipulates inherent chaos. Victims cannot identify power sources or dodge quickly enough the vectors that blindside them. In an amusing tale from *Thousand and One Nights* Hasan, a thief, pretends to be the merchant who owns a certain shop, so that the night watchman lets him in and actually watches him pack up and ship off several bales of goods. But with the help of the same watchman the rightful owner traces the goods to a khan, where he locates them under the thief's cloak. The merchant seizes the goods, and the thief, who has been following him, has the effrontery to ask for his cloak back. Smiling, the merchant complies. And Hasan of Bassorah, in another tale from the same collection, determines to get from certain boys a cap of invisibility and a magical rod that controls a jinn. So he sets up a running contest between them, the winner to have the rod; the loser, the cap. He throws a stone for them to chase, and as soon as they are gone, he walks off with the treasures he wants.[8] It appears that in the bright-shadow world any kind of break in the routine, any kind of stimulation, any freshening of mood is welcome and approved.

From all over Europe come stories about the master thief, a figure who delights in the most extraordinary moves, robbing people who know full well his intent. "For me neither lock nor bolt exists," claims one great representative of the breed; "whatever I crave is mine" (Magoun and Krappe, 616).[9] In this version by the Brothers

Grimm, the master thief is challenged to steal the very horse on which his challenger is riding, the sheet on which this same person and his wife are sleeping, and the parson and his wife themselves from the church. There is a slightly different version in Dasent about a youth who, in order to join a band of robbers, must perform some tricky robberies himself—stealing an ox from a man without his knowing it (which he does by diverting the ox driver by leaving a shoe in the road), a second ox (which he does by pretending to hang himself), and then a third (which he does by setting up a terrible bellowing).[10] In such cases, the victim seems to know exactly what is going to happen to him, but his attention is diverted in such an unexpected way that he has no resources with which to defend himself. The context he faces is a truly chaotic one: no matter how he faces it, unexpected vectors will assault him.

Traditional narrative, then, suggests certain attitudes toward property that differ radically from those commonly held by the civilized community, and these attitudes ultimately determine style. The actor puts makes unusual demands of power sources, realigns the vectors, shifts about elements in the physical context, generates a denouement entirely favorable to himself/herself. We are critical, call for his/her punishment, because he/she is transgressing certain principles associated with our network. But we are also intrigued and challenged, because we recognize that what the rogue is doing has definite implications for the enhancement of life on a grander scale. Thus in many traditional tales theft is regarded less as taking what does not belong to you and rather more as a question of what you can get away with, how far you can manipulate the structure, to what extent you can loosen it up or exploit its inherent chaos (i.e., find some loose vectors that you can make work for you). I try to get my students to stop thinking in terms of "Am I allowed to do that" (the two-dimensional network, with teacher, the dominant actor, in control) and to consider instead what they can "get away with" (three-dimensional thinking, which takes into account the possibility that the students may devise something that lies totally outside their teacher's frame of reference, something that will enhance the experience of the entire group). But only the truly nimble-minded ever attempt such transcontextual moves. A joke has a trigger that "switches the listener from one premise to another."[11] Moreover, traditional narrative implies that existing resources are in some sense available to everyone within the network and that holding onto resources, refusing to share them or put them to use, is itself a serious breach of morality. It is far better to join Saktideva at the gambling table (although you face ruin there) or, like Ma'ruf, fling gold coins about the streets (even if they are not exactly yours)! At its best, resource redistribution can mean something far more than greed, self-interest, and manipulation.

Bricolage

This ability to solve problems by using whatever resources the situation offers is characteristic of all the great rogues. Sometimes the material available is so limited that a version of the sky hooks—a solid structure of knowledge based on almost nothing—discussed in chapter 10 is required to handle the situation. The nimble-minded can see possibilities in the most unpromising bits and pieces that are scattered about the network, while the unimaginative draw back in horror from the thought of using a knife for a screwdriver, a bicycle for a stepladder, or a fairytale for insight into a real human situation. Yet Odysseus escapes from the cave of Polyphemus by clinging to the belly of a sheep, and Sindbad and Saktideva complete their journeys on the backs of great birds. Always there is that sense of extraneous movement to which Lévi-Strauss calls attention—"a ball rebounding, a dog straying or a horse swerving from its direct course"—and which the clever person can put to use (*The Savage Mind*, 16).

We can consider once again the exploits of our old friend Goha, just reviewed. In the stories we have looked at, the trickster has very little to work with except his mastery of his physical context and something his opponent has unwittingly supplied. Often this resource is nothing but the dim outline of a useful analogy. In the clothing store, Goha works with the confusion of the owner over the hurried exchange of caftan for culottes and perhaps his pride in having such an important customer, which makes him hesitate about demanding payment. In the case of the beggar and the butcher—the fact that smell and sound belong to the same category of phenomena, though a category normally only peripheral to commercial transactions. In the cases of the sheep and the clothes, of judgment day and blasphemer—the possibility of overwhelming individuals who have no imagination by applying a single metaphor to quite different situations and doing it so nimbly that the other fellow cannot keep up with your moves. For Goha, experience is enhanced, albeit in no particularly noble fashion: he secures what he seeks, and he gains some new mastery over his physical/psychological world.

From *Thousand and One Nights* comes the story of a young man who likes to make love to his father's wives, with his eye on two in particular. When the father, in the hearing of both women, sends his son for slippers, the young man calls back to his father. "One—or two?" It is not difficult to guess the man's response.[12] In other stories a lobster wins a race with a fox by hitching a ride on its tail; a flea defeats an ostrich by riding to the finish line in the corner of the great bird's eye; a cat gets at a ball by making the string to which it is tied oscillate ever more wildly until she can seize it; two men persuade a band of opponents that they are really very numerous by rolling stones down on them from several directions, sending out as many vectors as they can (Lüthi, 97; Afanas'ev, 310), and another army gains a great victory by developing one-way arrows with a special cut that will not accommodate the enemy's thicker bowstrings, rendering their reuse impossible (*Decameron*, 302). In all these cases one vector is made to serve two purposes.

In truth, bricoleurs fully exemplify the behavior of Waska and Schurka in "The Magic Ring": they search for their master, "looking always to right and left for traces . . . following up every track, making inquiries of every dog and cat they met, listening to the talk of every wayfarer they passed" (*Yellow Fairy Book*, 188), projecting as many vectors as they can. This general and loose approach to problem-solving, right down to seeking help from cats and dogs, is an essential part of nimble network-riding, an important generator of productive chaos, a key to important forms of life-enhancement. Something that one can put to use in one's situation—perhaps not the the most appropriate thing, but something—is out there for anyone with sufficient imagination and a willingness not to be limited by accepted techniques.

Exploiting Sets

In chapter 4 we examined the tendency of bright-shadow people to shy away from numbers and to look at the world, instead, in terms of significant groupings, and in chapter 11 we watched clever people solving problems by breaking up sets, chunks of the physical context, clusters of vectors rendered powerless by the clustering. Nimble people, masters of bricolage, create their own sets and impose them on others, aware that structures can be traps for the literal-minded just waiting to be exploited. Traditional narrative offers many stories about human folly (unskilled or uncomprehending use of the sets provided by one's network), and Clouston's *Book of Noodles* is a standard anthology. Cosquin prints the story of a peasant woman who gives a beggar a horse when he claims that he is going off to Paradise: he will carry with him a morsel of bread for her dead husband (I, 237). Of course, he keeps the horse, for the widow was unable to handle the set he offered her. Equally manhandled is the devil (sometimes seen as a simpleton), when he enters into a contest with a clever farmer: at first they agree that the devil will have whatever grows below ground, and the farmer plants beans; then they reverse conditions, and the farmer plants onions. No doubt the farmer will continue to shuffle his sets, always one step ahead of his opponent.[13]

Through the power of sets a nimble actor can persuade a greedy person to see one pig and a field of pig's tails as a field of buried pigs, and a full barrel and several empty ones as several full barrels. You can convince a rich farmer that a horse actually spouts gold, that a cooking pot never runs out, and that a whistle can bring the dead back to life. And you can persuade several brothers to burn down their houses and kill their wives—and do it in such a way that you alone benefit.[14] Foolish persons build on superficial patterns and apparent connections, but the nimble individual exploits sets that are organic to his network. Even when he is blocked, he can find tiny cracks in existing arrangements through which he will be able to move. The nimble person's expectations lead toward infinity; the stodgy person's, toward nothing at all.

Hiding Things

Nineteenth-century detective stories often recount cases necessitating the concealment of valuable material (or individuals)—and very quickly. Moreover (as in the case of Poe's "Purloined Letter"), what is hidden so effectively must also be immediately accessible. Or the garments of bathing women may be hidden by a young man who has his eye on just one beautiful girl. Such incidents seem to stretch the wit of nimble persons to the limit. There is a well-known Japanese story about a tanuku who was punished by his son for betraying his wife. The father is aware that the son is a threat but is not prepared for the fact that the boy does not adopt any disguise at all when he confronts his father: he simply lies in wait, while the father, thinking it likely that the son will have transformed himself into some very strong creature, attacks just such a powerful figure and is, of course, himself destroyed (*Japanische Märchen*, 46 ff.). In the Grimm Brothers' story "The Monkey" one hundred young men seek the hand of a princess who destroys any suitor whom she can spot after he has had a chance to conceal himself. Successful concealment is the price of her hand. One suitor hides in the egg of a raven, where he is observed immediately. Another is more successful in the stomach of a fish, but he too is identified. Only the braids of the princess's hair prove a safe spot, and the suitor who hides there gets the woman as his wife (612).

(A common trick among children playing Hide and Seek is to conceal themselves on the other side of the tree that serves as base, within inches of the person who is It.)

Where people take words and images seriously, metaphors can be instruments of concealment as well as devices for problem-solving/buffering, and of vector distortion as well as vector concealment. We have already encountered the famous story "The Monkey and the Tortoise" from *Kalilah and Dimnah,* where the intended victim saves himself by adopting, falling in with, the very metaphor by which the rogue had hoped to destroy him. In *Thousand and One Nights* three lawbreakers save their necks by coining metaphors that suggest, with studied ambivalence, who they really are. One claims to be the son of one to whom all necks bow, and he has in mind a barber, not God. Another claims to be the son of one whose ranks time does not abuse, and he is a seller of *fūl,* the timeless boiled beans of Egypt. The third claims to be the son of one who plunges through the ranks with a sword—a weaver, not a warrior (*1001,* Suppl. I, 47–48). Oona and Peter Opie discuss the interest of schoolchildren in these tricks, and their love of crooked answers (42), having the last word (45), either-way tricks (70), and embarrassers (71). The schoolyard is a training ground for rogues as well as for generals and admirals.

Moving About

Dancing, hint-reading, communication across great distances, personal commitment to some other individual, storytelling—these are some of the ways interconnections are sustained in traditional narrative by nimble people, and some of the ways through which others, who do not have their antennae out regularly, may find themselves threatened. Here it is affirmed that one can place himself or herself wherever he or she chooses in the physical context—a life-enhancing position that contrasts with the view of many that they are stuck here or being pushed around. The networks that make possible these activities are often three-dimensional, and anyone who seeks to navigate them must be prepared not only for moves sideways and forward/backward, but also for vertical jumps into quite new contexts. In Hesse's *Steppenwolf* Hermine, a creature of the bright-shadow world if there ever was one, speaks of Harry Haller's "crossing" her path to become her comrade, and certainly Haller's life takes on new dimensions—is radically enhanced—at that point. Indeed, at the masked ball described later in the novel, Haller observes his own personality "dissolving" in the gaiety of the experience and blending with all the other personalities there. The edges described in chapter 5 represent experiences of both connection and separation.

In the story of Saktideva, we encountered Princess Kanakarekha at a time when she was more or less mired in the city of Vardhamana, at the center of a tricky matrimonial situation. Later her lover finds her dead on a bier in the City of Gold, and then, after apparently being drowned, he discovers her alive at home and can pose the question "What are you doing here, when I saw you dead?" His mental leaps between two apparently unconnected realities match hers, and we may say that the rest of his story is his imaginative reconstruction of the events that led to this situation. His moves are not unlike those with which Emily Dickinson links Tunis and Massachusetts, Spring and Tyre, crossing both temporal and spatial boundaries in her imagination. Witty, alert combining of seemingly unrelated bits of data, a possible description of the imagination, is one key to movement across the bright-shadow network.

Many nimble riders are careful to place themselves at some spot in the network where their talents will be exercised fully: they are true edge-dwellers. Thoreau notes in the second chapter of *Walden* that "I went to the woods because I wished to live deliberately," adding in chapter 18, "I left the woods for as good reason as I went there." Deliberation intensifies liberation: the freedom he felt was a result of his commitment to a particular spot. Ma'ruf places himself behind the plow in the farmer's field; Saktideva chooses to enter the forbidden room; Psyche consents to life in a remote and forbidding palace. However, the most striking accounts of conscious placing are to be found in the books of the great travelers, whose reasons for going to Tibet or up the Amazon or around the world on a bicycle are clear enough to suggest intentionality and serious reflection.

Dodds identifies fluency, flexibility, originality, and elaboration as factors in movement to be considered in developing a model for assessing creativity-in-movement.[15] To this list I would add persistence and patience, even if one is by nature witty and nimble. Dimensions may be impossible to determine; distances, enormous. Indeed, the journey must be long if it is to lead to psychic changes and significant meetings, and sometimes boring if it is to effectively turn one in upon oneself. It may involve penetration into realms even those living along the road have never heard of, and perhaps heading toward a goal that itself is quite unclear. The quester in the Rumanian story of Aurora, the Dawn Fairy, continues his journey through the most ambiguous and undefined situations, revealing a capacity to endure the most extreme forms of disorientation, on the way to some kind of transcendence of his former self.

Wherever you locate yourself in the bright-shadow world, you will be hemmed in by regulations and interdictions, definitions, limitations, and barriers that do not appear to brook broaching. But the nimble rider discovers the crack in the system through which he or she can move. We have seen this happening in the story of Vishnu and Hiranyakasipu and in all the progeny of that remarkable tale. When the great nineteenth-century explorer Fred Burnaby heard that the Russians had forbidden travel to Central Asia, he determined, precisely then, to make his famous ride to Khiva and thereby produced one of the world's great travel books.[16] And when Gavin Maxwell sought to accompany Wilfrid Thesiger back to the territory of the Marsh Arabs in southern Iraq, Thesiger raised every possible objection—extreme discomfort, insects, disease, hostile inhabitants—and these problems seem only to have motivated Maxwell even more strongly.[17]

Disrupting Established Categories

Categories are boxes into which certain material is placed so that it can be linked with similar material. The concept sounds abstract, but as Greenfield and Bruner note, "no matter how rich the vocabulary available to describe a given domain, it is of limited use as an instrument of thought if it is not organized into a hierarchy that can be activated as a whole.[18] Real-world categories reflect, determine, and make possible an orderly view of the world, and deconstructionists have been busy breaking it up. Aristotle identified the categories as substance, quantity, quality, relation, place, time, position, state, action, and affection (feeling). When a sense of some new reality is emerging, new categories must be established to contain these new perceptions, and this is always a critical moment in the emergence of a new field or context. The psyche resists the process until finally it is forced to make the move. At the beginning of a course students often have trouble taking notes, because they do not yet see what the significant categories are. Right now, we are interested in the games and tricks that rogues play with established categories to befuddle the less nimble-minded.

Many stories on this theme are linked with Nasr-ed-Din Khoja, and it seems appropriate to illustrate this topic with stories in which he is involved (though the same motifs may, of course, be linked with still other rogues). One very common way of suggesting the passage between incompatible structures of reality is to describe the way dreams can spill over into the waking world. One night Nasr dreamed that a man gave him nine gold liras and that he, Nasr, haggled and asked for ten. When he woke up, he had no liras at all in

his hand, so he shut his eyes and agreed to take nine (58). The shut-
ting of the eyes is enough to move the actor from one reality to
another. Elsewhere, Nasr wakes up and asks his wife for glasses so
that he may see more clearly what he is dreaming (192). Such incidents take us back to the great dream of the traveler in Baghdad about
the location of a cache of treasure in Cairo—which actually proves to
be there. All such stories challenge one of the distinctions we mind
most carefully—between dream and reality, sleeping and waking.
Movement around the network becomes chaotic indeed when this
distinction is neglected—or it is marvelously enhanced.

In other cases, Nasr's nimble movement between incompatible
levels of reality gets him out of dangerous scrapes. A cadi condemns
him for holding a funeral for a sheepdog—until the cadi learns from
Nasr that the sheepdog willed him ten sheep. Then the cadi is ready
to pray for the dog's soul (*Tales Alive*, 248). Nasr suggests a bizarre
dish to the governor—honey and garlic. When the governor insists
Nasr himself eat the mess, Nasr demurs, saying that his recipe was
only a theory, that he never intended to turn it into a real dish (*Tales of
Nasr-ed-Din Khoja*, 125). And a neighbor is quite willing to accept the
fact that a cauldron he lent Nasr has had a baby (Nasr returned it with
a small saucepan inside) but balks when informed that the cauldron
has died (Nasr kept it for himself) (146).

Or you can make a point by forcing your hearer to cross category
lines that normally he or she keeps separate. This technique, as noted
earlier, relies heavily on the power of analogy. A man orders a carpenter to put the floors of his new house where the ceilings are and the
ceilings where the floors go: he is getting married and everything will
be turned upside down (158). And when Injili Chavush is accused of
warming himself at a fire that burned a mile away from the cold
minaret in which he has been sentenced to spend the night alone, he
responds by inviting his accusers for dinner and heating the soup in a
great cauldron over a candle (*Tales Alive*, 239). The analogy compels
his hearers to see the injustice of their accusation. In all of these cases
an attempt is made to transplant the vectors normally associated
with one reality to another. Such transfers do not always work when
something physical is being moved about (lira, glasses), but they
often succeed brilliantly (as metaphors in the hands of poets) when
concepts, attitudes, or information are involved. Powers of
communication—one way of moving about—are greatly enhanced.

To blur or destroy old categories is also to suggest the creation of
some new ones, containers for some fresh, suddenly prominent realities that have been separated out, some new file drawers into which
material can be thrown. Perhaps the most important recent work on

category formation has been done by George Lakoff and reported in *Women, Fire, and Dangerous Things,* to which reference has already been made. Lakoff argues that the categories we devise to contain our reality are based on—or at least reflect—"the bodily nature of the people doing the categorizing" (371) and certain imaginative process in which they are involved—imagining, metaphor-making, the exploitation of metonymies—rather than "the manipulation of abstract symbols" (xii) that relate us objectively, not subjectively, to the world. My argument, of course, is that traditional narrative both describes actors involved in highly imaginative processes of category formation and also encourages readers today to undertake this process for themselves. Lakoff's thinking here fits very nicely into the plea of F. D. Foster and D. T. Morgan for possibility thinking as opposed to actuality thinking.[19] I make the following suggestions about categories of reality important for traditional narrative.

1. *The network.* Into this file we dump all data about contacts, communication, relationships, and much that has to do with movement. Vector-related issues belong here, as does material about the way knowledge crosses great distances, about ESP, about relationships remembered, forgotten, recovered. When you find out how an actor moves about, whom he or she is touching, where he or she is going to or coming from, you have a substantial chunk of reality under control. This is a big file drawer, and vast leaps of the imagination are required to become aware of all the material that belongs in it. It is also not one that we pay much attention to per se. But it can help us make sense of much very diffuse material, and rogues see links that are invisible to many of us.

2. *Inbetwixities.* The great authority here is Pearce, with his cracked cosmic egg.[20] Filling in this category is a never-ending process, since every time new realities are created, new spaces between them appear. This category is designed to take care of the feeling so many of us have of being bumped or rubbed from all sides, of not really having enough room.

3. *Sets.* This category collects patterns and configurations as well as information about how they are formed and what impact they have on various contexts. What are the common groupings? How do they function? What powers do they generate? Sets are a critical part of the structures where they appear, and the nimble learn to manipulate them effectively.

4. What *moves* are made, typically, across the networks of the bright-shadow world? What patterns do they follow? What kinds of powers are implied by them? How do the nimble-minded exploit them? We recall that metaphor means "to carry across."

5. *Commitments.* What values do actors hold? What is the source of these commitments? How do these commitments affect behavior? What threats do commitments have to withstand? What happens when commitments clash? Grasping the plight of others is an act of the imagination.

6. *Personhood.* Here we find data that differ in many respects from the material we make use of in forming our sense of a person. Roles become more important than individuality and one's place in a set. Transformation or metamorphosis may take precedence over single identity. And the view of the person as a temporary coming together of isolated parts challenges our view of the stability of the individual. The origins of the stress on nimbleness are clear.

7. *Consciousness.* Here belongs material on sleeping and waking, remembering and forgetting, self-awareness and ignorance of self, goal-seeking and diversion from goals. It is a category without which traditional narrative could not exist.

8. *Style.* This category is obviously related to consciousness and personhood, but it is also important in its own right. Traditional narrative attends to the way an actor moves about his/her world, and that manner is an important source of our delight in the story, our identification with its themes.

9. *Possibility.* As the number of vectors increases, so do the ways in which they can be combined, and with every change in actors (new perceptions, new relationships), other vectors emerge.[21]

The very idea of reading the world seems to suggest order, clarity, and clean paths to the truth. Indeed these qualities lead us a good way into the bright-shadow world and enhance experience in many significant ways. But the tendency of the bright-shadow world to move toward chaos must also be kept in mind. Individuals are enchanted, fall asleep, lose battles with dragons, fail to answer riddles correctly, are baffled by certain metaphors. In this chapter I have tried to suggest some of the ways that one figure common to traditional narrative—the nimble rider—surmounts these problems and, after some fashion anyway, triumphs. But the moves he makes—manipulating the vision of others, twisting sets and patterns about, working with the most inappropriate tools—suggest how messy is the world over which he presides, albeit with greater agility than most. His "unreading" of the world is every bit as significant as many of the more elegant and structured readings we have encountered.

13 The World of the Bright Shadow

Throughout these pages I have argued that the basic structure of experience, as described in popular narrative, has important points of contact with normal, real-world experience. I have drawn many parallels between the actual junctures of lived life and events described in fairytales and folktales, tracing the inner workings of actors, vectors, power sources, and physical facts through to denouements that are often both instructive and profoundly satisfying. And I have noted how the concerns of many modern researchers in such fields as anthropology, religion, psychology, and social psychology touch upon the principal motifs of traditional narratives. But I have also argued—indeed, this has been a major concern—that in fairytale and folktale basic human experience is often transcended, transformed, or enhanced, pushed beyond the limits to which we are accustomed into areas that are sometimes bizarre and improbable, often challenging, enlightening, stimulating, even liberating. These stories offer the vision of other modes of life, other levels of experience—material, as I suggested in the first chapter, that we are badly in need of now, as we search for new images of humanness. I have tried to indicate how traditional narratives describe the pursuit of real-world themes beyond real-world boundaries and thus enrich human experiences and perspectives. This pursuit can follow many quarries—universal archetypes and motifs; aesthetic experiences; alternate moralities and altered states of consciousness; the mental creation of alternate worlds; the exploitation of human potentialities; the development of an awareness of the inner structure of experience—and the deconstruction of all of these.

A Review of Structural Issues

We have watched *actors* in traditional narratives reading their worlds, establishing sets, choosing (contrary to all the advice we are usually given) passive roles; we have seen them succumbing to enchantment or defying it; resisting diverting blandishments; exerting their wills; suffering through the tendency of their own personalities to dissolve or be absorbed by the world around them; drawing knowledge from the most unlikely sources; experimenting with numerous unusual life-styles and ways of moving about.

And *contexts?* We have seen thorny hedges blocking the entry to a castle where all the inhabitants are asleep, and heroes covering enormous distances on journeys that take forever—or are completed almost instantly—on magic carpets. A shoe will fit only one foot, and a pile of seeds must be sorted before morning. Stormy seas separate Odysseus from Penelope; a terrible desert and hard-hearted people block Moses from the promised land. Horses, dragons, foxes, and fish serve both as aides and threats. Individuals plow fields, tend sheep, sell animals at market. Everywhere there are physical facts to be considered, and for everyone who succumbs, another overcomes.

We have followed out many *vectors,* lines of force. Immense journeys by which solitary individuals carry power and knowledge from one spot to another. Contacts between distant persons that amount to something very like ESP. Ties of kindness and gratitude between humans and animals. Malevolence and egoism. Every kind of category disruption. Dreams, hints, and gestures through which information is conveyed. Interdictions and prohibitions by which individuals control those who come long after them, from other levels of reality. Linkages of loyalty and envy. Ironies joining events in unexpected ways. The determination to be recognized and accepted once again by loved ones.

The importance of *power* in mythology and religion spills over into the lesser realms of fairytale and folktale. We have looked at many forms of power but always come back to the suggestion that power lies in concentration: where there are intelligence, raw material, and will, power will be released if it can be focused. The experience of power is most noticeable in the lives of the great questers—Saktideva looking for the City of Gold, the third son searching for the ointment that will cure his father's eyes, Odysseus relentlessly pursuing his way home. It is symbolized by certain objects that are found, carried about, rubbed or cleansed, lost and recovered—a ring, a jewel, a lantern. And it is located in certain rare figures—Morgiana, wise foxes, a jinn—who are devoted to their masters. The means by which such power is transferred from fairytales to real-life merits careful study—i.e., how children who read or hear this material put it to use as adults.

Discussion of typical *denouements* merits more attention, for in looking at traditional narrative we have observed a rich variety of life-enhancing experiences, which are perhaps more readily available to us than is generally realized. Trollope wrote: "There are men whose energies hardly ever carry them beyond looking for the things they want," but this is scarcely true of fairytale and folktale, where many heroes push well beyond the aspirations they were taught to entertain. The gambler Saktideva becomes a "Man of Light," an exalted spiritual being. Ma'ruf, as his name implies, attains enlightenment, knowledge of ultimate truth. The third son extricates himself from his impossible position in the family structure and completes his quest. The jewel the ostrich swallows is found, brighter and more intense in hue than before. And King Kalinga escapes from a narrow, Puritanical morality into real enjoyment of his kingdom and the people around him. Traditional narrative, it has been argued here, exists to help us escape from the limitations of our own wishes into an arena of far broader possibilities than we had hitherto imagined.

Innumerable combinations are possible when these five structural elements are linked to the various issues (e.g., world-reading, edges, moral commitments) that have been considered in these pages. Yet it is possible (as I have demonstrated in appendix 1) to devise a limited number of short thematic statements that enable us to see at a glance the essential elements of a given story. Thus classification, comparison, and contrast are facilitated.

The Enhancement of Experience

When we attempt to erect an ethical position on the structural issues we have just summarized, we note, first, that a certain enrichment of experience is implicit in a sensitive and detailed reading of one's context, a process that provides for countless fairytale figures the basis for an experience of reality. The heroes and heroines of fairytales demonstrate a remarkable capacity to draw useful conclusions about their contexts and to grasp physical realities in a productive manner.

Experience is enhanced when the central actor is located (or locates himself or herself) between contexts as they are usually defined, in spots where the vectors are often difficult to identify. Enhancement lies in the actor's ability to work out his or her own position and dominate it intellectually, and in his or her continuing penetration of all its contradictions. Finding oneself "between" may elicit major changes in personality and moral commitment, and while the experience can lead to depression, it can also mean being "surprised by joy." Nowhere else is the personality so pushed and pulled in opposing directions, but nowhere does the actor who knows himself or herself have so much to gain.

Life is enhanced when actors are able to escape the dark drives projected by their own inner beings and the malign forces of the universe and place themselves under the influence of positive vectors. Their (re)alignment with existing power sources is signaled by waking up, remembering, casting off the bonds of illusion, recovering a sense of their goals, escaping purely mechanical processes. They reflect on their experience and consider options.

Life may be enhanced when an actor who seems powerless within his or her physical context is able to tap into hitherto unidentified power sources so as to carry out difficult tasks or escape undesirable situations. Special wonder attaches to an actor's ability to invoke his or her own will, generate luck, and focus or concentrate abilities, however small they may be.

The moral values advanced by traditional narrative differ significantly from those advanced in our world, and this implies different forms of life-enhancement. The central actor is seen as the servant of existent moral forces in the universe (Goodness); his or her deeds may affect a wide variety of issues throughout a particular network. Power sources are one's own sense of goodness and the proper balancing of subjective and objective factors, pragmatism and idealism. Restraint and attention to small, humble things are important. To us this situation appears confusing and ambiguous, because we are ill-tuned to the possibility that moral vectors are related to the tendency of the universe to respond to the actions of individuals. The physical environment contains an infinite number of neutral facts, waiting to be shaped by strong-minded individuals.

Life is enhanced when an actor assembles a personality for himself or herself out of bits and pieces of the physical and psychic context and whatever power is available, for whatever tasks lie at hand. Although the personality may then dissolve, even a brief experience of integrated consciousness is a gain for humanity. The physical context within which the personality emerges is quite rich, both affirming and challenging the ego, transient as this aspect of the actor may be.

Life-enhancement occurs when an actor employs unusual means of learning about his/her world and taps unusual power sources—dreams, words, sounds, gestures, rhythms; some inner voice. Thus, he or she can penetrate secrets thought to be secure, uncover intentions, learn what is going on in distant places, identify disguised individuals, get a fix on the future.

Life-enhancement lies, too, in dealing with the peculiar problems that occur in the bright-shadow world—making choices without adequate information (critical vectors are missing), being in situations without letting one's presence be felt, escaping overly rigid sets (dominated by only one kind of power), conflict management (controlling vectors for the benefit of all), finding things, escaping traps (hidden power sources), using metaphors (inventing vectors). Such activities reveal one's mastery of the psychological/physical context.

Nimbleness of response characterizes the actor who can handle readily the vectoral challenges posed by the network in which he or she must function, who can read the world quickly and accurately, navigate its borders, escape enchantment, uncover unusual forms of power, make productive but unusual moral commitments, pull himself or herself together at critical junctures, gather information where none seems to exist, solve problems the rational mind finds baffling, and move easily across networks. Inherent in such activities is a considerable enhancement of experience, and certain denouements are indeed characterized appropriately by the familiar phrase about living happily ever after. (This material is summarized in appendix 2).

The Postmodern Dimension

Implicit in these possibilities is that set of attitudes I have referred to as "postmodernism." The term—as those who have dealt with it know well enough—has been defined in all sorts of ways; I have taken it to apply to situations which can no longer be explained or legitimized by a single overarching narrative or a set of generally accepted concepts. There is no longer any established path through experience, any structure that can be relied upon. We have pursued the implications of this situation (as they are uncovered by traditional narrative) along many lines, particularly by suggesting that the world described in fairytales and folktales rarely has the grandeur of myth or epic, but that it is a matter of tiny, often domestic, details every individual must patch together in his or her own way. We have watched individuals making their ways across the edges of the known and the defined into the unknown, without guidance from familiar resources. We have watched them suffering enchantment—

the loss of capacity to direct their own lives. We have seen them putting together practical codes of morality out of the simplest and most naive responses, without any assurance at all that there is any overall scheme into which their moral behavior fits. We have watched individuals solving problems and collecting data with no instruments but their own wit and various odd bits and pieces lying about. And we have argued that the human personality—the self—which we take to be so stable, is also an assemblage of such bits and pieces, coming together briefly and dissolving just as quickly.

World-Making

A final issue remains: the suggestion that fairytales and folktales invite us to devise "other worlds and other seas," as the poet Andrew Marvell put it—imaginary worlds that may offer us some structure and may be useful as well to others.[1]

Mental world-making may involve bringing minor actors into roles of prominence and dismissing the "big names," or altering the role of an actor, or bringing one actor into some new relation with another, or changing some basic characteristic of an actor—all ways of renewing a situation. It may require identifying some new power source, which no one else has thought of tapping, or increasing/limiting the power that is flowing into a situation, or directing the power at some new angle, or even discovering that what was thought to hold the power is really powerless. Physical features may be transcended or suddenly recognized as more—or less—serious than had been thought. These features may be put to quite unorthodox uses or combined in unexpected ways with other physical forces. And as for vectors, there is no end to the changes to which they may be subjected: calm lines of force may be exploded; simple lines may be rendered complex; certain elements in the network may suddenly be connected or disconnected; long-broken ties may be restored; lines may be extended in new directions. Such are some of the structural possibilities of world-making to which fairytales and folktales call attention, possibilities that lie well within human grasp.

The most readily available instrument for the creation of mental worlds involves asking "what if" questions, consciously trying to escape from the normal categories and enter wholly new situations where there are new limitations and resources, where lines of force operate with which we have had little past experience and hitherto unimagined power sources can be tapped.

The speculative, what-if world is very much a world of play, requiring abundant wit of its participants, an attractive world of easy wish-fulfillment. Mathematicians have found this kind of activity particularly interesting. Witness Lewis Carroll's *Alice in Wonderland,* where many mathematical truths are twisted about into new forms; Edwin Abbott's *Flatland,* which describes a two-dimensional universe, and Dionys Burger's *Sphereland.* Isaac Asimov, who has made effective use of "what-if" questions, has explored worlds dominated by robotics;[2] Clifford Simak, worlds where time and space are distorted; Ursula LeGuin, a unisexual world (in *The Left Hand of Darkness*); and Frank Herbert, a world of paranormal perception (in *Dune*). For such activity, visionary thinking is essential, and it would appear that no real-world assumptions about reality need go unchallenged.

Imaging or image-making is another kind of mental activity by which we construct alternate realities, an activity that is often observed in traditional narrative. By "imaging" I mean the combining of all kinds of data into a coherent picture that becomes an individual's reality. Kenneth Boulding has gone so far as to suggest that the only reality we ever know consists of the images we form as we filter through our own "changeable value system" what we pick up from the world around us.[3] In the kind of imaging (or reimaging) of reality which I am speaking about here, the normal or everyday world takes a quite peripheral position.

The variety of disciplines that have found imaging and reimaging to be important—education, medicine, geography, economics, psychology, urban planning, athletics, futuristics—suggests that such vision is characterized by great breadth and comprehensiveness. My own feeling is that we can see the process unfolding most clearly in long texts—the stories of Moses and Black Elk, for example, or the return of Odysseus to Ithaca, or the accounts of Saktideva and Ma'ruf. In these cases we are observing the construction of a paradigm, a large model of reality formed of many small images, by which a comprehensive vision is presented and which may challenge opposing views popular at a given time.

Individuals who would like to use the technique of imaging to create a new reality for themselves (using fairytales and folktales as source material) are advised to make careful observations of a variety of phenomena which envelop or close around them—the old parts of cities; reflections in water; complex, many-floored libraries. They should become intimates of trees and small, frail things, for in these surroundings they can gather many useful images to incorporate into their visions. They should be alert to various intermediate states—

dawn, twilight, dozing, waking—for it is at these spots that consciousness has the most to learn, the most to absorb. They need to be perceptive and ready synthesizers and effective actors, with their hands on power sources, engaged in contacts with others, capable of handling the physical frustrations they are sure to encounter.

Yet another important mental world can be brought into being through the mental process of abstracting or drawing out from a great mass of material what is relevant or suited to one's particular purposes, constantly narrowing the range of what is selected, focusing ever more sharply in a single direction. Intensity of will is critical here, and the activity of the great questers, who exclude everything from their concern except a single goal, provides good illustrative material. Problems with the abstracting process arise when one admits into one's consciousness elements that do not contribute to the life-story one is creating.

The questers in "East o' the Sun, West o' the Moon" and "Golden Bird" stories ruthlessly eliminate all obstacles that stand in their way. First and second sons are invariably indicted for being too lackadaisical, unable to exclude from consideration pleasant options that do not fit in with the goals they are pursuing. We have observed the easy, diffused behavior of Saktideva until he makes his great commitment. Psyche, as she undergoes her final test, must not attend to the calls for help that threaten to distract her.

Inferred worlds are the most important part of this discussion, however: all around us are to be found hints and signs from which, if we have the will and insight, we can deduce the existence and the nature of dimensions of experience representing enhanced or transcendent aspects of normal reality. When I infer a world, I am "going beyond the information given" (to use Jerome Bruner's fine phrase), and my guesses, the possibilities I consider, will eventually be confirmed or rejected when I see more of the picture. Or discover that my inferences do (or do not) add up to a functioning whole. Or realize that they are leading in the wrong direction. Or that the picture lies beyond my comprehension at the present stage of my development. Inferring is not necessarily a systematic procedure, observes Gilbert Harman, for it may require dealing with half-disclosed material that at best I can only glimpse. And my inferences, my beliefs, my conclusions may depend heavily on my general attitude about affairs: "How things look is a matter of a certain kind of disposition to accept a certain kind of representation as one of [my] beliefs."[4] This, of course, is a theme that has run all through this book.

I first gained some sense of the power of inference through a passage from *Toxophilus, the Schole of Shoting,* a treatise on archery by the sixteenth-century humanist Roger Ascham. One bright and frosty morning, Ascham writes, he walked out into the snow and realized as it blew in currents of varying width and direction and speed that he was actually watching the wind.[5] Inspired by Ascham, I began studying the leaves of trees that grew in arid places—olive trees, for example, contrasting them with the leaves of tropical plants that enjoy an abundance of water. The tiny, almond-shaped leaves of the olive, gray-green in color and very hard, seemed to point to a climate of dry, hot days and the need of the plant to collect moisture from the cool night air. Once I learned this principle, I could infer a good deal about the worlds of maples and banyans—and the worlds of Spanish and Tunisian peasants as well. But since my eyes and mind alone were gathering data, I could not incorporate into my own being as much of these worlds as the trees or the peasants did. Whether wrinkled bark and skin were the results of the sun's heat or a way of dealing with it is the kind of question that would occur to a mind, not to a total organism. Nevertheless, the inspiration of Ascham did evoke in me a thoughtful, productive kind of behavior, and I went on to consider how we might use the peculiar formations of rock crystals and the brightly colored petals of flowers to infer facts about yet other worlds. And so I suggest that from the data we can gather from traditional narratives, a fair sample of which has been collected here, we can also infer much about the bright-shadow world.

Here our road divides.

We may take a sceptical, negatively deconstructive approach to the material before us, asking what is the absolute minimum we can infer from this material. The answers will be that stories about other dimensions of reality are popular with both children and adults because they offer an amusing, often (and probably erroneously) hopeful view of affairs; that kindness and generosity are probably good things; that an indirect approach to problem-solving may be useful; that at certain times various individuals are enchanted, rewarded, or punished; and that human attempts to understand or read the world often go seriously astray. Not particularly impressive stuff!

We will find a lot more data if, following Gendlin, we assume a believing, naive, childlike point of view (recognizing all the dangers that such a view opens up) and look for insights on a somewhat broader scale. So we pick out a few motifs from many available to us and see what we can infer from them about the bright-shadow world and the enhancement of experience it promotes.

The stunning successes of those who reflect, ruminate, observe passively and detachedly, and recognize the importance of sets, concatenations, analogues, anomalies, and ironies suggests the existence in the bright-shadow world of an infinite variety of details ready to be organized into patterns by human actors. No one of these patterns can be judged correct, though some are more attractive, more productive than others.

From the sense of the strange, the undefinable, the terrifying, which fairytales convey so very powerfully, from the many accounts we are given of being lost or in between or vulnerable, it may be inferred that signposts are rare in the bright-shadow context, that most paths entail some risk, and that most experiences tend to be ambiguous and hard to define. It would appear, too, that the psychic and spiritual rewards offered by the bright-shadow world lie in categories to which little attention has been paid by the modern world.

Stories about enchantment challenge our view that evil is largely a subjective or societal matter and suggest, instead, that there may indeed be malignant forces in the universe. These malignant vectors lure individuals from their goals, entangle them in various misadventures, doom them to the endless repetition of mechanical processes, induce sleep and forgetfulness. This malignancy can be observed first hand in ugly stepmothers and scheming wazirs, in those who are cruel to animals, and in the horrid way that husbands and wives sometimes treat each other and their children. The will to Evil is a reality in the bright-shadow world, against which all forms of Goodness need to be assembled determinedly.

From information we are given about moral issues, we can infer that morality in the bright-shadow world is a tricky blend of objective and subjective factors, and that individuals have more power to influence moral situations than we normally grant them. A concentration on the domestic virtues rather than on cosmic issues suggests the small scale of the bright-shadow world. A sense of balance and fitness that is almost Buddhist is pervasive.

The importance accorded style in the bright-shadow world confirms what we have already inferred about its loose network structure. Chaos and illegibility constantly threaten those who explore it. Nothing seems settled or nailed down—least of all what we refer to as "personal property." No accepted behavior, no established categories of reality, no popular metanarratives or language games go unchallenged. Though appearance and similarity mean much, depth sets often prove more important than surface patterns. Movements need to be traced carefully: individuals are constantly, surprisingly running into each other; indeed, the junctions or synapses of the network are busy places. And so much can be inferred from the importance accorded the rogue!

But readers can draw their own inferences. I have suggested some of the kinds of data traditional narrative provides for anyone who might wish to carry out this important exercise in world-making.[6]

My point about experience is lost, however, if it is reduced to a matter of data-gathering. Stories read and experience enjoyed are parts of the same continuum, constantly interacting. Stories grow from experience and help to determine it. Outside my office window at seven this morning, a tree emerged from the shadows of night, glowing in the dawn, almost seeming to will its peculiar shape. I read a letter from a former student whose sense of selfhood was being lost in her husband's. Later, looking for a particular book in the library, I stumbled by chance on something else, which proved to be just what I needed. In class, a student struggling out of the enchanted sleep of adolescence suddenly confronted me, adult authority, as an adult herself. The newspaper featured an article about someone downtown who was trying to seize some power. I used the word "five" in class and sensed the color blue. A friend decided that a particular course of action had to be taken and willed to take it. Fairytales I had read made each of these events something special. They became part of a world where King Kalinga has learned to reign at ease, where Black Elk is a living presence, Emily Dickinson an eloquent guide. The pieces of the mosaic are there, ready to catch the sunlight, for anyone with the courage and imagination to fit them all together.

Appendix One:
Analysis of the Structure
of Situations

Situations Related to Creating Alternate Worlds

The actor tells a story, speaking to a context, out of a context, relying on such powers as verbal skill, imagination, memory, and psychological understanding. He/she projects vectors of sympathy, humor, excitement, and suspense, and he receives vectors of support, approval, enthusiasm, and criticism.

The actor saves his/her life by storytelling, establishing the right to be in a certain context, indicating some mastery of power-sources and the control of important vectors.

The dominant actor listens to a story, projecting vectors of approval/disapproval, interest/boredom—i.e., he/she responds.

Listener/teller move together from context to context, growing less and less certain about where reality lies. Their sense of power sources grows confused, and they become unsure about the vectors available to themselves.

Situations Related to World-Reading

The actor is quietly observing his/her context, taking note of but not disturbing existent vectors. He/she calls upon the power of keen observation, free-floating attention, and the ability of the mind to try out various combinations.

The actor creates *sets* out of the vectors that come to his/her attention, thereby clarifying and organizing his context and sorting out available powers on the basis of perceived similarities. The actor is dominated by a drive to combine, to link. In the search for a strategy by which to deal with his context, the actor balances opposing impulses (i.e. vectors) to act vigorously and to respond passively. He/she may resist use of available power.

The actor faces anomalies and ironies—vectors unanticipated or desired. Inappropriate forms of power offer themselves. The actor who had intended to dominate is dominated.

As the actor moves about a network (context), he/she absorbs powerful vectors which connect him/her with other vectors.

Situations Related to Edges

The actor abandons one context, one power source for another, opening himself/herself up to new vectors and to a new context which resembles nothing ever experienced or postulated before. For a time he/she faces chaos, vectors apparently out of control.

The actor faces/makes (or may be lured into) a journey without a goal through an uncharted context, perhaps without comrades. On returning, he/she discovers how radically the sense of time and distance, form and relationship, have been distorted so that a once familiar context has altered completely.

The actor explores an unknown structure (such as a vast palace) that seems to exist between normally identified contexts. Certain parts of the structure are closed, but he/she penetrates them anyway, defying many vectors, discovering what is both strange and familiar.

Under the pressure of strange vectors, the actor becomes another actor, or at least assumes another's guise. He/she can be at ease in this new context only by making fundamental changes in appearance or essential being.

Situations Related to Enchantment

The actor is dominated/overwhelmed by obscure power sources, but gaining control of them he/she is gifted with extraordinary vectors which *work* in the new context.

An actor disregards forceful negative vectors (interdictions) and suffers serious consequences.

By remaining awake an actor identifies the source of harm to a particular context.

The actor is trapped or immobilized and cannot reach out for power known to be present in the context: by sequentiality (the same vector over and over again), sexuality (vectors that invite self exposure in an act of total vulnerability), by sleep (ceasing to maintain conscious control of available vectors), by forgetfulness (unawareness of vectors and power sources in the environment), by diversion (vectors other than those appropriate to a context are dominant).

The actor regains control of his/her life and the ability to function in a context and project vectors into it.

Appendix One: Analysis of the Structure of Situations   213

The perceptive actor frees another from the dominance of numbing vectors.

Situations Related to Power

The actor is a person who (perhaps by virtue of special birth) has amassed numerous powerful vectors.

Each actor in a sequence is more powerful than the one who preceded him.

By exerting will and/or intelligence the actor alters his/her context, making available once again such vectors as clear perception, the ability to assess situations accurately, and determination.

The actor manipulates/taps into power sources existent in a context (such as a tablecloth or donkey, a bequest, or other actors with special skills), and is thereby able to project into it vectors that alter it in his/her favor. These vectors include the power of focusing and concentrating attention.

The actor escapes a dominant set.

The actor generates good luck by combining in unusual ways (or recognizing an existent combination of) power sources and vectors in a context.

The actor competes with other perhaps lesser actors for a power source of enormous worth—a princess, for example.

The actor loses something essential to a process.

The actor travels across a physical context, apparently unaided by vectors or power of any kind.

The actor carries out a difficult/seemingly impossible task despite the constraints imposed by a physical context with the aid of other helpful actors—animals, for example.

The actor makes moral decisions out of an awareness of forces rooted in another dimension of reality, sensing acutely the vectors connecting him/her with other spots in a network.

The actor makes himself/herself an instrument/agent of vectors that sustain/support the context in which he/she lives.

The actor opts to maintain the balance of vectors and power sources in his/her world, making sure that no elements dominate or are exploited.

The actor participates eagerly in the context, making full use of available power, projecting and receiving important vectors. To the situation he/she imparts a personal "twist."

The actor is granted and makes certain wishes, often wasting available vectors.

Situations Related to Moral Commitments

The kindly actor is aided by beneficent vectors in a physical context: they open up new power sources.

The actor makes wise choices, weighing all the vectors in a situation and estimating their significance in a given context.

A careless (uncommitted) actor dissipates available power.

The actor organizes and directs available vectors in support of other actors who are encountered, learning to exert self against threatening powers.

Because of an actor's cruelty (i.e., the negative vectors he/she has projected into his context), the power in this context erupts and destructive vectors are released.

An actor faces and survives the onslaught of highly threatening vectors ("fear").

A good actor is punished; a bad actor, rewarded; a particular context does not support moral commitments.

Situations Related to Identity

An actor seeks the owner of some object (like a lock of hair or a shoe)

Two actors are jealous of a third superior individual, whom they see as a rival, and seek, by threatening vectors, to remove him/her from their context.

An actor transforms his/ her form (though retaining the basic personality) and thus escapes some negative vector in context.

The actor has a dream in which his/her personal identity is affirmed by ancestors and/or associates. This individual is blessed by various positive vectors and learns of communal power.

The actor (often a third or youngest son) says, "I am . . . " thereby emerging from obscurity, putting himself or herself at the center of certain critical vectors, and establishing a new physical/psychological context which will embrace all those with whom he/she is associated.

The actor extracts an identity from bits and pieces of a context, assembles power sources, and collects the vectors that are characteristically his or hers.

The actor chooses and develops a role., i.e., a recognized, identifiable way of being an actor.

The actor engages in boasting, i.e., lays claim to power sources, threatens to project vectors into a context, that he/she may not actually control.

The actor opens himself/herself up to new experiences, admitting vectors not before acknowledged, tapping new power sources, exploring new contexts (a deserted castle, for example).

The actor wills to be himself/herself, despite threats from hostile vectors, no help from normal power sources, and an indifferent context.

The actor explores alternate states of consciousness, i.e., ways of being in a context, evoking vectors from deep within, normally unrecognized.

The actor dissolves into a context: vectors dissipate, power sources dry up.

One actor is substituted for another, to the confusion of a third, who is either unaware of what has happened or cannot sort out the vectors. Another actor makes the critical connections.

Situations Related to Knowing

An actor enters a situation without being seen to be there, sending out very weak vectors which (at first anyway) are not picked up by others.

The actor sees through a disguise, i.e., spots another actor beneath various distorting vectors, or tracks someone through several metamorphoses.

The actor communicates by the most delicate vectors, vectors that are virtually undetectable (a hint or a voice), and another actor, highly intuitive, picks them up.

The actor conceals something, trying to secure it from vectors projected hostilly.

The actor is suspicious, wondering what unidentified vectors have appeared in the physical context, what unexpected power-sources have been tapped, what threats are developing.

The actor dreams, thereby evoking vectors either from the personal subconscious or from outside the self.

The actor dances, evoking strong rhythmic vectors from a power source and projecting them out into the world.

The actor assembles vectors into scenarios and metaphors, constructing imaginary counter contexts which an opponent accepts because they seem familiar, but which contain various unexpected vectors.

Situations Related to Typical Problems of the Bright-Shadow World

The actor chooses, sorting out vectors (which possibly are not what they seem) from a context and deciding on those most pertinent to his/her needs. The actor's best guide may be internal vectors (intuition).

The actor discriminates between useful power sources and those of lesser value.

The actor makes deductions about a context and the powers it contains, on the basis of certain obscure vectors.

The actor sets up a guessing game (i.e., offers to another actor a confusing set of vectors) and provides clues.

The actor penetrates a guarded or secret place, finding a way through a context where power sources are unclear and vectors ambivalent or obscure, perhaps to make contact of the most subtle kind with some figure therein.

The actor is assaulted by a new set of perceptions.

The actor locates himself/herself in a context criss-crossed by a maximum number of vectors.

An actor entangles another actor in vectors of the latter's own making, even going outside a context in the search for exploitable power sources.

The actor manipulates numerous conflicting vectors darting between various actors.

The actor makes a point by creating out of some context a set of vectors which determine the response of his or her opponents.

The actor finds what has been lost by recreating the vectors and context in which the object was originally lost.

The actor conceals a difficult message (vector) in an innocent-looking context.

The actor tries to trap another actor in certain vectors; the intended victim escapes by insisting that the vectors be taken seriously, and at face value, or by involving a number of other actors in the situation.

The actor asks or answers riddles, creating confusing verbal vectors for an opponent or working through such vectors launched by another, or imposing his/her view of things on the riddler.

The actor, who knows a context well, tricks or deceives the naive and inexperienced, by turning their own vectors against them.

Situations Related to Stylishness

The actor appropriates power sources belonging to other actors and evades whatever hostile vectors they dart at him/her.

The actor confuses (to his or her own benefit) less quick-witted actors by the sheer volume and variety of conflicting vectors he/she launches at them.

The actor invents vectors and power sources out of materials found in a context.

The actor hides things in the contexts most obvious to searchers.

The actor moves easily about a context.

The actor consciously destroys the sets of vectors by which opponents deal with their contexts and constructs new sets of vectors.

Summary

The number of situations described in literature and/or occurring in life is so great as to defy meaningful classification. Even limiting our analysis to the four factors used here, we get a virtually infinite number of possible combinations. Nevertheless, this analysis enables us to see "what is going on" in any story we look at, and by contrasting analyses of various stories we can significantly clarify our sense of structures (what makes a story work) and our grasp of life-enhancing elements.

This analysis enables us to link stories (on the basis of structure) that may at first, because of details, appear unrelated, providing the basis for a significant taxonomy.

It enables us to distinguish between fairytales/folktales and myth/saga, which yield up quite different formulae.

The sparseness of the formula forces the highest degree of abstracting and thus the broadest possible application.

Appendix Two:
Assessment of
Life-Enhancing Themes

Related to Creating Alternate Worlds

The storyteller constructs a new world, according to his or her own specifications, revealing mastery of such techniques as abstracting, re-imaging, speculating, and inferring. The listener's imagination is awakened and he moves into that world, to some degree, for some period of time.

Listener and storyteller learn to move between and to some degree master various levels of reality.

Related to World-Reading

The listener develops improved techniques of perceiving and observing his/her context, learns how to balance action and receptivity, and nurtures an allocentric viewpoint.

. . . begins to form fresh new sets and taxonomies from material unnoticed before or thought to be exhausted.

. . . notes the networks in which he/she lives and becomes involved in the on-going process of modifying and being modified by these networks.

. . . becomes aware of anomalies inherent in experience and the possibility of exploiting these anomalies creatively, developing a sense of the structure of situations and thus some means of exploiting them.

Related to Edges

The listener is encouraged to navigate various transcontextual situations.

. . . avoids the various buffers that are erected between human beings and between the known and the unknown.

. . . learns to take positions between normally accepted realities, reaching out consciously for the undefined.

. . . learns to desire.

. . . identifies journeys he/she must take.

. . . renders himself/herself vulnerable.

. . . forms a new definition of reality out of material originally regarded as untenable.

. . . becomes another person or assumes another's roles.

. . . explores new experiences of time and space.

Related to Enchantment

The listener gains, regains, maintains control over his/her life by asserting the will; by escaping illusions, sleep, forgetfulness, fixations, and automatic responses; and by pulling together the various parts of his/her personality and focusing them sharply.

. . . achieves a sexual relationship based on such adult values as mutual respect and shared responsibility.

. . . helps others to escape enchantment.

. . . learns to move synchronically, deriving all that he/she can from a particular moment, and transcontextually, from context to context.

. . . seeks to assure that the personality is formed slowly, deliberately, and that it does not achieve final form too quickly.

Related to Power

The listener is encouraged to recognize the power inherent in the charismatic personality, a personality which seems to be the product of an individual's inexplicable abilities, needs, and the pressure of something often perceived to be a divine command.

. . . discovers the capacity to exert his/her will and to project it into difficult situations.

. . . identifies comrades, tools, and physical resources suited to the problem/situation which he faces.

. . . is alert to the demands of a particular situation and is able to turn whatever resources he or she has into some useful instrument.

. . . develops highly specialized, sharply focused intelligence or diffuse, wide-ranging intelligence.

. . . develops a capacity to use unprocessed data and to identify areas where concern will be productive.

. . . learns to generate luck.

. . . has something to trade or bargain with.

. . . makes himself/herself an instrument of "higher powers."

. . . makes productive wishes.

Related to Moral Commitments

The listener learns not to base his actions on the demands of a role but enters into situations as an existent human being.

. . . exercises restraint in what he/she takes from a network, leaving most for others.

. . . learns not to dedicate himself/herself primarily to self-interest, though self-interest is not excluded as a factor. The primary concern is to manipulate vectors encountered for the benefit of the network.

. . . responds to the needs of apparently weaker, dependent actors, recognizing that the system is also concerned about them. He/she discovers that the supposedly inferior contribute to the well-being of the strong.

. . . learns that there are ways to handle even the most negative vectors.

Related to Personal Identity

In a complex and often diffused physical context, one actor is either struck by or manages to assemble vectors sufficient to enable him or her to tap into available power sources and to start to "perform." He/she is recognized by others, recognizes himself/herself, and becomes a dominant figure. In the course of this process he/she may

. . . compare or contrast himself/herself to others (this means self criticism and self-encouragement).

. . . create a personal script and be prepared for it to unfold in unexpected ways.

. . . make significant choices and thus gain a sense of power over personal experience.

. . . pull together the scattered pieces of himself/herself as unexpected elements emerge or as new situations develop.

. . . maintain thematic continuity with the past.

. . . compete with and best rivals.

. . . learn to be a story-teller, thereby making a social contribution, enhancing his/her own confidence, and inspiring others.

. . . open himself/herself up to the unknown.

. . . will to be a person.

. . . realize the enormous potential of the human mind by experiencing different modes of consciousness.

. . . come to see himself/herself as a changing combination of diverse elements from many different sources with a very limited time for creative action.

Related to the Knowledge Question

The listener may develop new ways of knowing—intuition, dancing, increased psychic vigor, dreaming, scenario-building, the ability to read hints and gestures and other non-verbal responses.

. . . may learn to let the world speak in whatever way it chooses.

. . . may realize that the richness of possible messages may be more important than accurate determination of them—i.e., being wrong can be an important source of insight.

Related to Problem-Solving

The listener may want to develop his/her choosing (i.e., decision-making) capabilities.

. . . substitute subtle contact for various confrontive modes.

. . . escape from rigid sets so as to explore unthought possibilities.

. . . master motivational psychology and various ways of gaining control over others—not always, of course, a welcome prospect.

. . . learn to manage conflicts so that both sides gain something of value.

Related to Matters of Style

The listener may recognize that nimbleness of movement, wit, liveliness, alertness, and attentiveness are already life-habits.

. . . may identify chaos as a source of productive experience.

. . . may discover that as *bricoleur* he/she can gain freedom from many of the constraints imposed by overdevelopment.

. . . may realize that all kinds of traditional sets and categories are opening up to reveal new possibilities.

. . . come to see the role of style in conveying meaning.

Notes

Abbreviations Used:

CE   *College English*
CL   *Children's Literature*
GCQ *Gifted Child Quarterly*
IJP   *International Journal of Psychiatry*
IJSLP *International Journal of Slavic Linguistics and Poetics*
JCB *Journal of Creative Behavior*
JHP *Journal of Humanistic Psychology*
JPT *Journal of Psychology and Theology*
PQ   *Psychological Quarterly*
PR   *Psychological Review*
PT   *Psychology Today*
SA   *Scientific American*

Chapter 1

1. An eloquent critique of contemporary values is to be found in D. E. Denton, *The Language of Ordinary Experience* (New York: Philosophical Library, 1970), a study of particular importance since it is directed at educational problems. See especially ch. 1, where Denton describes the destruction of important human values by the present "sociological-nomothetic orientation." Henry Glassie finds the modern world too individualistic, too materialistic, too progressive. See *The Spirit of Folk Art* (New York: Abrams, 1989), 26. See also Alfred Schutz, "On Multiple Realities," in *Collected Papers* (The Hague: Nijoff, 1962), I, 230, on "our world," and Erving Goffman's comments on Schutz in *Frame Analysis* (New York: Harper and Row, 1974), 6n.

2. See Howard Gardner, "The Seven Frames of Mind," *PT* 18, no. 6 (1984): 20ff., who suggests ways of escaping narrow Western ideas of intelligence; also J. C. Gowan and M. Olson, "The Society Which Maximizes Creativity," *JCB* 13 (1979): 194ff.

3. Michael Metzgar, *Fairy Tales as Ways of Knowing* (Bern: P. Lang, 1981), 8.

4. *The Uses of Enchantment* (New York: Knopf, 1976). See Harold Bloom, *New York Review of Books*, 15 July 1976; Schutz has comments (I, 236) about Don Quixote's response to his own earlier interpretation of events that parallel my feelings about Bettelheim. And see also Ruth Bottigheimer, *Grimms' Bad Girls and Bold Boys* (New Haven: Yale University Press, 1987), 168. See also Betsy Hearne, *Beauty and the Beast* (Chicago: University of Chicago Press, 1989), 220–21, and Jack Zipes, *Breaking the Magic Spell* (New York: Methuen, 1984), 160–78—a savage attack.

5. "By telling his child fairy tales the parent can encourage him to borrow for his private use fantastic hopes for the future, without misleading him by suggesting that there is reality to such imaginings" (126, 47, 50–51). Patrick Huyghe takes an equally cautious approach in "Imaginary Friends" (*Omni*, July 1982, arguing that the normal child can "easily distinguish" between real and fantasy worlds. Perhaps he or she can; the question is whether it is always desirable to do so.

6. See a variety of articles in *Psychology Today:* E. Hall, "Nobody Lives in the Real World," July 1974, 60ff.; M. A. S. Pulaski, "The Rich Rewards of Make Believe," Jan. 1974, 68ff.; Joan T. Freyberg, "Increasing Children's Fantasies: Hold High the Cardboard Sword," Feb. 1975, 62ff.; Ravenna Helson, "Through the Pages of Children's Books," Nov. 1973, 107ff.; and J. L. Singer, "Fantasy: the Foundation of Serenity," July 1976, 32ff., on the dire consequences of an undeveloped fantasy life.

7. A number of aspects of postmodernism are relevant to this material. Jean-François Lyotard, *The Postmodern Condition: A Report on Knowledge* (Minneapolis: University of Minnesota Press, 1984) notes an incredulity about all myths, language games, and metanarratives by which humans have lived. There are comments in D. R. Griffin, *Varieties of Postmodern Theology* (Albany: State University of New York Press, 1989) on the disappearance of universally acceptable forms of legitimation; the impossibility of any group's now telling another group what is worth their attention; a sense that it is the role of art to destabilize reality and encourage diverse narratives; and a new concept of knowledge based on nonsensate perception. Griffin and Houston Smith, *Primordial Truth and Postmodern Theology* (Albany: State University of New York Press, 1989), stress the development of a sense of the sacredness of human creativity. Writers in Gary Shapiro,

After the Future (Albany: State University of New York Press, 1990), stress the rejection of periodization (xii); radical eclecticism (90); the rejection of the traditional categories for a highly diverse pluralism (273); the denial of a privileged position to anyone (283); a new understanding of the role of the reader in writing (29–30); and a realization that reality is a series of "so many diverse conjunctions" (86). In several places Griffin has made an important distinction between relativistic/nihilistic postmodernism and more constructive forms. See, for example, *Primordial Truth*, xii. Writing from an architectural point of view, Charles Jencks in *What is Post-modernism?* New York: St. Martin's, 1986) stresses the interplay of the serious and the parodic in postmodernism: it is, he says, to speak innocently and yet to be aware that one speaks innocently. Jencks's analysis brings to mind the clearly postmodern dilemma of a marching band at a highly sophisticated university that has a football team but does not put any great stock in the game. How does the band, through its attire, capture just the right mix of bemusement and enthusiasm? A similar dilemma attaches to fantasy. Note is also taken of similarities between postmodernism and the concept of Experientialism as described by George Lakoff in *Women, Fire, and Dangerous Things* (Chicago: University of Chicago Press, 1987). See xii and following pages.

8. See David Bakan, "Speculation in Psychology," *JHP* 15, no. 1 (1975): 17–25. For Tatar, *The Hard Facts of the Grimms' Fairy Tales* (Princeton: Princeton University Press, 1987), xv.

9. E. Gendlin, *Experiencing and the Creation of Meaning* (Glencoe, Ill.: Free Press, 1962), has helped me understand what was happening with his assertion that "preconceptual experiencing" (21) is a basic factor in the development of a sense of experience, important because it is very concrete, leaves much unfinished business, and creates thought patterns based on feelings and images rather than on words and concepts (27–28).

10. *Surprised by Joy* (New York: Harcourt Brace, 1955), 16–17.

11. "Bright-shadow world" is technically a mythoform, a "culturally specific system of processes chosen from among the mythologemically [archetypically] dynamic processes of the consciousness' execution of acts and things." (R. P. Armstrong, *The Powers of Presence* [Philadelphia: University of Pennsylvania Press, 1981], 60). Although Shelley's use of the term has idealizing implications, in Lewis the phrase suggests so much that is strange to us that it is relatively free from metanarrative implications. *Omni* (Oct. 1981,

133ff.) published a Mobius Psi-Q Test, implicit in which is a description of the bright-shadow type, and (Oct. 1982) a parallel test on the capacity for "remote viewing." See June 1988, 65ff., for an article by Jessica Maxwell on fantasy-prone individuals.

12. See *Steps to an Ecology of Mind* (New York: Ballantine, 1972) and *Mind and Nature* (New York: Bantam, 1980, 127ff). Bateson links transcontextuality to the experience of the "double bind," where conflicting demands upon a person are made by opposing forces. "We are talking," he says, "about some sort of tangle in the rules for making . . . transforms and about the acquisition or cultivation of such tangles" (*Steps*, 272).

13. *Final Integration in the Adult Personality* (Leiden: Brill, 1964), 113. See also S. Krippner, "The Creative Person and Non-ordinary Reality," *GCQ* 19 (1972): 203–28.

14. *Against Method, Outline of an Anarchistic Theory of Knowledge* (London: NLB, 1975), 32.

15. C. Clausen, "Home and Away in Children's Fiction," *CL* 10 (1982): 141ff. discusses why children do or do not accept certain books; see also Brian Attebery, "*The Beginning Place*: LeGuin's Metafantasy," *CL* 10 (1982): 113ff., on the sense in which fantasy is true and on ties between fantasy and real-world experiences. Hearne quotes Margurite Loeffler-Delachaux: "The absence of archetypes or 'ancestral images' exposes with absolute clarity the false tale or the story invented by those naive writers who believe they can substitute their own imagination for the products of the universal psyche" (*Beauty and the Beast*, 19).

16. *Fairy Tales and After* was published in 1978 by Harvard University Press. For Davies, *The Manticore* (New York: Penguin, 1976), 63.

17. Erik Erikson, *Gandhi's Truth on the Origins of Militant Nonviolence* (New York: Norton, 1969), 120.

18. Jalal ad-Din Rumi, *The Mathnawi*, 3 vols., trans R. A. Nicholson (London: Luzac, 1977), I, 366.

19. *Phantastes: A Faerie Romance* (Grand Rapids, Mich.: Eerdmans, 1981), x.

20. *At the Back of the North Wind* (Ann Arbor: University Microfilms, 1966), 113.

21. See Griffin, *Varieties*, 14, on the importance of typifications, and Shapiro, *After the Future*, 89–90, on the importance of diversity.

Note is taken of the observation of Maria Tatar that various national versions of the same familiar story may "come out" quite differently (Ruth Bottigheimer, *Fairy Tales and Society* [Philadelphia: University of Pennsylvania Press, 1986], 110.).

Chapter 2

1. S. V. Propp, *Morphology of the Folktale*, trans. Laurence Scott (Austin: University of Texas Press, 1968).

2. Claude Lévi-Strauss, "L'Analyse Morphologique des Contes Russes," *IJSLP* 3 (1960): 122–49. No more useful than Propp's instrument is Marie-Louise von Franz's attempt to impose a quadripartite structure ("quaternion") on fairytales. See *Individuation in Fairytales* (Zurich: Spring, 1977), 21, for example.

3. Goffman offers a rich array of actors that reflect the importance of the con-artist in our society. Other social settings produce other dominant types of actors. See *Frame Analysis*, 28, 223, 130, and passim.

4. *German Folk Tales*, trans. F. P. Magoun and A. H. Krappe (Carbondale: Southern Illinois University Press, 1960), 174.

5. See M. Esther Harding, *Psychic Energy* (Princeton: Princeton University Press, 1963), 52; Schutz, *Collected Works*, I. 212; and Carole Douglas, "The Beat Goes On," *PT*, Nov. 1987, 36ff., on the various social rhythms that underlie speech and action. A splendid use of vectors can be found in the Fortuna-North chapter of Grass's *The Tin Drum* (New York: Vintage, 1964), when Oscar stands beneath high-tension lines carrying current all over Europe. Lakoff offers many examples of types of movement; see, for example, his analysis of "over" (416–61).

6. See Merleau-Ponty, *Phenomenology of Perception* (New York: Humanities Press, 1962), 145–46, 100–109; chap. 2; also ch. 2 of part 2, esp. 243ff. See also Johnston's discussion of points of resistance in Shapiro, *After the Future*, 69.

7. On Dilthey's analysis of experience, see V. W. Turner and E. M. Bruner, *The Anthropology of Experience* (Urbana: University of Illinois Press, 1986), 4ff.

8. Bottigheimer, *Grimms' Bad Girls and Bold Boys*, 35, 167.

Chapter 3

1. Carlos Castaneda, *Tales of Power* (New York: Pocket Books, 1974), 173.

2. John Dewey, *Experience and Nature* (Lasalle, Ill.: Open Court Press, 1958), 10.

3. Morton Deutsch and Robert M. Krauss, *Theories in Social Psychology* (New York: Basic Books, 1965), 30.

4. *The Psychology of Interpersonal Relations* (New York: Wiley, 1958), 70.

5. For Foucault, see *The Order of Things* (New York: Pantheon, 1970), ix; for Feyerabend, *Against Method,* 160; for de Groot, "Heuristics, Mental Programs, and Intelligence," in *Methods of Heuristics,* ed. R. and M. Groner and W. F. Bischof (Hillside, N.J.: Lawrence Erlbaum and Associates, 1983), 109–29.

6. *The Intentional Stance* (Cambridge: MIT Press, 1987), 48–49.

7. See Peter McHugh, *Defining the Situation* (Indianapolis: Bobbs-Merrill, 1968), for an account of the chief topics of world-reading—discovery of a theme, elaboration of the theme, taking responsibility for the process, discovering topicality and substantive congruency, etc. Schutz discusses the world of daily life, "the intersubjective world which existed long before our birth, experienced and interpreted by Others, our predecessors, as an original world" (I, 208) that modifies our actions and which we modify. Merleu-Ponty observes that "sense experience is that vital communication with the world which makes it present as a familiar setting of our life" (*Phenomenology,* 52). David Griffin's concept of *"soft-core commonsense notions"* is relevant (*Varieties of Postmodern Theology,* 33). See also Armstrong, *The Powers of Presence,* 13, on syndesis, "the basic process of apprehending and constructing the world."

8. See James Kritzeck, *Anthology of Islamic Literature* (New York: NAL, 1964), 93.

9. *Old Deccan Days* (London: John Murray, 1898), 50–59. This version bears only the most distant relationship to standard versions of the *Ramayana.*

10. See R. D. Gaymer, "You are a Camera . . . Some Aspects of Observation," *JCB* 19 (1985): 67ff., for suggestions about improving observational skills.

11. See T. B. Allen, "The Ultimate Party Line," *Smithsonian*, Sept. 1988, 82ff; also Barbara Rowes, "Techno-Kids," *Omni*, May 1983, 94ff.

12. Shah, *Tales of the Dervishes* (New York: Dutton, 1967), 51, 43, 140, 162, 127, 185.

13. *The Book of the Thousand Nights and a Night*, trans. Richard Burton, I, 189. References are to the undated edition published by the Burton Club in ten volumes and seven supplementary volumes.

14. See K. M. Briggs, *The Personnel of Fairyland* (Cambridge, Mass.: R. Bentley, 1955), esp. "A Dictionary of Fairies," 189ff.

15. See the forward by Andrea Rugh to Nayra Atiya, *Khul-Khaal, Five Egyptian Women Tell Their Stories* (Syracuse: Syracuse University Press, 1982). Also, E. M. Bruner, "Storytellers . . . shape and reshape their own lives and their culture as they tell and retell stories," "Introduction," in Turner and Bruner, *Anthropology*, 27.

16. *Jataka or Stories of the Buddha's Former Birth*, ed. E. B. Crowell, 3 vols. (London, 1895), I, 68, 93, 136, 219.

17. F. R. Kreutzwald, *Ehstnische Märchen* (Halle, 1869), 333, and June Singer, *Boundaries of the Soul: The Practice of Jung's Psychology* (New York: Doubleday, 1972), 142, a case study of a young man who came to similar terms with self and world.

18. J. B. Van Buitenen, *Tales of Ancient India* (University of Chicago Press, 1959), 113.

19. Stephen Toulmin, "The Recovery of Practical Philosophy," *American Scholar* 57 (1988): 337ff., raises a question about what philosophy has chosen to neglect at its various stages. See also Merleau-Ponty, *Phenomenology*, 56, on the breakdown of a traditional universe of thought and value, and Adam Smith, *Powers of Mind* (New York: Random House, 1975), 169, on learning to change models.

20. K. M. Briggs, *The Fairies in English Traditions and Literature* (Chicago: University of Chicago Press, 1967), 131.

21. Important critiques of naive psychology are to be found in C. W. Offir, "Floundering in Fallacy: Seven Quick Ways to Kid Yourself," (*PT*, April 1975, 66ff.); Cheris Kramer, "Folk-Linguistics: Wishy-Washy Mommy Talk" (*PT*, June 1974, 82ff.); and Alfie Kohn, "You Know What They Say . . . " (*PT*, April 1988, 36ff.), on the validity of certain familiar proverbs. For a discussion of the scepticism of world-readers themselves, see Iona and Peter Opie, *The Lore and Language of Schoolchildren* (London: Oxford University Press, 1959), ch. 11.

Chapter 4

1. Bateson, *Mind and Nature*, 55–56, and see George A. Miller, "The Magical Number Seven, Plus or Minus 2," in *PR* 63, no. 2 (1956): 81–97.

2. Gestaltists are interested in this phenomenon; see Deutsch and Krauss, *Theories*, 5, 16, 21–22, on how things are grouped.

3. See Axel Orlik, "Epic Laws of Folk Narrative," reprinted in Alan Dundes, *The Study of Folklore* (Englewood Cliffs, N.J.: Prentice-Hall, 1965), 133. The extreme dogmatism of Orlik's position has raised many eyebrows. A more temperate position is taken by Roger Sale, *Fairy Tales and After*, 43. On the traditional importance of three, see also Rudolf Arnheim, *Visual Thinking* (London: Faber and Faber, 1969), 211. Two is minimum, four is redundant, says Arnheim. Three evades contrast and suggests intertwining. And the great Indo-European mythologist Georges Dumézil found a tripartite social structure to be a basic element in cultures stretching from India to Ireland—the priest, the soldier, the farmer. See C. Scott Littleton, *The New Comparative Mythology*, 3d ed. (Berkeley: University of California Press, 1982).

4. Heider, *Psychology of Interpersonal Relations*, discusses the interplay of assimilation and contrast in grouping (182); see also Denton, *Language*, ch. 2.

5. *The Elementary Forms of the Religious Life* (London: Allen and Unwin), 142, 356. The relationship of some fairytales to myth is supported by the presence in the former of motifs (significance largely forgotten) from the latter: kinship with animals, taboos or interdictions, power, and of course correspondences.

6. John G. Neihardt, *Black Elk Speaks* (Lincoln: University of Nebraska Press, 1979), 169. See also R. F. Sayre, "Vision and Experience in *Black Elk Speaks*," *CE* 32, no. 5 (1971): 533ff.

7. *The Science of Fairy Tales* (London: 1891), 29–30. See Hosea 4:1–3 for an example of the concurrent collapse of spiritual, social, and natural *shalom* (well-being), a passage that lends biblical authority to the concept.

8. *Jataka* VI, 166–67, only one of several stunning cases. Montaigne observes that nothing is exactly like anything else: experts on eggs, for example, or playing cards, can observe distinctions that no untrained eye would ever see. See *Complete Works*, ed. D. Frame (Palo Alto: Stanford University Press, 1948), esp. "Of the Inconsistency of our Actions," 243, and "Of Experience," 815.

9. *Hitopodesa*, trans. Charles Wilkins (London, 1888); see 23.

10. *Tales of the Dervishes*, 191.

11. *Kalilah and Dimnah*, trans. Keith-Falconer (Cambridge: Cambridge University Press, 1885), 208 ff. In *Shadow and Evil in Fairy Tales* von Franz is particularly good on the dilemma of choosing between acting and not acting (Irving, Tex.: Spring Books, 1980), 119.

12. *Tuti-Nama: Tales of Parrot*, trans. M. A. Simsar (Cleveland: Cleveland Museum of Art, 1978), 291 ff.

13. Discussions of the now famous Prisoner's Dilemma problem are relevant here. See, among other sources, P. Watzlawick, *How Real is Real?* (New York: Vintage, 1976, 98ff.) and R. Frank, *Passions within Reason* (New York: Norton, 1988, 29–31 and passim).

14. Qur'an XII. In the Dawood translation, "Above those that have knowledge there is One more Knowing."

15. Assagioli, *The Act of Will* (New York: Viking, 1973), 157–59. An important element in the I-Ching world is KUN, the receptor, and in Pueblo (American Indian) thought, passivity is embodied in the concept of the Kiva. See Frank Waters, *The Man Who Killed the Deer* (New York: Pocket Books, 1971 [1942], passim.

16. Shah, *Tales of the Dervishes*, 13. A similar story appears in *Kalilah and Dimnah*, making a point about procrastinating.

17. *Egyptian and Sudanese Folk-tales*, ed. Helen Mitchnik (Oxford: Oxford University Press, 1978), 31–37. There is a version in Grimm, "The Turnip," 508.

18. Lüthi, *Once Upon a Time*, trans. Lee Chadeayne and Paul Gottwald (Bloomington: Indiana University Press, 1976), 53. Arnheim notes (*Visual Thinking*, 212) that among children "the exact quantity of elements" may be irrelevant.

19. *The Possible Human* (Los Angeles: J. P. Tarcher, 1982), 135.

20. *Donegal Fairy Stories* (Dover), 22; Italo Calvino, *Italian Folktales*, trans. G. Martin (New York: Pantheon, 1980), 114.

21. Amina Shah, *Arabian Fairy Tales* (London: Frederick Muller, 1969), 76ff., and *Tuti-Nama*, 256. There are opposing tales about someone who skillfully nurses something insignificant into great wealth. See *Jataka*, I, 19, about a merchant who constructs a fortune out of the corpse of a dead mouse.

22. *Indian Fairy Tales* (Dover), 105, and see the story of Baarlam and Josaphat (Loeb, 137) on the too-quick forgetting of advice from a nightingale.

23. Reinhold Niebuhr, *The Irony of American History* (New York: Charles Scribner's Sons, 1952), viii.

24. See, for example, "The Twelve Wild Ducks," in Dasent's *East o' the Sun and West o' the Moon* (Dover), 59.

25. *Illuminations*, trans. H. Zohn, New York: Harcourt Brace & World, 1968), 102.

26. Jules Brun and Leo Bachelin, *Sept Contes Roumains* (Paris, 1894), 312.

27. Stochastic sequences (sequences with a random component) are discussed by Bateson in *Mind and Nature*, 51, 163ff., and see Rob Stanish, "The Underlying Structure and Thoughts about Randomness and Creativity," *JCB* 20 (1986): 110–14).

28. Ursula le Guin, *The Left Hand of Darkness* (New York: Ace, 1969), 259–60.

Chapter 5

1. See Lakoff on fuzzy sets, where clearly defined categories begin to blend (*Women, Fire, and Dangerous Things*, 15, 21, 26, etc.). Also Victor Turner on marginal individuals, *Revelation and Divination in Ndembu Ritual* (Ithaca: Cornell University Press, 1975) and *Dreams, Fields, and Metaphors* (Ithaca: Cornell University Press, 1974).

2. See Rosemary Jackson, who paraphrases Todorov: "The purely fantastic text establishes absolute hesitation in protagonist and reader: they can neither come to terms with the unfamiliar events described nor dismiss them as supernatural phenomena. Anxiety then . . . is incorporated into the *structure* of the work to become its defining element" (*Fantasy: the Literature of Subversion* [New York: Methuen, 1981], 27–28); see also Todorov, *The Fantastic* (Ithaca: Cornell University Press, 1975), 30–33).

3. George Yúdice, "Marginality and the Ethics of Survival," in Andrew Ross, *Universal Abandon: the Politics of Postmodernism* (Minneapolis: University of Minnesota Press, 1988), 214–36.

4. See Judith Hooper, "Connoisseurs of Chaos," *Omni*, June 1983, 85ff., for an examination of academic interest in anomalies and

randomness, and James Glieck, *Chaos: Making a New Science* (New York: Viking, 1987). Also relevant is Geoffrey G. Harpham, *On the Grotesque* (Princeton: Princeton University Press, 1982), 14ff., on another kind of distinctiveness.

5. See D. W. Winnicutt, *Playing and Reality* (New York: Basic Books, 1971), xiii. See also Simon Grolnick's discussion of Winnicutt's theory of transitional phenomena in Bottigheimer, *Fairy Tales and Society*, 209–13.

6. *Ocean of the Streams of Story*, trans. C. H. Tawney (Delhi, 1880–1968), I, 195.

7. Cf. *Mathnawi* I, 269: "Hundreds of thousands of hidden (spiritual) kings are holding their heads high (in the region) beyond this world." And see Henri Corbin, *The Man of Light in Iranian Sufism* (Boulder: Shambala, 1978), ch. 2, "The Man of Light and His Guide." Black Elk is recognized as a "man of light" when he recovers from his trancelike state after his great visions. As a companion observes, "Just as I came in I could see a power like a light all through his body" (49). I like Stephen La Berge's term *oneironauts*, "dream-voyagers." See *Lucid Dreaming* (New York: Ballantine, 1985), 82.

8. This is the problem in the very old story of the king's son who wanders off into the world and forgets his true home. See Acts of Thomas, *The Apochryphal New Testament*, ed. M. R. James (Oxford: Clarendon Press, 1924), 411–15, and *The King's Son*, ed. by Robert Cecil et al. (London: Octagon Press, 1981), 3–4, 5–7, and Robert DeRopp, *The Master Game* (New York: Dell, 1968), 49ff.

9. *The Poems of Emily Dickinson*, ed. M. D. Bianchi and A. L. Hampson (Boston: Little Brown, 1944).

10. *Heaven and Hell, The Doors of Perception* (New York: Harper and Row, 1963), 33.

11. See, among many possible sources for Indian mythology, Veronica Ions, *Indian Mythology* (London: Paul Hamlyn, 1967), 51, and Benjamin Walker, *The Hindu World* (New York: Praeger, 1968), I, 432.

12. *The Tibetan Book of the Dead*, comp. and ed. W. Y. Evans-Wentz (London: Oxford University Press, 1960), 109.

13. P. W. Martin, *Experiment in Depth* (Boston: RKP, 1976), 140.

14. *English Fairy Tales* (Dover), 121.

15. Afanas'ev, *Russian Fairy Tales* (New York: Pantheon, 1945), 254. This is a translation of the text that provided the material for

Propp. See also Calvino, 263, and Hasan M. El-Shamy, *Folktales of Egypt* (Chicago: University of Chicago Press, 1980), 26. For Agamemnon, see Robert Graves, *The Greek Myths*, II, 55. For the Welsh material see the *Mabinogi*, trans. and ed. by P. K. Ford (Berkeley: University of California Press, 1977), 105–6.

16. *Jataka* I, 155. This motif bears a striking similarity to the incident in Bedier, *Tristan and Iseult*, when Iseult stations Tristan (disguised as a pilgrim) near her and after he carries her across a stream swears that she has been in no man's arms but his and her husband's.

17. *Tales of Power*, 185; *Briefing for a Descent into Hell* (New York: Bantam, 1972), 158; *At the Back of the North Wind*, 122; Shapiro, *After the Future*, 24, 108.

18. *Roumanian Fairy Tales*, collected by Mite Kremnitz, adapted by J. M. Percival (New York: 1885), 191–243.

19. A version of the Vishnu/Hiranyakasipu story; the Knight of the Dawn has the capacity of a Vishnu to place himself in the cracks between identifiable realities and the ability of a Saktideva to pursue his path unswervingly, no matter what barriers face him.

20. Dasent, *East o' the Sun, West o' the Moon* (Dover), 31.

21. On the theme of Krishna's mouth, see Wendy O'Flaherty, *Dreams, Illusion, and Other Realities* (Chicago: University of Chicago Press, 1984), 113, and for her comments on Lewis's use of this motif, 242. See also Susan Stewart, *On Longing* (Baltimore: Johns Hopkins University Press, 1984), Chapter 2, "The Miniature."

22. See Arthur Clarke, *Profiles of the Future* (New York: Harper and Row, 1958), ch. 9, "You Can't Get There from Here," an examination of the problem of dealing with the enormous pressures encountered as the center of the earth is approached. Clarke raises questions about the nature of impossibility and considers what it means to go deep within.

23. See the neat device in *Gilgamesh* of baking a fresh loaf of bread every day so that by observing how stale some of his bread has become the sleeper can gauge how long he has slept (Penguin, 114).

24. This famous story is retold in Surah XVII ("The Cave") of the Qur'an and is also to be found in Voraigne's *The Golden Legend*. See Hartland, *The Science of Fairy Tales*, chs. 7 and 8.

Chapter 6

1. See Rollo May, "The Problem of Evil: An Open Letter to Carl Rogers," *JHP* 22, no. 3 (1982): 10–21, asserting the continuing presence of the demonic in our world, and Rogers' reply, *JHP* 22, no. 4 (1982): 85ff. Tatar's *Hard Facts* is a survey of the various kinds of harshness encountered in the Grimm Brothers—physical violence, family problems, the oppression of women, etc.

2. See C. G. Jung, *Two Essays on Analytic Psychology,* Bollingen Series 20, (New York: Pantheon, 1953), 150–51, 236.

3. *Shadow and Evil in Fairytales,* 122, 144–46, 182.

4. The title of the German translation of Bettelheim's book, *Kinder Brauchen Märchen* (Stuttgart, 1977), avoids the ambivalence of the English title (*Children Need Fairy Tales*).

5. Karen Horney, *Neurosis and Human Growth* (New York: Norton, 1950), 87; Albert Schweitzer, *Out of My Life and Thought* (New York: Holt, 1949), 245.

6. Paul Goodman, in "The Aged Knight," in *Adam and His Works* (New York: Random House, 1968), deals with relatively normal people who have ceased to function effectively because of various "hangups" (itself modern slang for "enchantment"), such as problems of sexual frustration or being lost in an overly theoretical world.

7. Harding, *Psychic Energy,* 208; Gurdjieff's *Tales of Beelzebub,* that enormous and largely unreadable three-volume novel, touches frequently on the tendency of humans to be trapped by mechanical processes. And cf. Jean Houston on "nebbish": "If I tried it wouldn't happen, and if it happened it would cost too much. . . . Nobody really wants me, it's just that I'm the only one around. . . . Don't look back on your life. It's too sad. Don't look forward. It's too horrible. You could die at any minute. Just stay in the now where nothing ever happens anyway" (*The Possible Human,* 116).

8. Penguin *Odyssey,* 194.

9. See von Franz, *An Interpretation of Apuleius' Golden Ass* (Irving, Tex.: University of Dallas, 1980), 49–50, 84.

10. O'Flaherty, 161. Similar figures appear in the *Jataka* tales as she-goblins (II, 89) and ogresses (I, 233–34), confirming the importance of the sexuality-as-enchantment theme, which goes back at least to Circe.

11. Paul Pruyser, *A Dynamic Psychology of Religion* (New York: Harper and Row, 1968), 198.

12. Ibn Tufayl, *Hayy Ibn Yaqzun*, ed. Lenn Goodman (New York: Twayne, 1972).

13. See Harding, *Psychic Energy*, 7. Much the same point about sleep is made by Doris Lessing in *Briefing for a Descent into Hell*, the central figure of which is Charles Watkins, a Cambridge classicist who has grown cynical about his profession and forgotten that in the divine scheme of things he is a messenger from the gods, one of those sent from time to time to straighten out the world, only to have been subjected, as all infants are, to parental efforts to keep him quiet, always asleep. See also Arasteh, *Final Integration*, 180, Martin, *Experiment in Depth*, 35, and Schutz, 212.

14. Lefftz/Lemmer, *Grimms Märchen in Ursprunglicher Gestalt*, 33.

15. John M. Ellis, *One Fairy Story Too Many* (Chicago: University of Chicago Press, 1983), 152. This is Ellis's translation. Ellis's position has not gone entirely unchallenged. See, for example, comments by Tatar (114) and Zipes (273) in Bottigheimer, *Fairy Tales and Society*. In *Hard Facts* Tatar offers an extended discussion of the development of the Grimm Brothers' project. She argues that Ellis's problem is that he limits too strictly his view of folklore to "peasant culture" (24). See 28–32 for what she believes to be the heart of the issue.

16. Besides the versions already cited, see also *Yugoslav Folktales*, XI, ed. Nada Curcija-Prodanovic (London: Oxford University Press, 1957); Calvino, 92; Basile, *Il Pentamerone*, trans. R. Burton, New York: Boni and Liveright, 1927), ninth story of fifth day; and *Old Deccan Days*, 63. Perhaps the oldest version is the story of Sigurd's release of Brunhilde. See Lüthi's moving analysis, 22–34.

17. See "The Enchanted Deer," *Lilac Fairy Book*, 156. I draw no folkloric conclusions from the Lang texts here, using his versions solely as accounts of certain patterns by which human experience is (or has been imagined to be) structured.

18. Magoun and Krappe, 272; for the Swahili tale, Steere, *Swahili Tales* (London, 1870), 239.

19. Robert deRopp, *The Master Game*, 49. Reference has already been made to Robert Cecil's collection of related materials. For the Gnostic interpretation, see R. M. Wilson, *Gnosis in the New Testament* (Oxford: Blackwell, 1968), 19.

20. See Dörner's "Heuristics and Cognition in Complex Systems," in *Methods of Heuristics,* 100–101.

21. A well-known literary rendering is by Walter Pater, in *Marius the Epicurean,* and there is a superb contemporary retelling by C. S. Lewis, *Till We Have Faces* (1956). "Beauty and the Beast," with all its progeny, is the fairytale version. Useful psychological studies are by von Franz, *Golden Ass,* chs. 5–7; Erich Neumann, *Psyche and Eros* (1956), and Robert Johnson, *She: Understanding Feminine Psychology* (New York: Harper and Row, 1977). See also "The King's Hares" in Stith Thompson, *One Hundred Favorite Folktales,* (Bloomington: Indiana University Press, 1974), 258ff. Gathering and sorting, collecting and dispersing, consolidating and scattering are seen as fundamental dichotomies.

22. There are many versions of the golden bird story: *1001,* IX, 304ff.; I, 32; Grimm, 211, "The Gold Bird"; 356, "The Water of Life"; Calvino, 207, "The Sleeping Queen"; "The Black Horse," *More Celtic Tales* (Dover), 57. See also "The Farmer's Son, the Prince, and the Sister of the Sun," in *Lapplandische Märchen,* ed. J. C. Poestion (Vienna, 1886), 223; and "L'oeil qui pleure et l'oeil qui Rit," in Louis Leger, *Recueil de Contes Popularies Slaves* (Paris, 1882), and Stith Thompson, *One Hundred Favorite Folktales,* 231.

23. I have been told that the so-called "whirling dervishes," whose turning is actually far more sedate than a whirl, do not experience dizziness because they keep their attention centered within, paying no heed to the world that is passing around them.

24. Philip Glazebrook, *Journey to Kars* (New York: Atheneum, 1984), 106–7, discusses the fears that many travelers into difficult regions have felt—symptomatic of which is the anxiety about where in some remote region one will sleep and how one will get out after one has arrived. M. Konner, *The Tangled Wing* (New York: Holt, Rinehart, Winston, 1982), 208, relates fear to the exploratory drive; the desire to respond to challenge may override it. See also D. O. Hebb's classic article, "On the Nature of Fear," *PR* 53, no. 5 (1946): 259–76.

25. *Ocean of the Streams of Story,* I, 132. See also "A Lac of Rupees for a Bit of Advice," *Indian Fairy Tales,* 109–10; in Apuleius someone is ordered to guard a corpse all night with only an oil lamp for comfort (Loeb, 87). See also "The Sultan and the Four Strange Brothers-in-Law," Amina Shah, 1–12), and von Franz, *Golden Ass,* 35.

26. Calvino, *Italian Folktales,* 133, 177; Castaneda, *Tales of Power,* 185–86, 223; Giles, *Strange Stories from a Chinese Studio* (Dover), 16, 30.

Joseph Needleman finds theological significance in the motif: persisting in one's effort to find an answer to the great question, despite all temptation to cover it over or otherwise evade it (*Lost Christianity* [New York: Harper and Row, 1980], 167–171).

27. *Sometimes a Great Notion* (New York: Penguin), 322.

28. Note, on this matter, the human ability to apply steady pressure with the muscles and the capacity to command them to engage in quick, repeated, involuntary movement—reflexive rhythmia. What is striking about the latter process is that it is initiated and terminated voluntarily but becomes involuntary while it is going on.

29. *Individuation*, 116–17.

30. Wallace Shawn and André Gregory (New York: Grove, 1981), 74.

31. *Arabian Fairy Tales*, 137ff.

32. Two especially vivid accounts of ultimate escape from the bonds of enchantment are to be found at the end of Bunyan's *Pilgrim's Progress*, part 1, when Christian and Hopeful are conducted into the City by "the Shining Ones," and at the end of C. S. Lewis's *Great Divorce*, when the ghost consents to have the lizard on its back crushed by the Angel. Out of these two deaths the lizard emerges as a magnificent golden Horse, and the ghost as a glorious new-made man (New York: Macmillan, 1946), 101-3.

Chapter 7

1. De Groot, "Heuristics, Mental Programs, and Intelligence," in Groner, Groner, & Bischoff, *Methods of Heuristics*, 122; D. Dörner, "Heuristics and Cognition in Complex Systems, ibid., 102–3.

2. *The Roots of Coincidence* (New York: Random House, 1972), 85. The emphasis of the popular tale on lucky discovery of great power or wealth is more difficult for us to accept than the examples Koestler offers, though through technology such wealth and power become possible, but not usually instantaneously.

3. See "On Synchronocity," in *The Structure and Dynamics of the Psyche*, Bollingen Series 20, (New York: Pantheon, 1960), 423–25, 440–42.

4. *A General Theory of Magic* (London: RKP, 1972), 141.

5. There are many stories about rings that build palaces. See Afanas'ev, *Russian Fairy Tales*, 31; Basile, *Pentamerone*, 288, and *Indian Fairy Tales*, 93. Burton has a note on the history of rings (*1001*, Suppl. III, 72), and Clouston finds "The Ring and Fisherman" Talmudic in origin (*Popular Tales and Fictions*, London, 1887, I, 382.)

6. Frederic Macler, *Contes, Légendes et Épopées Populaires d'Arménie* (Paris, 1928), 89.

7. Leo Frobenius, *African Genesis* (New York: Stackpole, 1937), 97, 110.

8. Harding, *Psychic Energy*, 342. J. F. T. Bugental, "The Far Side of Despair," *JHP* 20, no. 1 (1980): 49–68, identifies spirit as "the dynamic principle which moves our impulses from their germination in intentionality toward realization" (56). Progoff puts the issue in Jungian terms: power results from "an harmonious complementation, a reciprocal balancing, in which the archetypes supply the basic psychic contents and set the direction while the ego and consciousness channelize, clarify, and guide the process as a whole to assist in actualizing the aims that the psyche unconsciously contains" (*Jung, Synchronicity, and Human Destiny* [New York: Julian, 1973], 91).

9. *Will Therapy*, trans. Jessie Taft (New York: Knopf, 1964), 221.

10. See also ch. 11 of Rollo May's *Love and Will* (New York: Norton, 1969) and Thelma Leaffer, "Wishing, a Universal Phenomenon," *JCB* 15 (1981): 36ff. I note the skill with which bright people advance themselves by creating desires. Sindbad, in his fourth voyage (*1001*, V, 39), visits a land where richly dressed people ride horses without saddles. He makes saddles for everyone and amasses great wealth.

11. *The Act of Will*, 70; M. E. P. Seligman, "Fall Into Helplessness," *PT*, June 1973, 43ff.; Harding, *Psychic Energy*, 38, on situations where requisite energy is lacking; and Goodman, *Five Years, Thoughts During a Useless Time* (New York: Vintage, 1966).

12. Basile, *Pentamerone*, 29.

13. See von Franz's very full analysis in *Individuation in Fairy Tales*, 1–58; see also "The Boy Who Had a Moon on his Forehead and a Star on his Chin," *Indian Fairy Tales*, 156; "The Promises of the Three Sisters," El-Shamy, 63; *Jataka* V, 230; and "The Twins with the Golden Star," *Roumanian Fairy Tales*, 30–41.

14. Cf. "The Rat's Wedding," in *Wide-Awake Stories*, ed. F. A. Steele and R. C. Temple (Bombay, 1884). This charming tale suggests

that we can control a great deal through the interpretation we put on affairs, but not everything. For a pipkin, a rat finds himself the owner of a buffalo. But unable to manage the beast, he goes where it wants to go and eventually gains possession of an abandoned bride—abandoned by men who kill and eat his animal. The bride's mother nearly fries him for supper, and he decides that he is playing out of his league.

15. See *The Bridge Between Matter and Spirit is Matter Becoming Spirit* (Garden City: Anchor Books, 1973), esp. ch. 44, "Life Is in the Thick of Things."

16. See Mary Caroline Richards, *Centering in Pottery, Poetry, and the Person* (New York: Columbia University Press, 1969), and Schachtel, *Metamorphosis* (New York: Basic Books, 1959), ch. 11, "The Development of Focal Attention."

17. *The Crack in the Cosmic Egg* (New York: Julian, 1971), 169. See also Neil Friedman, "On Focusing," *JHP* 26, no. 1 (1986): 103–16; Tom Treabasso, "Pay Attention," *PT*, Oct. 1968, 31–36, and Edward de-Bono, *The Mechanism of Mind* (New York: Viking, 1971), 88ff.

Chapter 8

1. Georg H. von Wright, *The Varieties of Goodness* (London: RKP, 1963), chs. 1 and 7.

2. References are to Lawrence Kohlberg, *The Philosophy of Moral Development* (New York: Harper and Row, 1981).

3. Significant challenges to current morality are to be found in M. E. P. Seligman, "Boomer Blues," *PT*, Oct. 1988, 50ff (on the by-products of "rampant individualism without commitment to the common good") and Alfie Kohn, "Beyond Selfishness," *PT*, Oct. 1988, 34ff. (caring for others is a deeply ingrained part of human nature).

4. See Berman, *The Reenchantment of the World* (Ithaca: Cornell University Press, 1981), 136ff.

5. "Faithful John," Magoun and Krappe, 22ff.; *Tales of the Dervishes*, 96–99; see also *Tuti-Nama*, 232, where a king, dying for the love of a woman, decides that if she will not love him, he must not force himself upon her: "Although I lose my life because of this passion, I will never be more cruel nor violate my moral beliefs and integrity."

6. Montaigne argues in his essay on repentence that some "sins" appear to be so deeply ingrained in the personality that we must assume them to be willed and intended.

7. *Small Is Beautiful* (New York: Harper and Row, 1975), 54.

8. Berman, *Reenchantment of the World*, 257. One thinks of Spain's ruining herself by her lack of moderation in what she took from the New World.

9. See Ellis, *One Fairy Story Too Many*, 193–94. He further notes that as changes were made in the Hansel and Gretel story, the father's role was softened and less and less did he appear to have been involved in the abandonment of the children.

10. Two views about the significance of these "forces": (1) that objectively they were or were not operating; (2) that my interpretation of the situation did—or did not—bring them into being. The actor's response may or may not be the key factor; at least we have raised the possibility.

11. *Sicilianische Märchen* (Hildesheim: Georg Olms Verlag, 1976), II, 183.

12. *Yuletide Tales*, ed. B. Thorpe (London: Bohn, 1853), 97.

13. *Orange Fairy Book* (Dover), 270; see also *Donegal Fairy Stories* (Dover), 234, about a large, unblessed cake.

14. *Gesta Romanorum* (Dover), 190. See W. Harman, "Rationale for Good Choosing," *JHP* 21, no. 1 (1981): 5–12, who argues for giving the creative/intuitive mind as large a role as possible in decision making.

15. Bateson, *Mind and Nature*, 213.

16. On fairness, see R. H. Frank, *Passions within Reason*, 162–84.

17. See the striking incident recounted in Max Wertheimer, *Productive Thinking*, enlarged ed. (New York: Harper, 1959), ch. 7, "Two Boys Play Badminton."

18. The bibliography is impressive, including *Encyclopedia of Islam*, III, 274; Amina Shah, 23ff.; *1001*, IV, 94ff.; *Tales of the Dervishes*, 91; an epic, *The Adventures of Hatim Tai*, trans. D. Forbes, 1830; and von Franz, *Individuation*, 59–125.

242 Notes to Chapter 8

19. Ignaz Goldziher, *Introduction to Islamic Theology and Law,* trans. A. and R. Hamori (Princeton: Princeton University Press, 1981), 91. See also von Franz, *Shadow and Evil,* 119.

20. See Harding, *Psychic Energy,* 463. Ernest Jones, in Dundes, *The Study of Folklore,* 88–102, argues that animals in folktales are really parents. Well, perhaps, but we have seen this way of thinking all too often, and it may be possible for us to recover another view, that ants are ants. The problem does not lie with the tellers of tales, but with us, who need to change our world view, not try out some tricky symbolism. When Black Elk talks about animal/human relations, it is clear that he means animals: "Once we were happy in our own country and were seldom hungry, for then the two-leggeds and the four-leggeds lived together like relatives" (Neihardt, 9). Benjamin (*Illuminations,* 102) observes that the many stories in which animals come to the aid of man suggest how much animals enjoy being aligned with man.

21. *Japanische Märchen und Sagen,* ed. D. Brauns (Leipzig, 1885), 59. For an analysis, see the discussion by Eugene Swanger in Fry, King, et al., *Great Asian Religions* (Grand Rapids: Baker, 1984), 150.

22. Cf. Dasent, 61, about kindness to raven, snake, and wolf, and Thorpe, 97ff., where cats help with the weaving.

23. Steere, 359, and *Ocean of the Streams of Story,* I, 183.

24. Cosquin, *Contes Populaires de Lorraine* (Paris, 1886), II, 227; *Yugoslav Folk-tales,* XXI; *Gesta Romanorum,* 170–71, and *Jataka,* II, 78, 197; III, 175; IV, 120; V, 84–85.

25. For the serpent as benign helper, see Harding, *Psychic Energy,* 264ff., and Colin Campbell, "Yoga in America: Who Really Owned Eden?" *PT,* Dec. 1975, 72ff: "The snake got a bum rap."

26. See Margaret Blount, *Animal Land: The Creatures of Children's Fiction* (New York: Morrow: 1975), ch. 7, and Mary Hill Arbuthnot, *Children and Books,* 3d ed. (New York: Scott Foresman, 1964), chs. 1 and 14; also Roger Sale, *Fairy Tales and After,* ch. 4.

27. See Ellis, 77; Magoun and Krappe, 217. One thinks also of Schmuh, in Grass's *Tin Drum,* who shoots twelve sparrows every time he goes hunting—with impunity. But on the day he bags a thirteenth, the other sparrows drive him to a terrible death.

28. For Cosquin, I, xxvi, xxxi, xxvii; for Hartland, *Science of Fairy Tales,* 295.

29. Von Franz, *Shadow and Evil*, 173.

Chapter 9

1. *Final Integration*, 17.

2. *The Dilemma of Human Identity* (New York: Aronson, 1977), 7; Jourard, *The Transparent Self*, rev. ed. (New York: Van Nostrand, 1971), 105.

3. See Rank, *Will Therapy*, 53; our sense of identity emerges from our sense of how different we are from others.

4. *The I* (New Haven: Yale University Press, 1985), 73.

5. Singer, *Boundaries of the Soul*, 145–46.

6. Jolanda Jacobi, *The Way of Individuation* (New York: Harcourt, Brace and World, 1967), 24; von Franz, *Individuation in Fairytales*, and Harding, *Psychic Energy*, 13 and n.

7. Yúdice discusses this work in "Marginality and the Ethics of Survival," in Ross, *Universal Abandon*, 226–29.

8. C. G. Campbell, *Tales from the Arab Tribes* (London: Lindsay Drummond, 1949), 71ff. We are reminded of the relationship between Perseus and Acrisius and of Odysseus' visit to his grandfather.

9. "The Descent of Ishtar to the Nether World," *The Ancient Near East*, ed. James Pritchard (Princeton: Princeton University Press, 1958), 80ff. See also *Tuti-Nama*, 230, and the English morality play *Everyman*.

10. Ornstein, *The Psychology of Consciousness*, 2d ed. (New York: Harcourt, Brace, 1977), 218, and von Franz, *Individuation*, 97–98, on the "falling apart of Adam," and *Interpretation of Fairy Tales* (Zurich: Spring Publications, 1975), 1, 2, where she asserts that all fairytales "describe one and the same psychic fact . . . what Jung calls the Self, which is the psychic totality of an individual . . . the regulating center of the collective unconscious."

11. Several similar cases are offered in the Turkish collection *Tales of Nasr-ed-Din Khoja* (London: Nisbet, 1923), 162–63, 186, 242–43, 250.

12. Such material supports a growing perception by feminist critics that the picture of women in fairytales is far from entirely

244 Notes to Chapter 9

negative: in many cases women are seen in a very positive light. For an examination of trends see Stone, 229–36, in Bottigheimer, *Fairy Tales and Society.*

13. *Jataka*, V, 18; see the discussion of the sticky question of identity in Castaneda, *Tales of Power*, 133; Rumi, *Mathnawi*, II, 45.

14. W. S. Walker and Ahmet Uysal are careful to provide material about the identity of their sources for *Tales Alive in Turkey* (Cambridge, Mass.: Harvard University Press, 1966), not so much, it seems, to prove the authenticity of the tales as to recreate the psychological setting of the act of storytelling; Renée Fuller, "Story Time," *Omni*, June 1980, 22ff., argues that the storyteller has a vital role in human development, being concerned with the most significant elements in human experience. Also, John Cech, "Breaking Chains: Brother Blue, Story-Teller," *CL* 9 (1981): 151–77, on the career and techniques of a famous storyteller who appeared in many parts of the country in the 1970s, always close to his audience. See also B. A. Babcock and G. and D. Monthan, *The Pueblo Storyteller* (Tucson: University of Arizona Press, 1986), about a tradition of storyteller figures in clay that was reawakened in the 1950s by Helen Cordero. One doll has over one hundred listening figures attached to it. Abrahams argues that it is now "possible to elevate the representative anecdote to the same place of importance as the rite of passage" (Turner and Bruner, *Anthropology*, 70).

15. Thus in Homer many figures are given names linked to the roles they play, and we never see them going beyond these roles. E. V. Rieu's translation brings this out particularly well, especially in *Odyssey*, Book VIII, when the names of the sailors in the Phaecian games are translated into their English equivalents.

16. See Magoun and Krappe, "The Brave Little Tailor," 79; "Jack the Giant Killer," *English Fairy Tales*, 99; Shah, *Tales of the Dervishes*, 43. For the Indian hero, Valiant Vicky, see *Wide-Awake Stories*, 89.

17. Macler, *Contes . . . d'Arménie*, 62ff.; also Cosquin, I, 258–59, "Le Cordonnier et les Voleurs." Jack Strong, Calvino, *Italian Folktales*, 358, squeezes out ricotta from a stone; see also "The Valiant Chattee-Maker, *Old Deccan Days*, 141ff., and *Jataka*, I, 205.

18. R. J. Trotter uses this motif as an entree to the social psychology of Muzafer Sherif, in "Harmony and Conflict in the Robbers' Cave," *PT*, Sept. 1985, 55ff.

19. For the complicated authorship of "Beauty and the Beast," see Jack Zipes, *Fairy Tales and the Art of Subversion* (New York: Wild-

man, 1983), 36–39. This important work studies the use of the traditional tale in the deconstruction of the European political system. More recent and very comprehensive is Betsy Hearne's *Beauty and the Beast*, cited earlier.

20. See Harding, *Psychic Energy*, 250, on "The Frog Prince."

21. See Stanton Peele, "The Question of Personality," *PT*, Dec. 1984, 54ff. Odysseus' narrative of his life history to Alcinous is the result of a careful selection of data. In the course of the narrative, "memory's flash bulbs" are popping in a controlled way. Also see D. C. Rubin, "The Subtle Deceiver: Recalling Our Past," *PT*, Sept. 1985, 38ff.

22. DeRopp, 49ff., discusses levels of consciousness; see also Joseph Campbell, "Kundalini Yoga: Seven Levels of Consciousness," *PT*, Dec. 1975, 77ff.

23. *Psychology of Consciousness*, 22ff. A basic statement of this theory is R. W. Sperry, "The Great Cerebral Commissure," *SA* 210, no. 1 (1964): 142ff.

24. *Psychology of Consciousness*, 43; von Franz, *Individuation*, 157, on voices; 89, on hunches; 115, on the war between right and left hands; *Interpretation*, 57, on the inventions of the unconscious; 69, on knocking out the superiority of the ego; 70, on the role of symbol and ritual. There is relevant material in Rumi, I, 136, 341, and esp. II, 350, and in Bruch, *Learning Psychotherapy* (Cambridge, Mass.: Harvard University Press, 1974), 29.

25. On the social conditions for storytelling, see the illustrations in Rowe's essay in Bottigheimer, *Fairy Tales and Society*, 66–70; also R. Schenda, ibid., 80–81.

26. Penguin, 198; Doris Lessing speaks of minds lying "side by side, fishes in a school, cells in honeycomb, flames in fire" (*Briefing for a Descent into Hell*, 96).

27. *The Dilemma of Human Identity*, 70, 73.

28. "The Joy of Work as Participation," in *Freedom and Culture* (Englewood Cliffs, N.J.: Prentice-Hall, 1959), 29.

29. *The Coast of Incense* (London: John Murray, 1953), 166. This is the third volume of the autobiography.

30. O'Flaherty, *Dreams, Illusion, and Other Realities*, 22.

31. *The Category of the Person: Anthropology, Philosophy, History*, ed. M. Carrithers, S. Collins, and S. Lukes (Cambridge: Cambridge University Press, 1985).

32. Carlos Castaneda, *A Separate Reality* (New York: Pocket Books, 1972), 106–7.

33. See *Varieties of Postmodern Theology*, 33; Shapiro, 72–74.

34. See Tatar in Bottigheimer, *Fairy Tales and Society*, 109.

35. See Harding, *Psychic Energy*, 205, on the possibility of many selves, and 325, on bodily disintegration. See also K. J. Gergen, "Multiple Identity," *PT*, May 1972, 31ff.; also Grass, *The Tin Drum*, when Oscar and his friend cut portrait photos apart and reassemble them in amusing ways, 49ff.

36. See Dasent, 63; *Ramayana*, trans. Buck (New York: New American Library, 1978), 104; for the "Monkey-Tortoise" story, *Jataka*, III, 88; *Kalilah and Dimnah*, 164.

37. On the substitution of a letter, see *Gesta Romanorum*, 51; *Brown Fairy Book*, 305–12; Magoun and Krappe, 111.

38. Magoun and Krappe, 321; in a variant in Thorpe, 240, the bride is able to tell her maid what she cannot tell her husband. The idea of telling your story to a stove suggests the modern technique of eliciting from abused children their stories by using a doll.

39. This story takes many forms—"Kamar az-Zamam and the Jeweler's Wife," *1001*, IX, esp. 270; "The Iron Stove," Magoun and Krappe, 454; "The Feather of Finist," Afanas'ev, 580; etc. In "L'Oiseau Bleu" the princess pays for bedchamber privileges with jewels (Mme. d'Aulony, *Les Contes de Fees*, 1708, 75ff.); in Grimms' "The Drummer Boy," 621, and in "Bushy Bride," Dasent, 322, the instrument is poetry.

40. *Noveaux Contes Berberes*, ed. René Basset (Paris, 1897), 18–20.

41. See especially *Ocean of the Streams of Story*, I, 17ff., where oil and lamp black is used as a marker, and *1001*, VI, 172, "The Lady and her Five Suitors." Also Dasent, "The Mastermaid," 71; Cosquin II, 6–7; and Voltaire's *Zadig*, XIII.

42. Leger, *Recueil de Contes Populaires Slaves* (Paris, 1882), 84. In "The King's Son and Messeria," Thorpe, 192, the hero must choose the same bride three times from a lineup; the shepherd of Myddvai, *Celtic Fairy Tales* (Dover), 58, chooses by a sandal strap; in *Ocean of the Streams of Story*, I, 360, S'ringabhuja must choose his wife from one hundred sisters (the one he is to pick will wear a necklace).

43. Helen Lynd, *On Shame and the Search for Identity* (New York: Harcourt Brace, 1958), 57.

44. According to von Franz, *Interpretation*, the Dummling "represents the new conscious attitude which is capable of contacting the feminine"; he is naturally led to the right attitude because he is naive and unsophisticated (46–50). See Afanas'ev, 97; *Donegal Fairy Tales*, 121; Dasent, 302, 396; Cosquin, II, 92.

Chapter 10

1. Schutz, "On Multiple Realities," I, 232. For Lévi-Strauss, "The Science of the Concrete," in *The Savage Mind* (London: Weidenfell and Nicolson, 1966), esp. 5.

2. Stories of this type include "The Sea King," Afanas'ev, esp. 435; "The Billiards Player," Calvino, 65; "The Grateful Prince," *Ehstnische Märchen*, 174–202; Grimm, "Foundling Bird," Magoun and Krappe, 185ff. See also Castaneda, *A Separate Reality*, 32, 43.

3. Of special interest, in the light of the identification problems just surveyed, is the fact that the ladle and the well might naturally be found where they were indeed found—by the roadside, though there was some unusual element about them that could have caught the attention of a discerning person. I think of waiting at a traffic light for the green signal—a point of light only a few inches across, obscured by trees and signs. A culturally unoriented observer might find it very difficult to determine what motivated me to start my car.

4. See also Frances Vaughan, *Awakening Intuition* (New York: Anchor Doubleday, 1979); M. R. Westcott, *Toward a Psychology of Intuition* (New York: Harper and Row, 1968); and Eric Berne, "The Nature of Intuition," *PQ* 23 (1949): 203–26. Berne asserts that "intuition" refers to a human capacity to "make judgments about everyday matters . . . by the use of functions whose processes are not ordinarily verbalised" (203). Westcott suggests that intuition means "reaching conclusions on the basis of little information which are ordinarily reached on the basis of significantly more information" (71).

5. See J. H. T. Bugental, "The Listening Eye," *JHP* 16, no. 1 (1976): 55–66; E. Gendlin and C. Tavris, "A Still Small Voice," *PT*, June 1970, 56ff. and A. Mehrabian, "Communication Without Words," *PT*, Sept. 1968, 52–55. Attention is called to Ursula LeGuin's moving account of the process of "foretelling" in chapter 5 of *The Left Hand of Darkness*, "The Domestication of Hunch." Faxe's foretellers cannot deal with all questions, but to answer those they can they do not need to know anything about the situation.

6. *Sagas from the Far East: Kalmouk and Mongol Traditionary Tales* (London: 1873), 160. Stith Thompson prints a closely parallel version, 344ff., and see Magoun and Krappe, 420ff.

7. *Folktales of Egypt*, 143–45. Such subtle, subconscious communication can develop among two people who become intensely focused upon each other, especially when sexual energy is involved.

8. See G. C. Dayton, "Perceptual Creativity: Where Inner and Outer Reality Come Together," *JCB* 10 (1976): 256ff.

9. *Lapplandische Märchen*, 248; the influence of the translation in Lang's *Brown Fairy Book* is acknowledged.

10. Heider discusses embeddedness, 37, as a key to knowing.

11. See Thomas Mann, "The Father's Face," in *Joseph and His Brothers* (New York: Knopf, 1948), 829ff. *Jane Eyre* (Penguin), 346; Castaneda, *A Separate Reality*, 55; LeGuin, *Left Hand of Darkness*, 65, 67, 147.

12. Lüthi, 14; in *Tales of Power*, 5, Don Juan tells Carlos that "knowledge is prowling around here" but that he must be careful not to try to make "convenient explanations."

13. *Phantastes*, 33. See also Paul Hawken, *The Magic of Findhorn* (New York: Harper and Row, 1975), esp. ch. 6, "Dorothy and the Devas"; also Lawrence Durrell's account of experiences with Egyptian dervishes in *Monsieur* (New York: Viking, 1975), 115ff.

14. See John L. Sherrill, *They Speak With Other Tongues* (Old Tappan, N.J.: Fleming H. Revell, 1965), and W. J. Samarin, "Glossalia," *PT*, Aug. 1972, 48ff. The relevant biblical text is Acts 2:1–11.

15. This subject is treated in Annemarie Schimmel, *The Triumphal Sun* (London: East-West Publications, 1978), and W. C. Chittick, *The Sufi Path of Love* (Albany: State University of New York Press, 1983). An older account of the dancing is to be found in J. P. Brown, *The Darvishes or Oriental Spiritualism* (1868) and legendary material in M. Onder, *Mevlana* (1977), and Shemsu 'd-din Ahmed el-Eflaki, *Legends of the Sufis* (London, 1981).

16. See *Meetings With Remarkable Men* (New York: Dutton, 1969), 161–63; Kazantzakis, *Zorba the Greek* (New York: Simon and Schuster, 1952), 70; and Gustaitis, *Turning On* (New York: NAL, 1969), 48.

17. See Elaine and Bernard Feder, "Dance Therapy," *PT*, Feb. 1977, 76ff., for a discussion of all that "the language of movement" can convey.

18. *A Mythic Journey: Gunter Grass's Tin Drum* (Lexington: University Press of Kentucky, 1974).

19. See *Dreams, Illusion, and Other Realities.* esp. chs. 1 and 2, and R. Caillois, "Logical and Philosophical Problems of the Dream," in *The Dream and Human Societies,* ed. G. von Grunebaum (Berkeley: University of California Press, 1966), 45.

20. Kilton Stewart, "Dream Theory in Malaya," in *Altered States of Consciousness,* ed. C. Tart (New York: Wiley, 1969), 159–67; and see the reply by Adam Smith, *Powers of Mind,* 211. Also, R. Ornstein, *The Psychology of Consciousness,* 142; Ruth M. Galvin, "Control of Dreams May be Possible for a Resolute Few," *Smithsonian,* Aug. 1982, 100–106; Stephen LaBerge, *Lucid Dreaming;* Douglas Colligan, "Lucid Dreams," *Omni,* March 1982, 68ff.; and, on daydreams, Eric Klinger, *PT,* Oct. 1987, 36ff., and J. L. Singer,"The Importance of Daydreaming," *PT,* April 1968, 18–26.

21. *More Celtic Tales* (Dover), 75, and von Franz, *Individuation,* 71–72, on the importance of teaching people about dreaming.

22. *Mathnawi,* III, 497, and see also the discussion of this story in Roger Caillois, "Logical and Philosophical Problems." An English version, "The Peddlar of Swaffham," is discussed by Jennifer Westwood in *Albion: A Guide to Legendary Britain* (Salem, N.H.: Salem House, 1985), 161–63. There is an account of veridical dreams in Rumi, II, 130–1, and in ch. 2 of O'Flaherty, *Dreams, Illusion, and Other Realities.*

23. *Jataka,* I, 187 ff. See also the account of a shared dream from the myth of Vikramaditya and Malayavati in O'Flaherty, 63–65. When two people dream the same dream, a sense of reality confirmed seems inevitable. There is scepticism, however, in the Danish tale "The Prince and Princess in the Forest" (*Olive Fairy Book,* 261), when the prince says that dreams don't mean a thing, to which the queen wisely responds, "Dreams always mean something."

24. See S. Krippner, "Access to Hidden Reserves of the Unconscious through Dreams in Creative Problem Solving," *JCB* 15 (1981): 11ff.

25. *The Tree Climber,* trans. Denys Johnson-Davies (London: Oxford University Press, 1966), 35.

26. *Ghosts in the Mind's Machine* (New York: Norton, 1983). See especially 127 for a model of the imaging process.

27. Kosslyn, 172, and F. A. Yates, *The Art of Memory* (Chicago: University of Chicago Press, 1966), 320ff.

28. *1001*, IX, 27–29 and note; *Tuti-Nama*, 298.

29. See Deutsch and Krauss, 186–87; and a number of articles in *Psychology Today:* Carin Rubenstein, "The Face," Jan. 1983, 48ff.; Paul Ekman, "The Universal Smile: Face Muscles Talk Every Language," Sept. 1975, 35ff.; F. A. Gelard, "Body English," Dec. 1968, 43ff.; E. G. Beier, "Nonverbal Communication: How We Send Emotional Messages," Oct. 1974, 53ff.; R. Rosenthal et al.,"Body Talk and Tone of Voice: the Language Without Words," Sept. 1974, 64ff.; see also Nasr-ed-Din Khoja, 104–5.

30. New York: Warner Books, 1966, 63. See also *Jataka*, III, 156; and a note by Burton on the language of signs (*1001*, Suppl. V, 107–8, 121).

31. Boccaccio, *Decameron* (Modern Library), 154ff., 34ff. See "The Vine-Dresser Deceived by his Wife" in *Disciplina Clericalis*, trans. W. H. Hulme (Western Reserve University Bulletin, May 1919), 27, and *Tuti-Nama*, 248–50.

32. Watzlawick, *How Real is Real?* (New York: Vintage, 1977), 103–5.

33. For the bell, *Old Deccan Days*, 40; for the rusting knife, *English Fairy Tales* (Dover), 132; for the oozing bladder, Calvino, 190; for the bleeding watermelon, El-Shamy, 164–65; for the winking eye, *Ramayana* (trans. Buck), 215; for the arm, Kazantzakis, *Zorba*, 296; for the tarnishing spoon, Afanas'ev, 555. The interest of the postmoderns in this theme may be related to their interest in Buddhism. See Griffin and Smith, 6, 47–48, 141, and passim, and Shapiro, 59–60. Networking is related to Von Bertalanffy's General Systems Theory (*A Systems View of Man* [Boulder: Westview, 1981]). For another approach to networking, see S. Milgram, "The Small-World Problem," *PT*, May 1967, 60–73.

34. On missing or not acting upon hints, see "The Twelve Dancing Princesses," one of whom suggests that something invisible is following them (her dress keeps catching and their boat rides low in the water) but never takes time to investigate (*Red Fairy Book*, 1ff.) Ali Baba recognizes the voice of the robber chief, but his intuition is overridden by all the disguises.

Chapter 11

1. The modern laboratory investigator goes to great lengths to ensure that his presence—and the test itself—do not distort the results. Polanyi, *Personal Knowledge* (New York: Harper Torchbooks, 1964), ch. 6, "Intellectual Passions," was one of the first to call attention to this phenomenon.

2. Lucretius (Penguin), 139; Charles Dickens, *Great Expectations*, ch. 38, refers to an "Eastern Story" about a set of pulleys that enable movement to be passed through several long passageways. And see my discussion of Wordsworth's *Prelude* (in *The Literary Moment as a Lens on Reality*, Columbia: University of Missouri Press, 1983) for another account of involvement in a series of reflections.

3. *Sinus*, a closed, twisting path. Lang includes this surprisingly erotic tale in his *Brown Fairy Book*. An introject consists of material such as a way of acting, feeling, or thinking, which you have taken into your system of behavior, but which you have not assimilated in such a way as to make it a functioning part of your organism. Acceptance is forced. See Perls, Hefferline, and Goodman, *Gestalt Therapy* (New York: Dell, 1951), 189. Cf. the behavior of Chundun Rajah, *Old Deccan Days*, 175, and the way Tristan makes his presence known to Iseult by floating bark and twigs onto the brook in Mark's garden (Bedier, Garden City: Doubleday Anchor, 64–66).

4. Mitchnik, *Egyptian and Sudanese Folktales*, 37ff.

5. *Strange Stories from a Chinese Studio* (Dover), 134.

6. David Chaffetz, *A Journey Through Afghanistan* (Chicago: University of Chicago Press, 1981), 13.

7. *Orange Fairy Book*, 268; this is a tricky blend of the random and the controlled.

8. *Orange Fairy Book*, 345. This is reminiscent of Fielding's comment about Parson Adams's proclivity for walking on obscure, narrow paths: "This track did he keep, as indeed he had a wonderful capacity for this kind of bare possibility" (Modern Library, 119). "Bare possibility" indeed—a perfect phrase for what is being attempted here! A useful technique, when one has lost something, is to do something else other than look for it—all the while, however, keeping one eye open to possible sightings.

9. *Decameron* (Modern Library), 365 (fourth story of sixth day).

10. *Disciplina Clericalis*, 30. This is genuine transcontextuality—playing with crossovers from one level of reality to another.

11. Ernest Schachtel, *Metamorphosis* (New York: Basic Books, 1959), 83, 220–21, 99–100); deBono, *Mechanism of Mind*, 177; and P. Watzlawick, *Change: Principles of Problem Formation and Problem Resolution* (New York: Norton, 1974), 77–91.

12. Shah retells this anecdote in *Wisdom of the Idiots* (New York: Dutton, 1971), 164; see also the section in Walker and Uysal, *Tales Alive*, "Perplexities and Ingenious Deductions," esp. 113.

13. See Minsky, "Jokes and the Logic of the Cognitive Unconscious," in *Methods of Heuristics*, 172, 181.

14. "How Ananda the Wood-Carver and Ananda the Painter Strove Against Each Other," in *Sagas from the Far East*. Also, W. J. J. Gordon, *The Metaphorical Way of Learning and Knowing* (Cambridge: Porpoise Books, 1971), and "The Metaphorical Way of Knowing," in G. Kepes, The *Education of Vision* (New York: Braziller, 1965), 95–103.

15. See J. and P. Opie, *Lore and Language of Schoolchildren*, "Half Belief," 222–25.

16. Mitchnik, 17. The riddle is interpreted as saying, "I spend one on my food, give my father one, spend one on my sons, and the last is for my daughter, from whom I do not expect repayment."

17. *Kalilah and Dimnah*, 110; cf. *Jataka*, I, 85.

18. Richard Bauman and A. Paredes, *Toward New Perspectives in Folklore* (Austin: University of Texas Press, 1972), 53.

19. *Magyar Folk-Tales*, ed. W. H. Jones and Lewis Kropf (Publications of the Folk-Lore Society, 1886), 232–44.

Chapter 12

1. F. J. Shaw, *Reconciliation: A Theory of Man Transcending*, ed. Sidney Jourard and Dan C. Overlade (Princeton: Van Nostrand, 1966), 108, discusses the self-expressive life-style, characterized by an individual's respect for his own resources. The entirety of an individual's approach to life may be summed up in the way he does one thing—such as playing golf. Particularly relevant is Shaw's theory of manageable dilemmas: the individual I have in mind is often in trouble but always escapes because he knows what he is good at.

2. Stanley Diamond, "Introductory Essay" to Paul Radin, *The Trickster* (New York: Schocken, 1972), xiii.

3. C. G. Jung, "On the Psychology of the Trickster Figure," Radin, 195ff. See also Richard Christie, "The Machiavellis Among Us," *PT*, Nov. 1970, 82–86, on the distinctly different mental make-up of gamblers who don't know when to quit, and F. Farley, "The Big T in Personality," *PT*, May 1986, 44ff., the thrill-seeking personality.

4. Goffman, *Frame Analysis*, 439ff.

5. Cecil, *The King's Son*, 40.

6. Van Buitenen, 187; cf. *Sagas from the Far East*, on Vikramadrit-ja, who was "exercised in all kinds of arts; and increased in strength, well favoured in mind and body. He learned wisdom of the wise, and the use of arms from men of valour; from the soothsayer he learned the cunning arts, and trading from sagacious traders; from robber bands he learned the art of robbery, and from fraudulent dealers to lie" (277). And cf. Igor Kusyszn, "How Gambling Saved me from a Misspent Sabbatical," *JHP* 17, no. 3 (1977): 19ff., on risk-taking, the motivation for gambling, and various theoretical concepts reflected in gambling.

7. See *Les Contes de Goha*, trans. E. J. Finbert (Paris, 1929), and El-Shamy, 219. The American Indian parallel is the heyokas, "sacred fools, doing everything wrong or backwards to make the people laugh": (*Black Elk Speaks*, 187). Also Nasr-ed-Din Khoja, 56.

8. This is "Fortunatus and his Purse," *Gray Fairy Book*, 74ff. The story of Hasan can be found in *1001*, VIII, 7ff.

9. Stith Thompson prints a Scottish version, 391. The term "master thief" is a nice play on the very heart of the bourgeois world, master carpenter, master weaver, master plumber, etc. The world of thievery adopts the usage and joins the respectability language game.

10. See Dasent, 232ff.; Calvino, 414, 424; and the Shifty-Lad Stories in *West Highland Popular Tales* (London: 1890), I, 330ff. There is a discussion of the master-thief motif in Clouston, *Popular Tales and Fictions*, II, 115ff. The motif is traced to ancient sources—Herodotus and Pausanius.

11. Cf. Koestler's theory of jokes, "From Humour to Discovery," in *The Act of Creation* (New York: Macmillan, 1964), 87ff., and Victor Raskin, "Jokes," *PT*, Oct. 1985, 34ff.

12. Suppl. V, 323; Cf. Calvino, 160 and note, where numerous analogues are suggested.

13. *Yugoslav Folk-tales,* XXVI. St. Peter is just as often a victim as the devil is. See also Dégh, *Hungarian Folk-tales,* 182–87. As so often happens, the same elements may add up to different results, or vice versa: 2 plus 3 plus 4 may have quite a different flavor from 11 minus 2. See deBono, 92, and Rank, *Will Therapy:* the therapeutic situation involves a patient, a therapist, and a particular theory of therapy; success or failure depends as much on the mix as on the significance of every element. This is the area of commutative mathematics, the study of the way *arrangements of numbers* do or do not affect results. Thus $2 \times 5 + 1$ does not yield the same result as $2 \times 1 + 5$. "The Mountain Path," in *Tales of the Dervishes,* 134, takes us into much the same issue. Both a truthful man and a liar make the same suggestion about how to reach a nearby village; the commutative element is related to the fact that the truthful man sees all the relevant issues, and in correct order; the liar misses important facts. See Gleick, *Chaos,* "The Butterfly Effect," 9–31.

14. *Santal Tales,* trans. A. Campbell (Pokhuria, 1891), 90–101.

15. P. Dodds, "Creativity in Movement: Models for Analysis," *JCB* 12 (1978): 265ff.

16. *A Ride to Khiva* (London: Cassell, 1876), 3–4.

17. *A Reed Shaken by the Wind* (London: Longmans, 1957), 1–4.

18. Greenfield and Bruner, "Culture and Cognitive Growth," *IJP* 1, no. 2 (1966): 102.

19. Foster and Morgan, "Piaget and Parables: the Convergence of Secular and Scriptural Views of Learning," *JPT* 13, no. 2 (1985): 101. Also Lévi-Strauss, 13–16, 35–38, and esp. 135ff., on creating new categories.

20. Pearce, *Crack in the Cosmic Egg,* esp. 9–10, on "empty categories."

21. An interesting attempt at category making is presented by Angelo Biondi and Nancy Kubik, "Ask . . . And You Shall Conceive," *JCB* 14 (1980): 235ff. They offer the following "stimulating new solutions": modification, adoption, rearrangement, magnification, combination, substitution, reversal, and re-application. And see J. L. Adams, *Conceptual Block-Busting* (San Francisco: San Francisco Book Co., 1976), 66, for other suggestions about flexible strategies.

Chapter 13

1. See my article, "Behavioral Implications of Mental World-Making," *JCB* 23 (1989): 1–13. This material is used here by permission.

2. Isaac Asimov, "And It Will Serve Us Right," *PT*, April 1969, 39ff.

3. *The Image* (Ann Arbor: University of Michigan Press, 1956), 14.

4. Gilbert Harman, *Thought* (Princeton: Princeton University Press, 1973), 182.

5. Ascham, *English Works* (Cambridge: Cambridge University Press, 1904), 112–13.

6. The world described here bears interesting similarities to that complex set of concepts Oswald Spengler calls "The Magian World View." See *The Decline of the West*, esp. chs. 12 and 14 of the abridged edition (New York: Knopf, 1962). See also Robertson Davies's novel *World of Wonders* (Penguin, 1977), 287; L. Durrell's account of the Gnostic universe in *Monsieur*, 168; Voltaire's *Zadig*, many elements of which correspond to the world of the bright shadow. Another parallel is to be found in the Islamic concept of *'alm al-mithal*, "the realm of images." And see also Black Elk's account of Crazy Horse's excursions into another world via dreams: "That is the real world that is behind this one," Black Elk observes, "and everything we see here is something like a shadow from that world" (85).

Index

A

Abbott, E., *Flatland*, 205
Accumulation Tales, 40–41
Active-Passive, as a behavioral issue, 34–38
Actors, as basic factor in narrative, 12–13, 16, 19, 23, 47, 97, 104, 199–200
Afanas'ev, A., 11, 60, 191, 233n.15, 239n.5
Aladdin, 61, 85–88, 123–24, 126, 167, 186
Ali Baba, 176
Alice in Wonderland, 31–32, 108, 205
Alternate Worlds, see World-making
"Ananda the Woodcarver, Ananda the Painter," 174–75, 252n.14
Anados (*Phantastes*), 50, 146, 152, 164–65
"Andras Baive," 154
Animal speech, understanding, 145–47
Anomalies (motif), 38–43
Appointments Missed (motif), 70
Apuleius (*The Golden Ass*), 67, 72
Arabian Fairy Tales (Shah), 77, 146, 156, 231n.21, 238n.31, 241n.18
Arasteh, R., 7, 68–70, 112, 118–19, 226n.13, 236n.13, 243n.1
Armstrong, R. A., 225n.11, 228n.7
Arnheim, R., 230n.3
Ascham, R. (*Toxophilus*), 207, 255n.5
Asimov, Isaac, 205

Assagioli, R., 89, 93, 231, 239n.11
Aurora, the Dawn Fairy, 56–57, 194

B

Baba Yaga, 96
Babcock, B. A., 224n.14
"The Banker and the Grain Merchant" ("A Long-Bow Story"), 170
Basile, *Pentamerone*, 27, 90, 236n.16, 239n.12
Bateson, G., 7, 156, 226n.12, 230n.1, 232n.27, 241n.15
Bauman, R., 252n.18
"Beauty and the Beast," 29, 122–23
Behavioral Possibilities, 2
Benjamin, W., 43, 119–20, 232n.25
Berman, Morris, 65, 102, 127–28, 240n.4
Berrenikov, F. (Russian folk hero), 12
Bettelheim, B., 3, 4, 65, 66, 95–96, 131, 134–35, 224n.4, 235n.4
"Bilar and Gobar," story of, 142–44, 153
"Bird Grip," story of, 72–73, 107, 186
Black Elk: Animals, Relation to, 146, 242n.20; *Black Elk Speaks*, 230n.6, 253n.7; Dancing, 148; Duplication, Experience of, 31; Goodness, Relation to, 96; Helpless-

Black Elk (*cont.*)
ness, 65; Other Worlds, 255n.6;
Power, 89
Boasting, as means of Establishing
Identity, 121–22
Boccaccio (*Decameron*), 158, 168, 191,
250n.31, 251n.9
The Book of Proof (Al-Jahiz), 18–20
Bottigheimer, R., 1, 14, 113, 224n.4,
227n.8, 233n.5, 236n.15, 244n.12,
245n.25
Boulding, K., 205, 255n.3
"Briar Rose" (Sleeping Beauty) story
of, 69–70
Bricolage, 190–91
Bright-Shadow World, 7, 16, 32–34,
183
Briggs, K., 26, 76, 154, 158,
229nn.14, 20
Bruner, E. M., 227n.7, 229n.15
Bruner, J. S., 195, 254n.18
Buddhism, 109
Burger, Dionys, *Sphereland*, 205
Burnaby, Fred, 195, 254n.16
Burton, R., 88–89, 239n.5

C

Caillois, R., 150, 249n.22
Calvino, Italo, 90, 145, 159, 231n.20,
234n.15, 236n.16, 237n.22,
244n.17
Carrithers, M., 245n.31
Castaneda, C., Alternate Worlds,
55; Internal Dialogue, 169; Intuition, 145; Vectors, Awareness of,
129; *Tales of Power*, 228n.1,
234n.17, 237n.26, 244n.13; *A Separate Reality*, 246n.32, 248n.11
"The Cat, the Mouse, the Ichneumon, and the Hunter," 172–
74
Categories, disruption of traditional, 195–98

Chaffetz, D., 167
Chandraprabha, 49
"The Charmed Ring," 107
"Childe Rowland," 55
Children's Games, 112, 130, 164,
186, 193
Chittick, W. C., 248n.15
Choosing (motif), 162–3
Cinderella, 164
Clarke, A., 234n.22
"The Clever Peasant Lass," 55
Communication across Distance, 33,
160, 250n.33
Concentration, focusing, 86–87, 93
Conflict-management, 20, 172–74
Connor, M. (Irish hero), 74
Contes . . . d'Arménie, 239n.6,
244n.17
Consciousness/Unconsciousness,
124–25; as a category, 198
Cosquin, E. (*Contes Populaires de Lor-
raine*), 109, 191, 242n.24
Covan (Irish hero), 104, 167, 169

D

Dancing, and enchantment, 74; as a
way of knowing, 147–49
Dasent, G. W., 75, 108, 189,
232n.24, 234n.20, 242n.22
David (Biblical), 133–34
Davies, Robertson, 9, 255n.6
DeBono, Edward, 153, 166, 169,
240n.17, 252n.11, 254n.13
DeGroot, Adriaan, 18, 79, 228n.5
Decameron, see Boccaccio
Deconstruction, 4, 183
Deducing, 156–58
Dennett, D. C. (*The Intentional
Stance*), 14, 18, 19, 36
Denouement of narrative, as struc-
tural factor, 14, 98, 201
Denton, D. E., 26, 223n.1
DeRopp, R., 49, 245n.22

Descartes, R., 25–26
Deutsch, M. and Krauss, R. M., 52, 59, 62, 120, 228n.3, 230n.2, 250n.29
Dewey, John, 17–18, 228n.2
Diamond, S., 184–85, 253n.2
Dickinson, Emily, 2, 53, 194, 233n.9
Dickens, Charles, 152, 157, 251n.2
Dillard, Edward, 149, 249n.18
Dilthey, W., 14, 227n.7
"A Discerning Old Faki," 166
Disciplina Clericalis, 168–69, 250n.31, 252n.10
Displaced Wife (motif), 131–32, 246n.39
Distance (as a factor in strangeness), 59
Diversions/distractions, 71
Donegal Fairy Stories, 231n.20
Dörner, D., 72, 237n.20, 238n.1
Dreaming, 149–151, 249nn.19, 20
Dumézil, G., 230n.3
Durkheim, E., 30, 78
Durrell, L., 255n.6

E

"East o'the Sun, West o'the Moon," 29, 47, 60, 206
Edges, challenges and dangers of, 45–62, 208, 219–20
Education, Modern, Critique of, 2, 140
Ego, 79, 112–17
Egyptian and Sudanese Folk-Tales (Mitchnik), 231n.17, 251n.4, 252n.16
Ehstnische Märchen, 60, 99, 103, 229n.17
Eliot, T. S., 31
Ellis, John M., 69, 236n.15, 241n.9, 242n.27
"The Enchanted Deer," 236n.17

Enchantment, 63–77, 208–220
English Fairy Tales, 233n.14, 244n.16
Enhancement of Experience, 3, 201–203, 219–222
Entrapment, 169–172
Erikson, E., 9, 110, 113–14, 226n.17
Evil, Nature of, in Bright-Shadow World, 63–77

F

Fairytales as stimulants to growth, 1–5; see enhancement of experience
"The Faithful Prince," 165
Faust/Mephistophiles, 65
Ferko, Tale of, 107, 159
Feyerabend, Paul, 7, 11, 17, 18, 139, 140, 160, 162, 226n.14, 228n.5
File-Comparison, 80
Finding Things, 175–76
"The Flight of Chance," 102
"Fly-Killer," 121
"The Folly of Jealousy," 155
Forgetting (as a motif), 71
Foster, F. B., 197
Foucault, M., 17, 25, 161, 228n.5
Frank, Robert A., 104, 231n.13, 241n.16
Frere, Mary, 19, 75, 154, 157
Freud, S., Freudianism, 3, 64, 187
Frobenius, L., 239n.7
"The Frog Prince," 245n.20

G

Generosity, 105
Gendlin, E., 6, 207, 225n.9
Gesta Romanorum, 104, 106, 242n.24, 246n.37
Gestures, Language of, 155
"The Ghostly Miser of Tangier," 77

"The Giant who had no Heart in his Body," 75
Giles, Herbert, 74, 166, 237n.26
Gilgamesh, Epic of, 68, 234n.23
Gilguerillo, 167, 169
Glassie, Henry, 223n.1
Glazebrook, P., 237n.24
"Gobar and Bilar," story of, 142–43
Goffman, E., 16, 48, 81, 149, 184, 223n.1, 227n.3, 253n.4
Goha (Sudanese wise fool), 185, 187–88, 190, 253n.7
"The Golden Bird," 72–73, 107, 206
"The Golden Lion," 133
Goldziher, I., 242n.19
Goodman, P., 235n.6, 239n.11, 251n.3
Goodness, nature of, 94–98
"The Goosegirl," 131, 145
Grass, Gunter, 149, 227n.5, 242n.27, 246n.35
Greenfield, P. M., 195, 254n.18
Griffin, D., 184, 224n.7, 226n.21, 228n.7, 246n.33
Grimm Brothers (*German Folk Tales*): 1, 98, 130, 227n.4, 236n.18; "Briar Rose," 69–70; "The Brave Little Tailor," 244n.16; "The Clever Little Tailor," 179; "The Clever Peasant Lass," 55, 174; "The Dog and the Sparrow," 108; "Faithful John," 98, 240n.5; "The Goose-Girl," 145; "Hansel and Gretel," 102–3; "The Juniper," 13, 64; "The Master Thief," 188–89; "The Monkey," 192; "The Riddle," 180; "The Three Army Surgeons," 129–130; "The Three Brothers," 55; "The Turnip," 231n.17; "The Two Brothers," 75; "The Two Travelers," 105; "The White Snake," 146
Gurdjieff, G. I., 148, 235n.7, 248n.16
Gustaitis, R., 148, 248n.16

H

al-Hakim, Tewfiq, 152, 157, 249n.25
"Hansel and Gretel," story of, 66, 102–3
Harding, M. E.: Animals, as Integrated Beings, 106; Consciousness, 72, 89; Emotional Training, 23; Enchantment, 64–65; "The Frog Prince," 245n.20; Intuition, 144; Multiple Selves, 246n.35; *Psychic Energy,* 227n.5, 235n.7, 236n.13, 239n.8, 242n.20, 243n.6
Harman, G., 206, 255n.4
Hartland, E. S., 31, 109, 230n.7, 234n.24, 242n.28
Hatim Tai (Arab folk hero), 105–6, 241n.18
Hawken, P., 248n.13
Hayy Ibn Yaqzun, 68
Hearne, B., 224n.4, 226n.15, 245n.19
Heider, Fritz, 17, 21, 24, 28, 33, 59, 230n.4, 248n.10
Herbert, Frank, 205
Hiding Things, 192–3
Hints, Reading of, 153
Hiranyakasipu (Incarnation of Vishnu), 54, 185, 234n.19
Hitopodesa, 35
Hoffmann, E. T. A., 61
Holland, N., 113–14, 243n.4
Horney, K., 235n.5
Houston, Jean, 40, 231n.19, 235n.7
Hungarian Folk Tales, 254n.13
Huxley, Aldous, 53–54, 233n.10

I

Identity, Personhood, 112–17, 198, 214–15, 221; Willed, 123–24; Discovering, 130–31; Threats to, 117–18; Establishing, 118–19; and Social Involvement, 125–30

Inbetwixities, as a category, 54–58, 110, 197
Indian Fairy Tales (Jacobs), 41, 107, 232n.22, 237n.25, 239n.13
Individuation, 114
Intuition, 140–47, 247n.4
Intelligence as a Power Source, 78–80
Interdictions, 49, 52, 75–77
Interiority, 60–61
"The Invisible Grandfather," 145
Irony, 42
Ishak of Mosul, 90
Ishtar, 117–18, 243n.9
Islandische Märchen, 167

J

Jackson, R. (on oxymoron), 54, 232n.2
Jacobi, J., 114, 243n.6
al-Jahiz, 18–20, 152
Jane Eyre, 145
Japanische Märchen, 192, 242n.21
Jataka Tales, 229n.16, 230n.8; Communication across Distance, 160; Deductions, 157, 250n.29; Distractions, 33, 34; Dream Interpretation, 151, 249n.20; Faulty Analogy, 53–54; Identity Issue, 119; Inbetwixities, 55, 58, 234n.10; Interiority, 60; Moral Allegory, 31; Passivity, 35; Perceptiveness, 22–24, 33; Pragmatic Viewpoint, 100–102; Unbalanced Treatment of World, 108–9; World-Reading, 22–23, 157
Jencks, C., 225n.7
Jephtha, Story of, 130
Joseph (Genesis), 115, 126, 145
Jourard, S., 113, 243n.2
Jung, C. G., 10, 31, 64, 81, 114, 235n.2, 238n.3, 253n.3
"The Juniper," 64

K

Kalila and Dimna, 36–37, 41, 142, 174, 177, 193, 231n.11, 246n.36, 252n.17
Kammerer, A., 81
Kanakarekha, 47, 50, 194
Kazantzakis, N., 148, 248n.16
Kesey, Ken, 74, 238n.27
King Kalinga, 100–102, 110, 201
Kindness to Animals, 106–10
"The King of the Snakes," 107
"The King of the Waterfalls," 154
"The King's Son," 71, 233n.8, 236n.19, 253n.5
Knowing, 138–160, 215, 222; Dancing as a Means of, 147–49; Deducing, 156–58; Dreaming as a Means of, 149–151; Intuition, 140–5; Language of Gestures, 135–36, 250n.29; Oblique Speech, 158; Scenario-Building, as a Way of Knowing, 151–53
Koestler, A., 81, 238n.2, 253n.11
Kohlberg, L., 95–105, 111, 240
Konner, M., 172
Kosslyn, S., 152, 249n.26, 250n.27

L

"A Lac of Rupees for a Bit of Advice," 41, 237n.25
Lakoff, George, 17, 197, 225n.7, 232n.1
Lapplandische Märchen, 154, 167, 237n.22, 248n.9
Lee, Dorothy, 126, 245n.28
LeGuin, Ursula, 205, 232n.28, 247n.5
Lessing, Doris, 56, 234n.17, 236n.13, 245n.26
Lévi-Strauss, 12, 138, 190, 227n.2, 247n.1, 254n.19
Lewin, K., 59

Lewis, C. S., 6–7, 9, 64, 107,
   225nn.10, 11; 234n.11, 238n.32
Lichtenstein, H., 112–14, 116, 117,
   126, 142, 185, 243n.2, 245n.27
Line-ups, Choosing From, 246n.42
"Lion's Track Tale," 177
Little Diamond, 46, 98, 138
"The Little Tailor," 121
"The Loan," *Wisdom of the Ancients*
   (Shah), 164, 252n.12
Luck, 80–84
Lucretius, 164, 251n.2
Lüthi, M., 40, 62, 179, 191, 231n.18,
   236n.16, 248n.12
Lynd, H., 246n.43
Lyotard, J.-F., 120, 128–29, 224n.7

M

Mabinogeon, 55, 234n.15
Macdonald, George, *At the Back of
   the North Wind*, 9, 19–20, 46, 55,
   98, 138, 150, 226n.20, 234n.17;
   Phantastes, 6, 9, 50, 112, 136, 146,
   148, 152, 164, 226n.19, 248n.13;
   Princess and the Goblin, 61
McHugh, P., 228n.7
Magic, as Power Source, 84–88
"The Magic Ring," 191, 163
Magoun, F. P. and Krappe, A. H.,
   see Grimm Brothers
Magyar Folk-Tales, 252n.19
Maqdad (North African folk hero),
   116–17
Martin, P. W., 54, 135, 233n.13,
   236n.13
Ma'ruf the Cobbler, the Enlightened
   One, 201; Identity Issues, 117,
   128; Intriguer, 126, 164; Luck, 82–
   84; as Paradigm, 205; Personal
   Power, 99–100; Positioning of
   Self, 61, 194; Risk-Taking, 190;
   Self-Interest, 104
"The Master-Thief," 188–89, 253n.10
Mauss, Marcel, 84, 127, 238n.4

Mechanical Processes, Entrapment
   in, 74–75
Menchú, Rigobertu, 115–16
Merleau-Ponty, M., 21, 23, 32,
   227n.6, 228n.7, 229n.19
Metamorphosis, 58–59
Metaphor-Making, 174–75, 193
Metzgar, M., 3
"The Miller's Four Sons," 187
Minsky, M., 187, 252n.13
Modern World, Nature of, 4; as
   Normative, 109–10; Critique of,
   223n.1
"The Monkey," 192–93
"The Monkey and the Tortoise,"
   129, 193
Monthan, G. and D., 224n.14
Montaigne, M., 230n.8, 241n.6
Moral Commitments, 94–111, 208,
   221, 198
Morgiana ("Ali Baba"), 79–80, 132,
   200
Moses, 35, 43, 46, 91–92, 118, 126,
   205
Motifs: Balance, Maintaining, 102–5;
   Being Diverted, 71; Choosing,
   162–63; Conflict-Management,
   172–74; Distance, 59–61; Edge-
   Dwelling, 208, 212, 219–20; En-
   chantment, Avoiding, 75–77; Entrapment, 74, 169–172; Escaping
   Sets, 165–69; Finding Things,
   175–76; Forgetting, 71; Greed and
   Generosity, 102–5; Hints, Picking
   up, 139–40; Identity, 112–137,
   214, 221; Inbetwixities, 54–58; Intelligence, 78–80; Interdictions,
   75–77; Kindness to Animals, 106–
   9; Knowing, 215, 222; Luck, 84;
   Magic, 84–88, 98–100; Making
   Contact, 164–65; Metamorphosis,
   58–59; Missing Appointments, 70;
   Morality, 208, 214, 221; Obstacle-
   Flight, 30; Out-of-Body Travel, 62;
   Persistence despite Danger, 73–
   74; Personhood, Gaining, 132–6;

Personhood, Loss of, 130–2; Petrification, 75; Power, 213, 220; Problem-Solving, 222; Riddling, 179–181; Roguery, 208–9, 184–90; Role-Making, 120–1; Same/Different, 30–34, 80; Sexuality, 66; Sleep, 68; Story-Telling, 119–20; Telling Someone Something, 176–77; Vulnerability, 53–54; World-Reading, 208, 211, 219; Youngest Son, Emergence of, 133–34, 172–73, 107, 206

Moving About, 193–95, 197

Muhammad, 62

Mu'tazilites, 106

My Bookhouse, 6

"My Dinner with André," 76, 238n.30

N

Narration: Nature of, in Fairytales, 5; Structure of, 5, 11–12; Role of Actors in, 12–13; Vectors, 13; Power, 13; Physical Context, 14; Denouement of, 14; Parallels in Contemporary Thinking, 5; Role of in Expanding Experience, 3

Nasr-ed-Din Khoja, 166, 185, 186, 195–96, 243n.11, 253n.7

Needleman, J., 238n.26

Networks, 41, 48, 197

Neumann, E., 124

Niebuhr, Reinhold, 232n.23

Nimbleness, 183–198

Noveaux Contes Berberes, 246n.40

Numbers, Interest of traditional narrative in, 27–30

O

Objective and Subjective Factors, Conflict Between, 29

Oblique Speech, as a Means of Communicating, 158–59

Obstacle-Flight, 30, 247n.3

Ocean of the Streams of Story, 233n.6, 237n.25, 242n.23; Behavior as Clue to Personality, 154, 157; Conflict Management, 172–74; Contemplation, Art of, 166; Helpful Animals, 107; Kindness to Animals, 108; Magic, 84; "Saktideva and the City of Gold," 47–52; Sexual entrapment, 67; Vetala tales, 74; Witnesses, Clever Use of, 171–72

Odysseus, *Odyssey*, 66–67, 117–18, 119, 123, 154, 169–70, 190, 200

Oedipus, 92

O'Flaherty, Wendy, 60, 67, 127, 150, 234n.21, 245n.30, 249n.22

Old Deccan Days (Frere), 19–20, 154, 157, 228n.9, 236n.16, 244n.17, 251n.3

Opie, Oona and Peter, 179, 193, 229n.21, 252n.15

Orgies, as a psychological "edge," 59

Orlik, A., 230n.3

Ornstein, R., 118, 124–25, 169, 243n.10, 245n.23, 249n.20

Out-of-Body Travel, 62

Ovid, 105

P

Panchatantra, 27, 41

Participating Consciousness, 98–100

Pater, W., 237n.21

Pearce, J. C., 93, 240n.17, 254n.20

"The Peasant, the King, and the Sheikh," 155

Pentamerone (Basile), 27, 90

Persistence despite danger, 73–74

Personhood: loss of, 130–32; emergence into, 132–134; as a category, 198

Perunto and Vastolla, Story of, 90
Petrification, Psychological State of, 75
Physical Context of Narrative, 14, 19, 97, 200
Pilgrim's Progress, 238n.32
Polanyi, M., 251n.1
"Pome and Peal," 90
"The Poor Man's Bowl," 40
Possibility, 197–98
Postmodernism, 4, 34, 120, 134, 138–39, 183, 203–4, 224–25n.7
Power, 13, 19, 78–93, 97, 200, 213, 220
Pragmatism, 100–102
Problem-solving, 222
Problems Typical of the Bright-Shadow World, 161–182
Progoff, I., 239n.8
Propp, V., 11–13, 227n.1
Prusyer, P., 68, 69, 236n.11
"Psyche and Eros," 72, 76, 96, 107, 122, 194, 206
"Punchkin," 75
Punishment for Cruelty to Animals, 108–9

Q

Qur'an, 231n.14, 234n.24
"The Qur'an Reader and his Wife," 141–42, 144

R

Ramayana, 186
Rank, Otto, 89, 239n.9, 243n.3, 254n.13
Recueil de Contes Populaires Slaves, 237n.22
Reading the World, 16–26, 208, 211, 219
Richards, M. C., 240n.16

Riddling, 179–181
Rip van Winkle, 61
Rogues and Roguery, 184–190, 208–9
Role-Making, 120–21
Roumanian Fairy Tales, 159, 234n.18, 239n.13
Ross, A., (Universal Abandon), 232n.3
Rugh, Andrea, 22, 229n.15
Rumi, Jalal ad-Din (Mathnawi), 9, 34, 35, 50, 148, 149–50, 153–58, 177, 226n.18, 233n.7, 249n.22

S

Sagas from the Far East, 140–41, 248n.6, 252n.14, 253n.6
"Saif-Baba, Tale of," 146–47
Saktideva, 47–52, 56, 60, 96, 126, 128, 135–36, 159, 180, 189–90, 194, 200–1, 206
Sale, Roger, 9, 226n.16, 230n.3, 242n.26
Samudratta, 48
"The Sandalwood Merchant, Tale of," 178–79
Santal Tales, 254n.14
Satyavrata (the Fisher-King), 48
Scenario-Building, 151–53
Schachtel, E., 169
Scheherazade, 119
Schimmel, A., 248n.15
Schumacher, E. F., 102
Schutz, A., 5, 69, 138, 223n.1, 224n.4, 227n.5, 236n.13, 247n.1
Schweitzer, A., 235n.5
"The Secret-Keeping Little Boy," 180
Selz, Otto, 79
Sept Contes Roumains, 232n.26
Sets and set exploitation, 38–43, 165–69, 191–92, 197
"The Seven Sleepers of Ephesus," 61–62
Sexuality, 59, 66–67

Shakespeare, 131, 162–63, 176, 177–79
"The Sham Prince, or the Ambitious Tailor," 170
Al-Shamat, Abu ad-Din, Story of, 24
El-Shamy, Hasan M., 60, 132, 141–42, 234n.15, 248n.7
Shapiro, G., 224–25n.7, 226n.21, 227n.6, 234n.17
Shaw, F. J., 252n.1
"Shifty-Lad" stories, 253n.10
Sicilianische Märchen, 133, 241n.11
Sidi Nu'uman, Story of, 67
Simak, C., 205
Similarity/Difference, 30–34, 80
Singer, June, 114, 229n.17, 243n.5
"Six Make their Way in the World," 70
"Sky hooks," 156
Sleep, 68–71
Smith, Adam, 229n.19
Soleri, P., 93, 240n.15
Somada and Bandhamochini, Story of, 67
"Soria Moria Castle," 154
Spengler, O., 255n.6
Stark, Freya, 126–27, 245n.29
Steppenwolf, 126, 193–94
Stewart, Kilton, 150
Stewart, Susan, 234n.21
Storytelling and Identity, 119–20
Strange Stories from a Chinese Studio, 74, 251n.5
Strangeness, 53–62
Structural Analysis, 199–201; Accumulation Stories, 40–41; Aladdin, 85–88, 123–24; "The Banker and the Farmer," 170–71; "Beauty and the Beast," 122–23; "Bilar and Gobar," 142–45; Black Elk, 114–15, 146; "Briar Rose," 69–70; "The Cat, the Mouse, the Owl, the Ichneumon and the Hunter," 172–74; "The Child Carried Off by an Eagle," 174–75; "The Cook and

his Girl Friend," 168; "A Discerning Old Faki," 166; Displaced Women, 130–32; "The Dawn Fairy," 57; Enchantment theme, 65–66; Flight and Transformation stories, 139–40; "The Four Distinguished Suitors," 171–72; "Four Men Search for Happiness," 37; Fly-Killer tales, 121–22; Stories about Goha, 187–88, 190; "The Golden Bird," or "Bird Grip," 72–73; "How is Wealth Gained?" 36–37; "Invisible Grandfather," 145; The Story of Ishtar, 117–18; "The Story of King Kalinga," 100–2; "The King and his Storyteller," 168; Little Diamond, 19–20, 23–24; "The Loan," 171; "The Magic Ring," 163; The Story of Maqdad, 116–17; Morgiana ("Ali Baba"), 79–80; "The Murdered Prince," 140–45; "Ma'ruf the Cobbler," 82–84, 99–100, 104; Nasr-ed-Din Khoja tales, 195–96; Odysseus, 123; "The Ostrich and the Jewel," 19–20; "Perunto and Vastolla," 90; "Pome and Peel," 90–91; "The Poor Man's Bowl," 40; Portia's Suitors, 162–63; Psyche (and Eros), 72; Rama and Luxman, 19–20; Saif-Baba, 146–47; Saktideva and the City of Gold, 50–2; "The Schoolboy and the Baklava," 166; "The Secret-Keeping Little Boy," 180; "The Seller of Sandalwood," 178–79; "The Sultan and the Cobbler," 175–76; "The Three Brothers," 58; "The Tale of the Three Fish," 39, 40; "The Qur'an Reader and his Wife," 141–45; "The Wazir and the Painter," 150–51; "When Death Came to Baghdad," 35–36; "The White Parrot," 91–92; "The White Slipper," 167. See also Actors, 12–13; Vectors, 13; Power Sources, 13;

Structural Analysis (*cont.*)
Physical Context, 14; Denouement, 14
"The Sultan and the Cobbler," 175
"The Sultan and the Four Strange Brothers-in-Law," 237n.25
Style, 183–86, 216–17, 222; as a category, 198
Subtle Contact, 164–65
Synchronicity, 81, 238n.3
Swahili Tales, 236n.18

T

Tales Alive in Turkey, 196, 244n.14, 252n.12
Tales from the Arab Tribes (Campbell), 116–17, 155, 157, 158
Tales of Ancient India (van Buitenen), 35
Tales of the Dervishes (Shah), 21, 35, 43, 98–99, 146–47, 229n.12, 231n.10, 240n.5, 241n.18, 244n.16, 254n.13
Tatar, Maria, 5, 52, 227n.21, 235n.1, .236n.15
Telling Someone Something, 176–77
Thievery, 186–90
Thesiger, W., 195
Thompson, Stith, 105, 121, 187, 237n.22, 253n.9
Thoreau, H. D., 26, 68, 194
Thousand and One Nights, 229n.13; B. Bettelheim on, 3; Accumulation Theme, 41; (Clever) Deductions, 157–58; Dreaming in, 150–51; Escaping Sets, 166, 178–79; Finding Things, 176; Intelligence in, 79–80; Interiority Theme in, 61; Life-Patterns in, 24–25; Luck, Treatment of, in, 82–84; Magic, Treatment of, in, 67, 85–88; Malignancy in, 96; Metaphor-Making in, 193; Precipitous Action, Danger of, in, 35; Resources, Lack of,

in, 92; Roguery, Treatment of, 188, 190–91; Sexuality, 67; Strangeness, Theme of, 21, 46; Subjective Factors, Operation of, in, 98, 99–100, 132; Will, Treatment of, 88; Misuse of, 92
"The Three Brothers," 58
"The Three Fishes," 39
Tibetan Book of the Dead, 54, 233n.12
Tiidu, Story of, 24, 128
"Le Tisserand Intelligent," 155
Todorov, T., 232n.2
Tolkein, J. R. R. (The Hobbit), 46; *Lord of the Rings*, 172
"Tontlawald, A Tale of the," 60, 103
Toulmin, S., 229n.19
Triplicities, 28–29
Tufayl, Ibn, 236n.12
Turner, V. W., 227n.7, 232n.1
Tuti-Nama, 37, 118, 159
"The Twelve Dancing Princesses," 250n.34
"The Two Brothers," 75
"The Two Caskets," 104

V

Van Buitenen, J. A. B., 35, 229n.18, 253n.6
Vectors, Role in Narrative, 13, 23, 83, 97, 200
Verne, Jules, 61
Vishnu, 54
Voltaire, 255n.6
Von Franz, Marie-Louise, 64, 75, 111, 124, 130, 227n.2, 235n.9, 237n.21, 238n.29, 242n.19, 243n.6, 245n.24
Von Wright, Georg, 94–95

W

Wagdu (Will), 88–89
Waters, F. (*The Man who Killed the Deer*), 129

Watzlawick, P., 169, 231n.13,
    250n.32, 252n.11
Wertheimer, M., 241n.17
West, Rebecca, 156
"What the Rose did to the
    Cypress," 165
"The White Parrot," 91–92, 130, 159
"The White Slipper," 167, 169
"When Death Came to Baghdad,"
    35–36
"The White Wolf," 130–31
"The White Snake," 146
Wide-Awake Stories, 165, 239n.14,
    244n.16
Will, 87, 88–93; and Identity, 123–24
Williams, Charles, 64
Wilson, R. M., 236n.19
Winnicutt, D. W., 233n.5
Wisdom of the Idiots (Shah), 170–71
    ("The Loan")

"The Wise Little Girl," 55
Wiseman, Mary, 17
Witnesses, Clever Use of, 170–72
World-Making, 5, 7, 204–9, 211, 219
World-Reading, see "Reading the
    World"

Y

Yúdice, G., 46, 243n.7
Yugoslav Folk-tales, 236n.16, 242n.24
Yuletide Tales, 241n.12, 242n.22,
    246n.38

Z

Zipes, Jack, 1, 78, 236n.15, 244n.19
Zorba the Greek, 148